Economic Populism and Institutional Reform

In response to the global crises in recent decades, many countries – both developed and developing economies – have resorted to populist forms of economic policy instead of undertaking meaningful institutional change.

This book explores two forms of economic populism in particular (wage populism and exchange rate populism) and demonstrates that these types of policies result in high inflation, unstable exchange rates, and chronic macroeconomic problems. The book opens with an elucidation of the institutional economics approach – drawing on Commons and Veblen, and foregrounding laws, rules, norms, regulations, religions, and traditions – which sheds particular light on economic populism. The book also explores the different forms of economic populism that have been seen throughout the world including policies in the United States, Brexit in the United Kingdom, the response to the Yellow Jackets in France, the populism of various countries in Latin America, and regulations in China. Delving deeper, two case studies are explored in greater and comparative detail: Argentina and Turkey. In these countries, which have followed similar patterns, it is shown how following a path of economic populism has prevented the much-needed institutional reforms from being enacted. The book argues that adopting populist economic policies may prove popular in the short term but prevents and ignores the longer-term project of institutional reform, which is needed to provide greater stability. Finally, the book also looks at the types of institutional and policy reform that may be required to prevent economic populism from taking hold.

This book will be of interest to readers in economics, political economy, politics, and other social sciences who are grappling with issues around populism in all its forms.

Emre Ünal obtained his bachelor's degree from the Department of Economics at Istanbul University. He also pursued a master's degree in economic theory, with specific emphasis on the institutional aspect. He successfully obtained his PhD from the Department of Economics at Kyoto University. Presently, he holds the position of associate professor at Firat University, specifically in the Department of Economics, located in Türkiye. While evaluating the book, he dedicated a portion of his time as a research fellow at the Faculty of Engineering at Kyushu University, Japan. He was employed at various universities and made visits to numerous institutions. He conducted research on growth models and institutional reforms, focusing on nations in East Asia and Europe. His areas of study include institutional economics, input–output analysis, East Asian economies, new technologies, energy economics, and financial economics. He authored publications in prestigious academic journals. He analyzes the institutional aspects within the framework of the global context. He tries to discover novel regulations aimed at mitigating economic obstacles. He proposes that conflicts within the market can be identified via institutional reforms.

Routledge Frontiers of Political Economy

The Myth of the Global Market
A Marxist Critique of Neoliberalism
Giulio Palermo

Government and Economic Growth in the 21st Century
A Classical Liberal Response
Edited by Juan E. Castañeda

Political Economy in Middle East and North-Africa
Why Institutions, Rents and Power Matter in Economic Reforms
Rachid Mira

How Economists Think
A Kantian Interpretation of Mainstream Economics
Steven Buccola

Economic Populism and Institutional Reform
Emre Ünal

For more information about this series, please visit: www.routledge.com/Routledge-Frontiers-of-Political-Economy/book-series/SE0345

Economic Populism and Institutional Reform

Emre Ünal

Routledge
Taylor & Francis Group
LONDON AND NEW YORK

First published 2025
by Routledge
4 Park Square, Milton Park, Abingdon, Oxon OX14 4RN

and by Routledge
605 Third Avenue, New York, NY 10158

Routledge is an imprint of the Taylor & Francis Group, an informa business

British Library Cataloguing-in-Publication Data
A catalogue record for this book is available from the British Library

ISBN: 9781032571560 (hbk)
ISBN: 9781032571584 (pbk)
ISBN: 9781003438090 (ebk)

DOI: 10.4324/9781003438090

Typeset in Times New Roman
by Deanta Global Publishing Services, Chennai, India

Contents

Preface

In the field of institutional economics, this book is founded on the fundamental concepts and principles that serve as its foundation. Neither any political movement nor any political party is intended to be criticized in this piece. In this book, an attempt is made to write it using scientific procedures, objective approaches, and classical principles. The most essential point that the book makes is that economic failures should not be centered on the strategies of political parties but rather on the institutional forms that have been developed for a long time before a party comes to power. It draws inspiration from the democratic institution of the Commons approach and the technocratic ideology of Veblen. The book suggests that a third system, which is referred to as economic populism, may arise as an outcome of modifications in institutional forms. To put it another way, there is the possibility of a third path in nations where democratic institutions are in place for the people, but where antagonism also grows as a response to elitism. In light of this, a democratic market needs to be organized according to the principle of power equilibrium between the various economic entities. The approach of Commons is more dependent on the presence of a balance of power between workers and industries, while the Veblen paradigm is more focused on elitism that is supported by industrialism. The book makes the essential suggestion that the definition of populism needs to go beyond its common traits, where it is comprehended by political ideology and the personality of those in leadership positions on the political spectrum. Populism may extend beyond the confines of a political party and expand into the very core of institutional forms. Populism can be grounded on the principles of institutional economics. The book explores the persistence of chronic economic difficulties despite changes in political parties and their philosophies governing the nation. It can be determined from this that political ideologies are not the only factors that contribute to economic difficulties. It also attempts to explain why, even when a political party changes power, the next administration keeps making the same errors and fails to implement any new reforms. This book provides a fundamental response to this issue by arguing that, given the existence of economic populism, as long as there is no essential institutional change, it does not matter which party is elected. The policies that are similar will continue to be implemented.

It is thus possible to trace the origins of economic populism back to institutional reforms, which resulted in an imbalance of power in the market. Institutional reform, which led to path dependency and a lack of institutional complementarity in economic policies and regulations, is the root cause of economic populism. In a sense, the policies of a political party are not the only factor contributing to economic populism. Two nations, notably Argentina and Türkiye, were investigated to further explain this idea. During the period of import substitution industrialization, these two nations pursued institutional reforms to strengthen their domestic markets by providing the working class with more power and to advance their industrial development. This constituted the establishment of the wage–labor relationship. Within the context of wage–labor relations, John R. Commons placed an emphasis on the legislative role that governments play, which led to the establishment of collective bargaining for labor organizations. Therefore, the working class gave up on the concepts of socialism and cooperative production. The power dynamic between the working class and industry witnessed a significant shift as a consequence of this institutional innovation. Strong ties between the working class and the government were developed as a result of the institutionalization of wage–labor relations. The establishment of the wage–labor relationship granted significant authority to the working class, thus impacting the economic policies of the government. This event marked the beginning of the rise of economic populism. In addition to causing a profound path dependency, which led to persistent inflation and unstable exchange rates for decades, this institutionalization constituted a significant barrier to economic stability and became a major obstacle to economic stability. This alteration led to an imbalance of power between the working class and industries. After that, governments continued to implement expansion ary policies, but they performed this without taking into account the productivity of the economy. This is due to the fact that they wanted to appeal to the people by implementing expansionary policies while avoiding the creation of fundamental institutional reforms. Democracy has the potential to slow down institutional reforms since political parties are concerned about the outcomes of their elections. Furthermore, since neoliberal policies do not attempt to reach a consensus in the market, it might be difficult to put them into practice. This is because neoliberal policies are not democratic in nature. To provide the groundwork for institutional reform, there needs to be a consensus that develops between the working class and the industries. To create a scientific approach to the wage–labor relationship that is founded on a robust growth model that is more advantageous for countries, fundamental institutional reforms are required to make a reduction in the number of persistent issues that are plaguing the economy.

Acknowledgments

Without the assistance of my PhD supervisor, Professor Hiroyuki Uni, with whom I collaborated at Kyoto University, it would not have been possible to develop the present edition of this book to that level. Even after I had finished my dissertation in 2016 on institutional economics and input–output analysis, he continued to support me. When we last met, I was working in the Faculty of Engineering at Kyushu University. At the time, I was not only thinking about the technocratic elitism of Veblen, but I was also working on new technological projects. These projects made me question whether or not the power of elitists could be held by future advancements. However, Professor Uni shared with me his intention of Commons and his democratic approach to the institutional reform. There is a potential for economic populism to emerge as a result of the imbalance of power that exists between the working class and the industries. This might lead to the people getting more dependent on the policies of the government. He proposed the concept that the Commonsian approach can be founded on scientific methodology, which would not only have the potential to make him democratic but would also bring him closer to the scientific collectivism of Veblen. Consequently, this concept compelled me to engage in the investigation of robust growth models and examine the relationship between the dynamics of productivity and wage. In other words, the conversation I had with him became an inspiration for me to create the concept of pluralism and the means by which conflict can be reduced in terms of institutional economics. I am grateful for his support.

I wish to convey my sincere appreciation to Professor Kota Kitagawa, with whom I had the opportunity to study at Kyoto University and whose supervisor was also Professor Hiroyuki Uni. By providing comments and engaging in a conversation on the wage–labor relationship, he embraced my idea. He provided me with a copy of his work in Japanese. I could comprehend the core aspects of his idea. The process of policy formation in Germany and Japan in terms of institutional economics was specifically outlined in his work, which provided a complete overview of the process. Within the context of this comparative perspective, the creation of policies and reaching to a consensus provided motivation for comprehending the democratic process of institutional reform. During the meeting that we had at Otemon Gakuin University to talk about the institutional approach to economic populism, he expressed his notion about the process of commission and consensus that should be built in order to reduce disputes between economic entities.

I would like to express my gratitude to three reviewers who remained anonymous and offered various perspectives on populism. The first reviewer to the study proposed the establishment of democratic policy formation in both developed and developing nations. Using this concept, the book was able to include the scientific methodology and the consensus-building process to construct an institutional reform. The second reviewer provided criticism on the democratic stance of the countries examined in the book. The concept revolved on the notion that these countries lack democratic governance. Therefore, it is challenging to analyze the phenomenon of populism in these nations. However, this argument prompted efforts to enhance the concept of economic populism. If economic populism exists, it is necessary to make efforts within democratic institutions to achieve a balance and minimize conflicts among economic entities. Populism can develop as a result of democratic elections in which the people have a voice. For the presence of populist policies, it is essential to have democratic institutions since populism is an inherent aspect of democracy and serves as a counterforce against elitism. Furthermore, the nations that are being evaluated for these instances also have a significant role in the presence of populism in literature. Therefore, this study does not just address these nations in terms of politics but also as part of economic populism. Hence, it would be extremely difficult to disregard the historical advancements in democracy in these nations and label them as undemocratic. The third reviewer highlighted the influence of ideologies, such as fascism, on the formation of populism. The comment offered a method to delineate economic populism using the framework of institutional economics. Furthermore, I would like to convey my appreciation to the Routledge Editor, Andy Humphries, for his invaluable assistance. His remarks offered a distinct guidance to enhance the themes explored in the book. Finally, I wish to express my gratitude to Firat University, where I am employed, for providing me with a complimentary and comfortable setting to pursue my academic endeavors.

I wish to acknowledge my sister and mother for their unwavering support and inspiration to finish my work. Their assistance always motivated me to advance in my academic pursuits. In addition, I would like to express my gratitude to my wife for her patience and support during the process of writing the book. Her remarks and assistance were of great use to me in enhancing the themes and constructing the sections of the book.

1 Introduction

The rise of economic populism can be attributed to institutional reforms due to their potential to disrupt institutional complementarity, create path dependencies, diminish the balance of power, and erode power separation. The process of globalization, coupled with technological improvements, brings about significant transformations in economic conceptions from an institutional perspective. This phenomenon leads to an increased significance of economic populism, which in turn influences the political landscape of both industrialized and emerging nations. Economic populism is linked to an absence of equilibrium in power dynamics. This strategy is in direct opposition to pluralism. The institutional approach attempts to attain a state of equilibrium among the different economic entities. Economic democracy is hindered if institutions are designed in such a way that they can only provide support to one particular group of economic actors. Hence, pluralism can be regarded as a fundamental premise of institutional economics. It ensures that all players in the economic system are not excluded or perceived to be unimportant. Alternatively, it can be utilized to provide optimal assistance to each individual group. It is possible to undertake institutional reforms to lessen the impact of economic populism. However, for these reforms to have a significant impact, they must not be used for political advantage. Populism has traditionally been a highly debated matter in both the realms of politics and economics. That does not entail that populism is a destructive philosophical approach. The mobilization of the nation has the potential to make a positive contribution to the development and growth of the economy if it is utilized in the proper direction. This occurs after the trauma of war, which has the potential to unite people in the pursuit of specific ideals that they share. Nevertheless, populism has a generally unfavorable reputation all across the globe in the modern era. This notion is used by the government in an effort to reinforce its power, as is the case in the majority of nations. This pertains to the political position of the populist movement.

Within the realm of economics, there exist two clearly differentiated forms of populism. First, populism, if effectively applied and utilized, has the capacity to promote progressive advancement within a nation. Specifically, governments can utilize populism to implement substantial institutional changes and stimulate economic growth, provided that there is no political risk or competition among political factions. This specific form effectively complements extremist ideologies. Nevertheless, due to its highly authoritarian and radical nature, there is no political

DOI: 10.4324/9781003438090-1

party prepared to construct an alternative system among this form. Amid challenging conditions, the government promotes unity and urges society to exert even greater effort. Therefore, there is an absence of political risk, and the administration is not at risk in any form. Steering society toward specific desired results is not a challenging task. Second, when populism is confronted with political risk, it has the capacity to generate economically disadvantageous outcomes. Governments exhibit reluctance to advocate for modifications in established institutional frameworks when there is a potential for political repercussions. When a significant number of people in an economy gain influence, governments have a greater ability to manipulate economic factors such as wages and the currency rate to accomplish their goals. One might infer that economic populism is prevalent when there is a significant increase in wages and an overvalued currency, both aimed at reducing inflation. This is a prevalent problem in emerging economies, such as Türkiye and nations in Latin America.

If a trend toward backward populism emerges, it can result in a notable level of economic path dependency and an absence of institutional complementarity (Ünal, 2020). In the field of politics, this term can also be referred to as retrograde populism, which denotes a style of populism characterized by xenophobic, antiprogressive, traditionalist, and extreme theocratic ideologies. This form of populism can be regarded as a movement that aims to restore the traditional values of the general population (Canovan, 1981; Anselmi, 2018). Individuals have the capacity to resist change and progress due to the potential clash with their cultural heritage and the benefits they derive from it. This approach may receive support from a populist political party that is dedicated to garnering backing from a substantial number of constituents. Economic populism may lead to a deceleration in the pace of institutional development. Furthermore, it frequently fails to consider growth models or the actual dynamics of an economy. It is crucial to bear in mind that any legislation enacted by populism has the propensity to result in a long-lasting economic disaster. Governments frequently avoid implementing innovative institutional reforms due to the associated political risks. If a government modifies the institutions it controls, it might potentially weaken its economic prowess and provide doors for a rival political party to seize power. Populism, in its fundamental manifestation, can incite competition among political parties, regardless of their ideological leanings toward either the left or the right. Consequently, there is a hesitancy among parties to initiate structural changes in the economy. Politicians prioritize pushing their own political agendas over the collective interests of the country. Populist economic policies are independent of the type of political system in place. The primary consideration is whether the government implements institutional reforms, regardless of the associated political risks. Dornbusch and Edwards (1991) analyzed populism from an economic standpoint. Their research focused on the growth of macroeconomic populism in Latin American countries (Kaufman and Stallings, 1991). The main inference drawn from their research was that governments can prioritize real wages to promote populist initiatives. This results in a significant increase in inflation, which subsequently causes a decline in real wages. Margaret Thatcher's policies in the United Kingdom were regarded as a manifestation of authoritarian populism, and they were implemented in opposition to the trade unions and welfare programs of the era. Her objectives encompassed the reduction of inflation and the establishment of a flexible labor market (Jessop, 1990; Jessop and Sum, 2006). Rodrik (2018a) explored the emergence of populism in Latin America and Europe as well as the diverse reactions of countries throughout the world to globalization. Aytaç and Öniş (2014) analyzed Argentina and Türkiye as two distinct nations in terms of the political populism that prevails in each nation. From the dawn of the modern era, the idea of populism has been a part of political discourse. The increasing digitization of the world, the growing tendency of globalization, and the implementation of more uniform regulations have collectively led to an elevation in the significance of economics for individuals. Therefore, it is increasingly imperative for governments to consider a range of economic measures. Failure to address economic issues could lead to widespread social and political turmoil across various regions of the world. Institutional actions that target economic populism can enhance the functionality of an economy by eliminating potential causes of instability arising from conflicts of interest.

The emergence of populism is not a recent phenomenon. Significant developments are being realized in many regions worldwide. Rather than focusing on implementing institutional changes, several industrialized nations' governments have endeavored to align their policies with populist tendencies. For instance, the secession of the United Kingdom from the European Union (EU), commonly referred to as Brexit, was primarily driven by a populist revolt against alterations to long-standing institutions rather than a simple desire to depart the EU. The economic and political actions taken by the United States against China exemplify the refusal to embrace institutional reforms that, if put into effect, could enhance the country's position as a strong competitor in global commerce. The Yellow Vest Movement in France finally precipitated the emergence of economic populism. The French government made a commitment to fulfill its campaign promises of increasing the nominal minimum wage, reducing the rate at which taxes are raised, and providing economic benefits to the middle-class population. Recent years have witnessed a substantial amount of attention devoted to studying populism in Latin American economies. Throughout the entire book, a greater amount of discussion is focused on the occurrences of populist acts that are comparable to the ones outlined.

There is no universally accepted definition of populism. The concept of populism can manifest in several ways, contingent upon the particular circumstances. This could be derived from philosophical principles, methodologies, or even contemporary trends that are prevalent in the collective awareness of the public. Populism is feasible to embrace several definitions, which may change depending on the expectations of societies. Despite this, there are still a limited number of definitions of populism that are widely acknowledged. Müller (2016) asserts that populists harbor a profound aversion toward established institutions. Their impatience with the rules and bureaucracy stems from their desire to promptly reach their conclusions and accomplish their aims. Politically, populists align themselves with the uninstitutionalized majority of society. Moreover, as stated by Weyland

(2001), populism can be associated with the charismatic qualities of leaders who possess the ability to attract substantial support from extensive segments of the population. However, it was unanimously acknowledged that assessing the populism of a government is a challenging task because of the multitude of diverse domains and policies related to it. According to this work, there is no establishment of formal structures occurring in the relationship between populist governments and the masses that they represent, and there is also no association with the involvement of intermediary organizations. Roberts (2007) focused on the prominent characteristics of politicians to attribute populism to them. It was concurred with the concept that populism is distinguished by a departure from a homogeneous perspective on political, economic, and institutional systems. Barr (2009) explains that the definition of populism can vary based on the specific administration, movement, and the approach of its supporters. Moreover, populism can exhibit distinct geographical characteristics, as witnessed in European populism and Latin American populism. According to Anselmi (2018), populism is a flexible kind of propaganda that adjusts itself over time in reaction to shifts in the political environment. Within the realm of democracy, it serves as a tool to challenge established powers, albeit no longer regarded as a radical ideology. Given this, it is infeasible to disentangle the populism of the contemporary era from democracy. Therefore, populism is not a viable approach to addressing the crisis that democracy is currently facing. Conversely, it is an unavoidable outcome of representative democracy. Populism has the potential to follow several evolutionary trajectories and is capable of adjusting to emerging technological and social advancements. Novel concepts have arisen within the domain of politics, encompassing populism on a global scale. These arguments demonstrate that populism can significantly influence democratic processes and the people.

Modifying the economic necessities of societies is notoriously challenging. Despite ongoing technical advancements, the fundamental cycle of consumption, distribution, production, and reproduction within the capitalist system may remain unchanged. The working class may experience a process of transformation that makes it more flexible, but the economic requirements needed to sustain a certain quality of life will persist in comparable patterns. Popular sovereignty cannot exist independently of economic measures. Governments frequently prioritize populist economic policies to enhance their authority instead of implementing the essential institutional changes required. Institutional economics posits that the government plays two essential roles in the economy. Reforms are required both at the institutional level and inside the government to address its function and impact on the economy (Boyer, 1990; Boyer and Hollingsworth, 1997). While states may be geographically dispersed and have diverse economies, the phenomenon of populism tends to exhibit similarities throughout nations. Most studies have primarily concentrated on the political implications of populism rather than its economic dimensions. Unlike prior studies, the concept of populism extends beyond the politics of a nation or the characteristics of its leaders. This book aims to illustrate that populism can largely result from institutional changes and contemporary forms. It appears that institutions have the ability to create a system that can be manipulated by populists. This suggests that well-established institutions can be exploited as a rationale for populist interventions. Regardless of a change in government, nations lacking the determination to implement significant institutional reforms may persist with the same unsuccessful economic policies.

Economic populism refers to the use of economic measures by a government to attract and mobilize large groups of people to gain support, without considering the potential negative effects such as high inflation or imbalances in the overall economy. There are no policies that can be deemed rational or realistic in any capacity. Common elements include substantial wage rise, an overvalued currency, elevated inflation, the lack of a clearly defined economic model, and impractical expansionary policies. The fundamental characteristics of the populist movements in Argentina and Türkiye share these similarities. A more precise elucidation of populism can be ascertained within the realm of economics. In the realm of politics, terms like nationalism, conservatism, fascism, and other ideologies remain exceedingly vague and challenging to delineate. Economics allows us to observe the concrete manifestation of populist policies through factors such as wages, currency rates, taxes, fiscal policies, and monetary policies, all of which have the potential to influence economic activity. Furthermore, the emergence of economic populism may occur, but it can also be alleviated by the reformation of existing institutions.

As a consequence, this type of populism is strongly associated with an absence of power equilibrium, historical reliance, a deficiency in institutional compatibility, and the division of power among economic agents. It exhibits an attitude that opposes pluralism and democracy, similar to political populism. Therefore, economic democracy is nonexistent. It strives to disregard the requests originating from firmly established industries that are dominated by elites. In other words, it disregards the contributions of other economic actors when making decisions related to the economy. As a natural result, there is an absence of fair allocation of power among the participants. It is antithetical to a command economy that is handled realistically and a free market economy. This populism takes its cue from the demand brought forth by the economy. The working class, lobbyists, and unions are prominent societal groups with the capacity to express their economic requirements and assert their demands. When a demand is supported by a substantial majority of the people, it is considered a popular demand, and populist administrations are expected to meet this need. The populace plays a crucial role in democratic systems, with the working class being the demographic most inclined to support populist political movements. There exists a mutually reinforcing connection between the government and the working class. The populist movement arises as a reaction to the demands of the people. The populist economic movement relies extensively on the existing institutional framework. In particular, during the era of import substitution industrialization, the emergence of the working class in production units after migrating from rural areas led to the strengthening of the constitutional guarantee of the wage–labor relationship through modifications in the institutional framework. Populism can be viewed as a concrete type of constitutional restructuring. Upon the establishment of the wage–labor relationship, the intermediary that previously existed between the government and the working class was removed. Consequently, this caused a shift in the allocation of authority. Furthermore, the elimination of power separation resulted in the eradication of the power disparity between the working class and the industrialists. Populism should be regarded as a form that is institutionalized. The reform of institutional frameworks is the fundamental factor that leads to the emergence of populism. As a direct result of this, economic populism is a form of institutionalization that has been kept hidden throughout the entire history of economic transformation. The origins of economic populism can be attributed to alterations in institutional frameworks that were implemented to benefit powerful and developing factions. Therefore, economic populism can be defined as a form of populism that relies on unstructured policies and a one-sided approach, contrasting with the principles of pluralism. It provides the rationale for the government to implement expansive policies that are not linked to a constructive growth model. There is no comprehensive mathematical formulation that can be applied in the process of policy development. It is a tool through which the government communicates with large groups of constituents. It does not depend on the presence of pluralism, the interdependence of institutions, functioning economic activity, or productive output. Economic populist policies are based on heterodox economic principles that may not have been applied or evaluated in alternative contexts.

This book explores the connection between economic populism and institutional reform from a variety of perspectives. The discussion is on the origins of economic populism as well as how it evolves in response to the formulation of policies. Argentina and Türkiye are being considered as potential candidates for the position. These nations were selected because, over the course of many decades, they have provided a consistent representation of the pattern of economic populism. In addition, the growth models of these two countries will be analyzed and juxtaposed to ascertain the extent to which their distinct institutional forms are complementary (Boyer, 2005). Populism is a crucial concept in social science. However, economic populism has been overlooked up until this point, despite the fact that it plays a significant part in the development of nations. The roots of economic populism can be studied from the perspective of institutional economics. This approach is based on a variety of authoritative sources, including religious tenets, secular guidelines, and statutory mandates. Given this, it is essential that any investigation into the origins of economic populism should focus on the governmental-initiated institutional changes. In both Argentina and Türkiye, there have been modifications made to the legislation governing the wage–labor relationship. As a consequence, the connection between the working class and the government was solidified. Institutional economics, in the view of J.R. Commons, is an effective approach for achieving power balance. In the event that this does not occur, there will be conflict as well as economic instability. The delicate balance of power in an economy can be thrown off if just one of its individuals becomes more powerful than the others. In each of these economies, the working class has a more advantageous position in the power dynamic. The involvement of the working class in the negotiation process of contracts with various companies was the primary emphasis of Commons. By the formation of trade unions, the growing working class strengthened its status. The employees were given the opportunity to participate in the process of decision-making. Thus, the working class entered the judicial system, just as the lords and capitalists had done with the King to safeguard their own property rights and businesses. While deciding on reasonable practices, the working class needs to be taken into consideration. Any action carried out by members of the working class that results in material deprivation and forces others to submit to the control of arbitrary authority should be condemned. In this way, Commons provides us with the legal underpinning of power when there are several actors in the market. A pluralist approach to economics is regarded as a significant concept of institutional economics. Both populism and elitism are rejected by this philosophy. Balance of power and separation of powers are crucial conditions that must be maintained. In other words, the institutional approach focuses on establishing a democratic foundation for the sustaining of an optimum power balance. It does not underestimate the requirements of the industrial sector or the needs of the working class. Even if one side has less power than the other to exert stress, it works to build a balance of power among the various economic actors. Populist governments generally make an effort to institutionalize the individuals for their own interests. In Argentina and Türkiye, the working class has been a major force that has contributed to the election of populist regimes. Governments or political parties can often pursue campaigns aimed at attracting the support of the working class and can dismiss the interests of the industrial sector. This runs against the institutional basis of the separation of powers and the delicate balance they need to function. In institutional economics, the government ought to act in a manner that serves the best interests of the nation.

Notwithstanding Veblen's assertion that the government can be molded to meet the requirements of the industry. Nonetheless, the government was a power structure that preserved the interests of the business class or elites in the capitalist economy. The perspective that Veblen takes is more closely associated with elitism. He focused his attention on the ability of the industrial might of a society to alter the course of economic development toward the improvement of scientific collectivism. This indicates that there needs to be at least some degree of power balance between the various economic activities. He claimed that engineers had the potential to be at the forefront of industrial growth and to have an influence on society as well as the economy. He made reference to a technical kind of elitism. In spite of this, he was a proponent of the notion of scientific collectivism. In contrast to what Commons and Veblen emphasized, the situation in Argentina and Türkiye is considerably different. Nonetheless, the concepts put out by Commons and Veblens include the answers that these countries want to find a solution to their current economic predicament. In the realm of economic activities, there is neither a balance nor a clear division of authority to be found. The populism that exists is well ingrained. The working class and the government are connected in a way that is quite straightforward. It means that pluralist forms of institutional economics are not supported. Their economies have been harmed as a result of persistent macroeconomic issues. In addition, they adhere to economic policies that are designed to rein in spiraling price increase across the economy. Remarkably, despite the fact that most developed countries have successfully eradicated the fundamental problem of inflation, these two economies continue to struggle with the issue. Exploring the impact of economic populism, which relies on institutional changes, can help other developing or developed countries address the macroeconomic problems caused by populist policies implemented by their governments. Economic populism, in the context of institutions, entails the confrontation between governments and essential institutional reforms. The efficacy of institutional reforms may be impeded or compromised by the impact of economic populism.

Here are the crucial inquiries: First, let us clarify the precise definition of economic populism and its relationship to the study of institutional economics. The second inquiry is to the diverse manifestations of economic populism. Furthermore, what were the specific institutional developments that led to the emergence of economic populism in Argentina and Türkiye? Finally, what specific institutional improvements or policy adjustments are necessary to mitigate the impact of populist politics on macroeconomic decision-making? This book aims to uncover the answers to the questions. A multitude of works have been published, drawing upon the principles of populism and institutional economics as their fundamental basis. Ünal (2016a, 2018) analyzed the transformation of the Turkish economy from an institutional perspective. Moreover, this book aims to be a pioneering investigation on the phenomenon of economic populism in Argentina and Türkiye. It endeavors to elucidate the connection between economic populism and institutional reform, distinguishing itself from previous studies that just focus on political aspects. It also explores how institutional changes can influence the economic performance of nations. The detrimental effects of populism on national economies will be explored. It is thus possible to comprehend how economic populism renders institutional changes ineffective. Consequently, dysfunctional governments that prioritize economic populism may lead to a lack of institutional complementarity and path dependency. Populism remains common in certain nations due to the absence of institutional structures, which not only leads to the collapse of a government but also creates opportunities for future economic populists. Removing institutional problems and establishing a functional economic relationship that is free from the clientelist policies of populist regimes is crucial. This may need the development of a new strategy. In my perspective, it is accurate to describe populism as a chameleon entity that adapts to the prevailing circumstances in nations. It is challenging to classify a political party as either left wing or right wing only based on its supported programs. It is not unexpected for a right-wing political party to embrace principles typically associated with the left, or for a left-wing party to do the opposite. A policy can be deemed successful if it is both implementable and attractive to a significant portion of the population. Therefore, economic policies are not bound by any certain ideology, which makes them well-suited for adopting flexible and adaptable approaches, equivalent to chameleon policies.

Populism can persist as a viable political strategy in the modern era as long as there is an established base of supporters. A multitude of populisms, characterized by diverse economic frameworks, can arise in response to various concerns.

According to Panizza (2005), populism may be defined as an anti–status quo rhetoric that categorizes the political arena by separating the country among the people and other groups. Antagonism, rather than any specific sociological classification, serves as the defining characteristic of this connection. Nevertheless, within the framework of this book, this refers to an institutional form that originated from a particular type of institutional revision. Regarding this matter, for Commons, it is essential to maintain a power equilibrium among economic participants, even if one of the actors is comparatively less strong than the rest. Therefore, pluralism acts as the fundamental basis for the institutional approach. Others are not excluded, nor do they become adversaries of the economy. Instead, it creates a democratic structure in which they can engage and collaborate toward a common objective. The balance of power serves as the basis for the development of the separation of power among the actors. There is no central authority that governs economic activities. There is a harmonious cohabitation that attains an ideal equilibrium among the individuals. Notwithstanding this, Veblen emphasizes the significant role of industries in their evolving function and the dynamic relationship they have with the government. He highlights the lack of equilibrium between the entities, as the government prioritizes the interests of enterprises. Populism renders this entire set of concepts obsolete. It is unrelated to the evolutionary process of industries, Schumpeter's theory of creative destruction, or the institutional arrangements of the economy that foster pluralism. The populist movement rejects the established systems of checks and balances and the division of power. It is in contrast to the practice of participating in multiple economic activities because this notion does not provide fair access to the market for all potential entities. Alternatively, it may be employed as a justification to propose amending the constitution to reduce the number of intermediaries between the masses and populist policies. Populism plays a significant role in institutional economics, and the most effective approach to counter it is by introducing institutional reforms. In the absence of any alterations, nations with a populist political orientation may persist in experiencing a conventional form of economic existence. During the era of import substitution industrialization, Argentina and Türkiye had a significant influx of people migrating from rural regions to urban production hubs, where they congregated and formed communities. The elites played a crucial role in propelling the expansion of the industrial sector. In the context of this work, industries refer to the other. This is the concept that Veblen addresses when he discusses those belonging to the upper class. The working class was the primary source of the generated wealth, while business activities were a form of political manipulation that appropriated such wealth. In other words, they are the privileged and highly skilled individuals.

In the absence of government engagement in the market, or when government involvement is restricted to favoring specific industries, it becomes feasible to establish a direct connection between the working class and various industries. This suggests the absence of both power stabilization and the division of powers. This represents a Veblen-style dynamic in which companies capitalize on labor for their own advantage, without any government intervention to protect workers' rights or advocate for constructive institutional reforms. Therefore, it is necessary to consider institutional economics when analyzing economic activities. Both Argentina and Türkiye underwent a crucial phase of preliminary industrialization, which necessitated their respective governments to implement institutional reforms. During the 1960s, significant constitutional amendments occurred in the wage–labor relations of both countries due to the worker rights movement and popular sovereignty. Subsequently, there exists no intermediary level of communication between the government and the people. This suggests the absence of any entity capable of establishing a state of balance. The omission of certain industries resulted in the formation of a mutually beneficial connection between the government and the working class. Inflation became a persistent problem, hindering the completion of industrial progress. Additionally, the collapse of currencies resulted in two once-promising countries falling behind in their industrial evolution. It is crucial to recognize that political and economic issues are not the primary cause of the rise of populism. Various conditions might provide as inspiration for political parties. The emergence of populism might be attributed to institutional deficiencies or incomplete implementation of improvements. Hence, it is imperative to conduct a comprehensive examination of institutional changes and institutional forms to precisely delineate the concept of populism.

2 Institutional economics and its forms

The patterns of institutional economics are present in all societies and economic systems. The field of institutional economics has a considerable historical background because institutions are founded on customs, culture, norms, regulations, or laws. In its contemporary interpretation, institutional economics originated from the contributions of classical economists such as Adam Smith, David Ricardo, and Karl Marx, although it was not explicitly defined during that era. The significance of Karl Marx's ideology lies in its analysis of the inherent deficiencies of the capitalist system and its proposal of an alternative way for societal organization. Marxism facilitates the assessment of the social and economic changes that have happened due to the inherent contradictions inside capitalism. An institutional approach is a methodology that may be utilized to examine these matters and build novel standards that can potentially aid in the development of economic stability. Consequently, it differs from both Marx's revolutionary economic remedies and Adam Smith's laissez-faire market system. The main goal of the institutional approach is to establish the ideal state among all the actors, thereby enabling the economy to function efficiently. The concept was initially introduced in John R. Commons's book *Institutional Economics* published in 1934. The book extensively examines the allocation of power across various institutions, which is a central issue. Interactions can take place between customers and manufacturers or between workers and industries. To restore this harmony, the authority to enact institutional modifications in an economy is typically held by either the authorities or the judicial system. In the absence of such action, instability and crises are unavoidable outcomes. The book's institutional perspective is rooted in the concepts outlined by Commons regarding the allocation of power. Additionally, the work draws inspiration from various institutional methodologies, like the Regulation Theory. This theory created concepts and frameworks to explain institutional phenomena, with a particular focus on economic crises. It posits that when a crisis arises, it is primarily caused by inherent flaws in the structure and functioning of institutions.

The theory of regulation originated in France. The expansion began as an outcome of the investigations conducted by economists who gathered in a specialized research center with a particular emphasis. Researchers have divergent viewpoints on facets of economic crises. Aglietta (1979) is widely recognized as one of the leading scholars who advanced the institutional approach to the study of economics in his book titled *Theory of Capitalist Regulation*. Nevertheless, the institutional

DOI: 10.4324/9781003438090-2

approach remained limited in its scope when compared to other branches of economics. Scholars required a significant amount of time to develop the fundamental principles of institutions and their interconnectedness with market economies. Despite Commons publishing his book in 1934, the institutional approach did not gain widespread popularity until the 1980s. This arose from profound economic problems that affected developed nations. Historically, when a nation's economy experienced a crisis, the transmission of that crisis to other countries was far more challenging. Both developed and developing nations experienced a range of economic crises due to the rapid industrialization and expansion of capitalist economies during the 1960s and the 1970s. The incidence of these events aided scholars in acquiring a more profound comprehension of economic policies.

The institutional economics approach diverges from the mainstream and dominant economics that is predominantly taught at academic institutions, which is mostly based on orthodox economics. The study of fundamental economic principles begins with the concept of scarcity and aims to achieve an optimal and efficient allocation of resources through the natural progression of production and consumption. Hence, any regulations aimed at fostering the advancement of economic relationships may be regarded as impeding market dynamics. Institutional economics diverges from that condition due to the inclusion of markets as part of institutions. This inevitably became a focal point for institutional economics. The comprehension of institutional economics was complicated due to the misinterpretation of its concepts. There are multiple potential explanations for the term regulation. The notion that regulation and deregulation are mutually exclusive has resulted in conceptual challenges. Regulation is commonly understood as the state's control of natural monopolies and involvement in the market to offer a range of social services. However, this impression has caused challenges in comprehending regulation. In the context of institutional economics, regulation encompasses not only the perspective that the economy is shaped by laws and government intervention but also a framework that examines overarching economic mechanisms and elucidates economic determinants. An institutional approach may also focus on examining the economic and noneconomic outcomes that result from alterations in the organization of market interactions. This phenomenon is not limited to the subject of economics but may also be observed in several other subfields of research, where it may serve as a response or remedy to political considerations.

Institutional economics has the potential to initiate discussions on an accumulation regime and the mode of regulation it utilizes (Boyer and Saillard, 2002; Jessop and Sum, 2006). The lack of a descriptive accumulation regime in developing countries can be attributed to the fact that their industrial expansion is still evolving. In contrast, when Fordism and Toyotaism were the prevailing economic practices in the United States and Japan, respectively, developed economies were perceived differently. These tactics were widely acknowledged as the definitive attributes of accumulation regimes. Emerging nations can be analyzed based on the growth models they utilize. These nations lack influential companies that can have a substantial impact on global culture. The institutional objectives of these countries can be inferred by examining growth models. The regulatory approach represents the fundamental theoretical framework prevalent in evolutionary and institutional economics. This definition can be employed to delineate the approach. This field of research examines the connections between the constantly evolving organizational structures of capitalist economies worldwide (Jessop and Sum, 2006). The patterns of accumulation regimes and modes of regulation in industrialized countries are clearly evident. These economies have undergone industrialization. Consequently, a connection arises between the production and consumption patterns. These nations have experienced diverse stages of transformation. Emerging countries are relatively new to industrialization, and their manufacturing methods are limited to low and medium levels of sophistication. Agriculture remains crucial, as a significant proportion of individuals' income is allocated toward the expenditure on food. The working class in industrialized nations tends to concentrate their skills and expertise in administrative and technological domains. In emerging nations, a substantial proportion of the labor force consists of individuals with limited educational attainment who receive only the minimum wage. Given the absence of accumulation regimes in these nations, it becomes necessary to elucidate the mechanisms behind the productive processes functioning within them.

Although the institutional approach was first developed in economics as a means of achieving the best possible equilibrium between multiple players, it is applicable to a wide range of other disciplines and may thus transcend the confines of the economic framework. This is due to the fact that a transformation in the variables that constitute institutions not only affects the political, social, and cultural aspects of a country but also other fields. The political systems, social norms, and cultural traditions of a nation all combine to produce institutions that are exclusive to that nation. Crises were the impetus for the first stages of the creation of institutional economics. The Great Depression highlighted the capacity of nations to modify their production strategies and establish new laws and norms inside an economy to avert stagnation. Furthermore, the institutional approach became increasingly popular throughout the 1970s due to consecutive economic crises that occurred worldwide, coinciding with governments' efforts to address rising inflation and macroeconomic instability. Due to technological improvements and revolution in accumulation systems, it is crucial for capitalist economies to adapt their institutional structures to align with the realities of the global economy. Nevertheless, it was evident that the previous regulatory measures were no longer effective. Outdated institutional forms required renovation. In the 1970s, worsening economic instability resulted in a succession of crises that had the potential to change the established balances created by Keynesian regulatory policies. In response, economists initiated a search for novel solutions and embarked on the development of a fresh conceptual framework for institutional economics. Capitalist economies underwent a transformation of economic activities as they introduced new labor organizations and production methods. This is the core principle of institutional economics, and it endows capitalist economies with the potential to innovate new institutional adjustments to reorganize themselves in response to changing economic and environmental circumstances. Hence, this is closely related to evolutionary economics since industries played a significant part in this economic development. In the 1970s, the crises that were occurring in the developed nations were thought to be Keynesian crises. This implied that the economic framework that had been constructed during the Great Depression was itself in a state of crisis. The inability of Keynesian economics to explain the operability of the law of supply and demand presented an opportunity for a theoretical challenge to explain the crisis via the institutional approach. This, in turn, paved the way for politicians to resolve economic crises through the implementation of novel reforms. The institutional approach offered fresh explanations and a theoretical framework for economic crises. This approach was aimed at investigating economic stability within the context of competent institutional forms, rules, and norms that could offer long-term protection for markets (Amin, 2000). A representative instance of how the economy's institutional change effectively resulted in a favorable economic cycle is Fordism. Fordism is a post–World War Second economic system that emerged in developed nations, commonly referred to as the 'Golden Age.' The defining trait is the establishment of a circuit in which increasing productivity resulting from production modernization and economies of scale leads to better wages, greater consumption and investment, and subsequently to further productivity growth (Fujita et al., 2023).

The objective of the institutional approach is to provide an explanation for the contradictions and paradoxes that exist within capitalist economies to generate new combinations that function in harmony with one another. The role of the government is to act as a vehicle to correct inefficiencies in the economy and to exercise control over various institutional forms. The government needs to implement new guidelines for the area that include rules and regulations designed to keep the economy running smoothly. In other words, the government takes on the function of a regulator in the process of establishing new institutional forms. At the same time, it has the ability to ensure the ongoing existence of the forms that it generates. There is a strong connection between the various institutional forms and the procedures of the government. The structure of government is one of the essential forms that permits economic ties to persist. When a government has control over the economic instruments, political factors have the potential to be employed in ways that are counterproductive to the interests of the market. It has been determined that developed capitalist countries may serve as models for other nations. They make sufficient data and research readily available, which allows one to understand their economic structures. In this sense, an institutional approach can be directed toward developing countries to fill the gap, and it can be employed to explain the economic transformation in conjunction with contributions from related disciplines such as history, sociology, and political science. The history of fundamental economic advancements in capitalist countries is a critical concept that is covered by this approach. Developments are able to occur in modes of production that are sometimes sluggish, while at other times they emerge via violence and chaos. These kinds of transitions pose substantial challenges for both the government and society. The institutional approach also refers to the past for guidance in establishing future initiatives in light of contemporary realities. The identification of prospective issues in the economy can be made possible via the use of historical research. Market economies exist as evolutionary structures, with definite borders and growth models give rise to continuing production and reproduction processes. The connection arises from the close interaction between crises and reproduction. While market economies are susceptible to unrest, crises, wars, and pandemics, institutional approaches have the capacity to provide room for change and new forms of organization.

There are three fundamental perspectives that are necessary to comprehend modern market economies. The classical approach, which is the most widespread, holds that sustaining the capitalist mode of production can be achieved without undermining the concept of general equilibrium. It has been argued that an economy's overall efficiency may improve if its policies are more focused on promoting free market competition. The Keynesian perspective, as the second viewpoint, argues that while capitalism may not always be stable and flawless, it may nevertheless attain equilibrium if the market is appropriately regulated. The Marxist perspective, which is the third one, maintains that the reproduction of the system is accomplished by the manipulation of external elements. In this regard, a novel perspective is required, one that must be founded on institutional economics. The presence of institutional forms within an economy is what ultimately leads to sustained production processes. The government is able to take on a regulatory role in the process of revitalizing markets and stabilizing the system (Boyer and Yamada, 2000). A new mode of regulation must be designed to ensure that the structural or institutional forms that fall within the established parameters of the mode of regulation are compatible with a new regime of accumulation. It is important that each country and social structure be evaluated based on its own unique realities. It is necessary to make use of the tools provided by history, statistics, and economics to determine the mode of production. Conjectures about the economy need to be subjected to a critical evaluation (Lipietz, 1987). It is essential to recognize that mere knowledge of economic principles is inadequate to completely grasp the functioning of institutional structures; political concepts are also necessary. Both an institutional approach and an economic populist approach can be utilized concurrently to evaluate the structure of an economy.

The political economy and institutional approaches could offer a novel viewpoint on the issues that arise in the economy. Nonetheless, the importance of technological revolutions is something that cannot be overlooked. The adoption of new technologies may also be regarded as a driving force behind institutional changes in the economic sphere. This phenomenon gives rise to new patterns of economic development and methods of production. Moreover, it results in the establishment of new social norms and regulations. Because of this, the components of law, philosophy, religion, culture, art, and tradition are all susceptible to change. This indicates that existing institutional frameworks are amenable to modification. They may serve newly formed societies and environments. Every aspect of the dynamics is interconnected. This does not imply that improvements in technical capabilities and institutional forms are the only factors that can govern and influence economic systems. Changes in the forms can sometimes emerge spontaneously and independently of any authority, even if the process takes decades. The existence of government is frequently inevitable, as economies are not always afforded the opportunity to undergo natural and evolutionary transformations during their development. It is crucial to remain vigilant for these alterations. Conducting investigations on the factors that cause economic systems to deviate from growth models is critical. These provide insight into the internal mechanisms of crises and transformations. Analyzing economies with a discerning perspective serves as the initial step for this approach, which establishes a methodical pathway connecting the origins of crises to their outcomes. Many of the ideas in institutional economics may be traced back to Karl Marx. These ideas that have been passed down from previous generations are very useful for understanding the problems that are occurring in the modern world, assessing the new social and economic situations, and developing an overarching framework within this setting. Understanding what these concepts signify helps grasp what institutional changes have entailed and how the mode of production has evolved. Furthermore, the developments under consideration are tightly interconnected with these notions. The phenomenon in question arises due to the gradual modifications that occur in the process of these concepts.

Institutional economics is a field that defies simple categorization. It is difficult to specify what can be considered an institution because of the lack of clarity. Institutions can refer to both written and unwritten rules, conventions, laws, traditions, religious standards, cultural values, or anything else that influences the interaction between individual activities. Commons (1931) brought to light the fact that many different ideas can be interpreted as distinct types of institutional economics. The terms collective action, liberty, and expansion of individual activity may all be used to describe institutions. Its shapes may be subject to both disorganized custom and organized concerns at the same time. The core concepts underlying institutional economics are collective activities and contractual agreements. Collective actions can be performed by a variety of different entities, including families, labor unions, employer associations, states, and so on. The control of individual actions can result in a gain or loss to another or other individuals. The degree of liberty that economic actors experience may be altered by a contract. Nevertheless, the core principle is to strike a balance between individual activities that are governed by a contract and collective actions. Commons asserted that an employer is exposed to the liberties of the labor who would want to work or not, and the labor is exposed to the liberties of the employer to hire or dismiss employees. Both parties are vulnerable to the liberties of the other. What an individual must, can, or has the option to do or not do governs their behaviors. The liberation of individual activities that are generated from coercion is what institutional economics aims to accomplish. Collective individual actions are capable of causing pressure, discrimination, and an uneven distribution of power. Liberation is achieved by the imposition of collective sanctions. Individual action may be defined as the engagement in economic activities to facilitate power distribution. The collective actions of economic organizations can be far more powerful than the actions of political organizations. Institutional economics is therefore an art that determines what individual actors can, must, may, may not do, or vice versa. It is subject to the jurisdiction of customs and concerns, both of which are derived from the operational regulations that govern economic activities. It can refer to the actions of various economic actors. Institutional economics can relate to anything that is extra or crucial to classical or hedonic economics. It might be a form of economic behavior. In contrast to the free market philosophy, institutional economics emphasizes the importance of collective rather than individual activity, management rather than equilibrium, and control over the economy. Institutional economics can be viewed as a critique of other economic theories, particularly those that are founded on either socialism or capitalism. In spite of this, Commons implies that institutional economics need to combine lessons learned from communism, anarchism, syndicalistism, fascism, capitalism, and unionism. It does not belong to any ideology since institutional economics provides a framework that allows for the investigation of various conflicts and potential rules that may be used to stabilize the relationship in any kind of economic system. Institutional economics are able to operate under a variety of economic systems, including but not limited to capitalism in the United States, communism in China, corporatism in Japan, populism in Türkiye, and others.

J.R. Commons had a significant role in advancing the theory that forms the foundation of the institutional approach. A significant number of scholars employ this methodology, which entails examining the essence of the state and the historical changes that have occurred, not only in the realm of economics but also in the domains of art, business, and architecture. Investigations have taken place in an effort to understand how market economies develop in response to the circumstances that already exist. In my view, institutional economics can be described as an evolutionary process of institutional forms that develop in response to the needs of economic operations. Institutional economics is a concrete form for individual actions that uses scientific methodology to search for an optimal level. In light of this, the study of institutional economics is founded not just on morals, norms, or rules but also on mathematical models and scientific procedures. Institutional economics is a mathematical formula that can establish the optimal balance, govern economic behaviors, generate new laws or norms for reducing individual interests, and build economic democracy. Confirmation and recognition of the mathematical formulation employed to construct a reasonable value are required. It ought to be a compulsory order that does not serve the interests of the individuals involved but rather the interests of the country. The concept of reasonable value is one example of institutional economics in its concrete form. It is not just for the purpose of protecting the interests of a particular actor. It offers a useful concept for the liberation of individual actions that are based on collective control. This is a separation of power between the individual actions.

Institutional complementarity

The concepts of institutional forms and growth models can be regarded as the fundamental pillars in the field of institutional economics. Due to significant changes in the development model, the institutional frameworks enable the capitalist mode of production to acquire the capacity to reproduce itself through reforms. To establish this authority, the government undertakes reforms to modernize the obsolete regulatory instruments, norms, and rules that could hinder the exercise of power. It sets out novel rules and standards that are appropriate for the fresh expansion. The term competitive regulation style was established to refer to the regulatory approach that emerged during the period of time when the classical perspective was the dominant one, commencing with the beginning of the Industrial Revolution. The economic system's development process incorporated the principles of classical thought, fostering a competitive framework. Due to the alterations in the process of acquiring a new production style in 1914, specific regulations had to be revised to ensure the continuation of the capitalist mode of production. The regulatory style that emerged in the aftermath of the Crash of 1929, commonly referred to as the monopoly regulatory style, was a direct consequence of these transformations. This is due to the changes in the way wealth is accumulated, which has led to various measures being taken to ensure the continued existence of the capitalist system of production. The regulating mechanism is being standardized to align with the accumulation regime, thereby maintaining capital accumulation. There is no certainty that the regime of accumulation and the mode of regulation would be able to reach a consensus or that a regime of accumulation can live with the norms of the mode of regulation (Lipietz, 1987). The term mode of regulation refers to the institutional structures that enable capitalism to continue in its present state. It consists of a collection of rules, which can be either formal or informal, that systematically arrange aspects of social interaction into a cohesive framework. Therefore, it includes the institutions and regulations that are responsible for maintaining the reproduction and maintenance of a specific accumulation system. It can be divided into the following categories: Various factors, such as laws, governmental policies, political practices, industrial regulations, administrative management, norms of negotiation and bargaining, consumption culture, and social expectations, all contribute to the overall outcome. A well-defined growth model ensures a harmonious balance between consumption, output, and capital accumulation. This is achieved by establishing an acceptable harmony between the institutional forms and the growth model. If reproduction can occur without any obstacles, it serves as proof that the capitalist system is capable of accumulating capital and that the capitalist mode of production possesses the capacity to sustain itself through reproduction. The presence of complementary institutional structures is essential for achieving economic stability. This concept implies that economic instruments synergistically complement each other and function cohesively. Therefore, the potential for economic instability could be reduced.

Institutional complementarity denotes the harmonious coordination that exists between fiscal policy and monetary policy. An expansionary fiscal policy may lead to an increase in inflation. In response, the monetary policy needs to intervene by raising interest rates to curb inflation. This merely provides a temporary reduction in the rate at which prices are increasing. In a scenario characterized by consistently elevated inflation, this method ultimately becomes ineffective. This indicates that the two political institutions lack sufficient institutional complementarity. To keep control over inflation, governments should abstain from implementing expansionary fiscal policies. If the current institutions do not adjust to their surroundings, any attempt at institutional reform will inevitably be unsuccessful. To elucidate this argument and enhance its clarity, I would like to employ an instance. In countries where traffic lights are still being developed, a red light indicates that cars are required to stop immediately. This alteration to the established procedures aims to organize traffic to minimize the probability of traffic congestion. However, if cars fail to adhere to traffic lights indicating a red light, it might be concluded that there is a lack of institutional complementarity in traffic. For any institutional reform to occur, the new standards must be acknowledged and accepted across the whole economy. The implementation of institutional changes in emerging nations can be likened to the installation of traffic lights. Despite being designed to disrupt societal conventions and create a novel atmosphere, there is a potential for individuals, governments, and businesses to use it only for their own interests. To achieve success, modifications to current institutional forms must be implemented in a way that fosters institutional complementarity. When there is a strong alignment across economic functions, a nation should expect to advance its development more efficiently and systematically. Institutional complementarity does not entail the autonomy of central banks but rather requires their collaboration with the governing bodies of their individual countries. Evaluating distinct institutional forms in isolation from one another presents a challenging task. One has the potential to exert a substantial influence on the other. Modifications in the processes of production affect the organization of labor, while labor itself affects both earnings and the demand for goods. On the other hand, the levels of wages and demand can have an influence on output, which subsequently has the potential to affect economic growth. Every variable is interconnected in a chain; however, each link in the chain is distinct and has a unique purpose in resolving crises. By taking into account all of these aspects, one may witness the transformation of growth models aimed at preserving the economy from crises as well as the specific modifications that occurred in various institutional forms. Nevertheless, the catastrophe can be averted with the effective regulation of the current forces. This technique involves acquiring insights into the necessary actions an economy must take to overcome economic crises through the implementation of institutional reforms based on robust principles.

Path dependency

Path dependency is a problem in institutional economics where it becomes impractical to effectively implement a change in existing rules or norms. Properly enacting institutional reforms can be a difficult challenge for a government when considering the working class. Governments typically avoid taking risks by disregarding institutional improvements that may contradict the interests of the working class. For instance, the existence of a larger quantity of state-owned companies could be a substantial obstacle to the process of privatization in emerging countries. The intensification of conflicts and the organization of demonstrations aimed at opposing the implementation of specific economic reforms can lead to suppression, direct conflict, and potentially even casualties. This is precisely the sequence of events that took place in China when it initiated the implementation of institutional reforms in the late 1980s.

Path dependency refers to the concept that once a nation has chosen a certain course of action, the costs associated with changing direction are significantly high. Although there may be more opportunities to make other decisions, the existing structures and systems in place make it difficult to easily change the first decision (Levi, 1997). Path dependency is characterized by the notion that it is difficult to reverse the consequences of decisions taken at significant junctures. These crucial times effectively bind nations to certain trajectories of progress. Decisions made at crucial turning points create institutions or structures that have a strong tendency to remain unchanged and are not readily altered, making it challenging to reverse the chosen route (Mahoney, 2001). Some nations experience a strong path dependency in economic advancement. What are the reasons for the persistent weakness of institutions in Türkiye and Argentina and their failure to provide a more conducive framework for economic development? Furthermore, what factors contribute to the superior performance of East Asian countries compared to these two nations? The primary issue lies in the failure of these nations, or similar ones, to effectively facilitate reform and implement institutional reforms over an extended period of decades. There exist multiple potential answers to these inquiries. Some scholars can justify their beliefs based on their cultural and religious backgrounds, while others can emphasize the differences in their economic perspectives. The utilization of wealth and income distribution is being employed as an instrument in a constant struggle for power inside governments. Argentina and Türkiye have both exhibited path dependency in regard to wages and exchange rates. The governments of these two nations are reluctant to implement measures to confront institutional issues. The presence of path dependency or prior institutional changes can result in governments acquiring greater authority and a wider range of economic instruments to serve their own objectives. When confronted with a clear path dependency, it is necessary to employ a carefully constructed political strategy to achieve a reform or, more specifically, a revolution. Institutional forms have a tendency to remain unmodified for extended periods of time. These forms may have emerged far earlier than anticipated within a growth model, and even if the model is modified, the institutions typically persist. Nations can accomplish exceptional achievements such as attaining sovereignty, establishing democratic systems, making substantial progress toward modernization, and establishing trade unions. The persistence of an institution can be attributed to political contention. Institutions may have difficulties in sustaining a robust harmony of power among various constituents when they encounter transformations and evolution as an outcome of the progress of time and evolving patterns.

Cultural and religious beliefs are major contributors to the phenomenon of path dependency. Altering people's ways of life and their ideas in a society is not a simple task. The modification of these two significant variables is a challenging and protracted process. While it is tough to alter ideology as well, it is not as challenging as changing one's cultural or religious values. However, a power struggle occurs beneath the umbrellas of culture, religion, and ideologies. The likelihood of it being based on path dependency is high. Belief, culture, and, perhaps most crucially, philosophy all play a role in power conflicts. It is possible for the distribution of wealth and income to be a driving force. Insufficient political determination exists to undertake the necessary risk to revamp outmoded institutions. Path dependency can also form the foundation for the policies that the government can adopt. This is a valid justification that might be employed to mobilize resistance against the proposed policies. To reduce the probability of developing a reliance on a certain path of action, a country should strive to enhance its institutional frameworks and avoid enacting regulations that impede the market's capacity to operate efficiently. Following the decade of the 1980s, there was a change in the populist tendencies that were prevalent (Roberts, 2007). Following the transformation away from closed economic policies and import substitution industrialization, neoliberal policies emerged as the prevailing economic ideology. The populist politicians who assumed power adjusted their policies to align with the coming era of technological progress. During periods of economic crisis and transition, populism can assume a distinct function from its previous manifestations. These stages result in the decline of established institutions or elites, creating an opportunity for the mass constituencies to assume power and become the driving force behind demanding change. Taggart (2000) asserts that the populist movement does not bring about revolutionary transformation. It aligns with the reformist worldview but lacks the ability to bring about profound or transformative change. To sustain its stature, governing ordinary people requires exceptional leaders. That is completely reasonable. The issue of path dependency, however, is being ignored. The inability of populists to enact significant reforms derives from the obstacles posed by entrenched systems and well established conventions. As populists are constrained by the desires of their large voter base, they persist on this path until a disastrous collapse ensues.

3 Political economic approaches to power

Commons and Veblen

J.R. Commons was concerned with the power dynamic that exists between the various economic entities that were present in a particular economy. Commons (1934) states that the establishment of a stable economy necessitates an authority capable of bringing individuals to a consensus and minimizing conflicts. The government or the legislators are responsible for the establishment of this authority, which operates as a decision-making process (Gruncy, 1973). The conclusion that can be drawn from the viewpoint of Commons is that social discontent can never be resolved in the absence of an institutional strategy. In an economy where there is a lack of political will, conflicts of interest might arise between different individuals. If there are two individuals in the economy, the government may utilize its authority to establish a balance that eliminates power conflicts that would otherwise arise from each individual acting according to its own interest. Commons (1934: 342–345) underlined the government's ability to facilitate collective bargaining with labor organizations to mitigate conflicts in the workplace. The ideology of socialism was abandoned when governments began allowing members of the working class the liberty to bargain for higher wages. This lured people away from the notions of cooperative production. In the context of the connection between industries and employees, legislatures have the position to play a role. This unexpected outcome was also used as a critique of both liberal economists and communist economists due to the fact that they were unable to predict the role that institutions would play. Karl Marx was unable to anticipate that capitalism would be able to make a resurrection with the assistance of institutional reforms. The demands of workers were not taken into account throughout the evolution and competitiveness of industries. The labor legislation that was passed in opposition to the power of industries was what made possible the forced recovery. Countries that operate under a capitalist economy witnessed advancements in their labor regulations. According to Commons (1925a), even in the same year that Marx and Engels were drafting the Communist Manifesto, the United Kingdom was attempting to establish labor regulation that restricted the amount of time that women can work in a day to ten hours. It was also mentioned that even in Germany, where Bismarck was exerting all of his power to create control over socialists and trade unions, he was introducing the most advanced legislation that protects labor against overexploitation by capitalists. This was carried out to curb the influence of these factions. It was noticeable that Marxist socialism and the beliefs it espoused

DOI: 10.4324/9781003438090-3

were brought down by institutional change. In this regard, Marx was incapable of imagining the growth and evolution of trade unions, which structured their forms in opposition to the powers held in the industries of developed economies like the United States, the United Kingdom, France, and Germany. The progressive movement attempted to limit the number of hours that workers were had to put in as well as to compel wages beyond their natural and market-determined levels. Marx held the notion that dismantling capitalism as a system of economic production was the means by which the working class could make progress toward achieving its rights. Nevertheless, this class recognized the feasibility of upholding rights while concurrently conducting production within the capitalist system through the establishment of a fair distribution of authority grounded in ethical principles and consensus. Consequently, the class had the advantage of being positioned within the industrial system to get favorable working conditions, such as shorter work hours, improved earnings, and guaranteed employment. If they were able to secure their rights, they were willing to become staunch advocates of the system. Through its authority in legislation, enforcement, and legal interpretation, the government is capable of preserving the advantageous aspects of capitalism while curbing its detrimental features.

Veblen (2004) asserts that a constitutional government can be considered as a business government and therefore should not be relied upon to produce effective regulatory and economic policies. He expressed skepticism over the capacity of the constitutional government to offer genuine leadership (Tilman, 2007). He also argued that the government is inclined to prioritize the objectives of companies over those of the broader public (Atkinson, 2007). The constitutional government is a business government, and political parties represent nothing more than various circles of business interest (Plotkin, 2012). In institutional economics, the government functions as a political instrument. In the case of Commons, the government has the ability to strive toward the creation of a balanced connection between individuals. According to Veblen, the role of the government is limited to that of a guardian of the interests of corporations (Spithoven, 2018). Veblen explains how a government may be accommodating to the needs of corporate organizations. In his view, the role of the government is to investigate various potential opportunities leading to the expansion of existing enterprises within the economy. He analyzed market conditions from the perspective of industries to determine how capitalist industries function and how the government maintains their interests. In contrast, the governments of Argentina and Türkiye have traditionally granted the working class a significantly higher level of authority. Business interests have been disregarded due to concerns about diminishing their political influence. Consequently, the issue is approached in a distinct manner in both countries. Furthermore, the intricate harmony of sovereignty that Commons delineated is not functioning as planned. Given the ongoing development of these economies, it is impractical to expect the presence of major corporations that can exert more influence on government policies than the working class. As an outcome of growing disparity, the working class wields a more significant influence on government policies. Nevertheless, through implementing structural modifications in wage-labor dynamics and reducing the prioritization of corporation interests, governments can potentially serve as a tool for substantial assistance to the working class. The working class includes those employed in various segments of the labor force, including workers, public servants, and individuals earning the minimum wage, throughout all production sectors. The wage–labor relationship and the nature of competition have an impact on transfer payments and public expenditures. The government's implementation of laws, regulations, and rules has a crucial role in determining the prevalence of different institutional forms. Consequently, a change in the growth model could result in various alterations in the structure of institutional forms. The government has a crucial role in both establishing and advancing the growth model as well as resolving any potential crises that may arise. The major institutional vehicle that is responsible for creating changes in the forms that institutions adopt is the government. When a government is founded on an ideology, other institutional forms have to be altered to conform to the political vision that underpins the authority. The ideology is adaptable and may be modified to fit the needs of society. The government is in charge of controlling the power. When political groups come to power, they bring about changes in the way institutions are structured, which in turn produces new elites. Roberts (2007) noted that populism's political popularity in Latin America went through periods of both prominence and obscurity. A form of state-led capitalist growth known as import substitution industrialization was at the center of populism's engagement in Latin American politics. It provided the government with the authority to utilize and extend benefits to constituencies who were working class or lower class. According to Mudde and Kaltwasser (2012), populism is a political style that is characterized by the promotion of a specific kind of connection between political leaders and voters. Populism is designed to attract people who experience a sense of alienation from their government. This relationship is founded on a strategy of appealing to large groups of people, which may be characterized by a lack of strict principles or a willingness to take advantage of opportunities to secure electoral victory or exert political influence. This political relationship is formed through the utilization of institutional forms. The examination of institutions brings us into direct contact with norms, regulations, and other sets of entitlements that shape and influence individual actions. In both economics and politics, individual acts constitute a common element. The distribution of power has the capacity to influence action. However, consensus can be attained in both economics and politics when the market is influenced by the free will and active participation of a significant number of individuals.

The concept of Commons symbolizes pluralism, which is another name for democracy and the formulation of its policies. The concept of pluralism refers to an institutional framework that competes with populism and elitism. It is not against the desire of marginalized groups or minority communities. It expresses disapproval toward social hierarchies driven by the pursuit of economic gain through rent-seeking. It ensures the inclusion of all segments of society in the formulation of policies and their active involvement in the decision-making process. Consequently, the system establishes a state of harmony, even in situations where specific social classes lack the capacity to exert influence over decision-making processes. There are no restrictions on the involvement of underprivileged organizations or communities in politics. This perspective is essentially in conflict with the populist approach to the formulation of policies. The philosophy of Commons, as well as the field of institutional economics, revolves around the reasonable process of policy formation that is built on diversity and conflicting values. Nonetheless, it is essential to comprehend that institutions perform the dual function of freeing and limiting the acts of individuals. The current institutional forms should be regarded as a reflection of scarcities, purpose, values, economic strategies, and political processes. Individuals will begin participating in activities that are more cost-effective after the necessary institutions have been established. Commons described this mechanism using arguments for reasonable value. The difference between reasonable and unreasonable demands, as well as between willing and unwilling obedience, may be a source of conflict. For the purpose of understanding populism, which is a structure that is antagonistic to pluralism, the concept of the reasonable (democratic) process of policy formation must be utilized and developed. One other interpretation refers to this concept is collective democracy (Chasse, 2017). In a world where resources are scarce, disputes are resolved by the authorities according to standards of reasonable value and reasonable practices. The necessities for freedom, equality, and the balance of competing forces gave rise to these principles, and these principles relied upon all of the competing interests of economic actors. The disagreements over scarcity provide the government with the justification to use legislative tactics to achieve the reasonable stability of capitalism (Commons, 1925a). It can be essential to make use of the theory of reasonable value, which evaluates economic actions in light of ethics, public welfare, and the national public interest in modern economies. The term reasonable value does not refer to the opinions of individuals that are deemed to be reasonable. There is a possibility that several perspectives held by numerous individuals may be considered to be reasonable. The reasonable value is a choice that has been legitimized by the central authority and is formed in such a way as to decrease the number of conflicts. It should be objective, measurable, and obligatory (Commons, 1936). A decision that protects the national interests should be pursued if it is reasonable and optimal. It is well known that each nation has different priorities that shape its democratic process. Different leaders and voters in various nations have different ideas about the function of institutions. However, a bargaining transaction can influence four parties: buyers, sellers, disappointed buyers, and disappointed sellers. Persuasion and coercion are notions used in bargaining. Persuasion will prevail when bargaining power is equal (Bromley, 2006). If not, there will be coercion in the bargaining process. Therefore, reasonable policies should be created by taking into account economic activity, requirements of the general welfare, and national interests.

According to Commons (1924), wage bargaining and industrialism should take into account the free will of the working class without imposing any kind of deprivation. There should be a reasonable distribution of power between the employer and the employees doing the actual work. There is no truth to the assertion that industries are the owners of labor or that labor is the property of industries. The free worker may choose whether or not to take a job. There is no responsibility that emerges on the side of the employer to continue employing him, and there is also no obligation that develops for the worker to remain in their current position. In most scenarios, there cannot be any situation in which the employer is able to fire an employee for disobeying a work order or being enjoined from his job. Hence, the employment contract is a renewal of agreements at any moment based on the continuing of what is regarded to be reasonable. On the side of the employer, there ought to be good service, and on the side of the employee, there ought to be satisfactory working conditions and satisfactory compensation. The contract needs to include a clause stipulating that it is predicated on each moment that the worker continues to create and that the employer approves his work. The worker does not have ownership rights to the position, and the employer is under no obligation to continue to employ him. Since the worker is consistently providing a service that the company is actively accepting, the worker has the liberty to continue bargaining with the employer. The ongoing renewal of the contract is a requirement that must be fulfilled. There is no power that can be exercised over other individuals. The mutual understanding of two parties serves as the foundation for the contract. Workers have the ability to actively pursue job opportunities in the labor market. While a worker is employed, he continues to produce goods and engage in bargaining since these two activities cannot be separated. The worker must maintain a high level of production to preserve his right to negotiate. As long as the worker continues to contribute anything, he retains this privilege. His technique of negotiating is contingent on his providing something for the employer, and whatever he produces must be of a quality that is consistent with the standards of his method of bargaining. The goodwill of the employer is the worker's property, and the good will of the worker is the employer's property. Furthermore, if one party is privileged while the other is not, this indicates that the privileged party does not rely on the other party's willingness to cooperate but rather on the unavailability of other options. As long as there is no goodwill shown by either side, there will not be a healthy balance of power in the sense that we understand the concept. Commons specifically asserted that the court has a responsibility to ensure a balance between employees and industries that aim to terminate workers who join a trade union. Associations of workers, as opposed to associations of property owners, may be formed and have their rights protected via legislation. This legislation has the potential to create a power dynamic that is more equitable among economic entities. Even though one group is far weaker than the other, the pluralism principle still holds true. It was brought to the attention of Commons that the employment contract is written in accordance with an understanding. The will is not a meaningless choice. While doing one activity rather than another, there need to be options for varying degrees of power rather than just one.

The will does not possess the capacity to exercise its freedom of choice by selecting nothing. It needs to decide on anything since resources are limited. It is required to choose the option that is superior than the others. If the option being considered is a desirable one, then the intention to change is genuine and open to being swayed by rational argument. The will is coerced when the alternative is not a preferable one. The employees are looking for protection from both physical aggression and economic pressure. The conditions of the workers drew criticism from the Commons. The government does not condone the use of coercive economic tactics. Because of its severe punishments and many inducements to conformity, such as the dread of becoming impoverished, industrial government is the foundation upon which economic coercion is constructed. The working class strives to realize its ideals via the establishment of protections against the political and financial influence of employers. While he made the point that there is evidently a need for a new equity, which ought to be the equity that would protect the employment in the same way that the earlier equity protected the industries. A strike is a tactic that may be used by a trade union to coerce an employer into accepting the conditions of the union's demands. This is accomplished by using the union's economic strength to threaten the employer with a financial loss. The court has the authority to approve an injection if it believes that the public significance of the interests of the industries is higher than those of the trade unions. It is within its power to deny the intervention request if it is of the opinion that the public significance of the labor union is higher than that of the employers' organization. Both the union and the employer have the potential to be the party that causes harm in any scenario. The court evaluates the advantages to the general public as well as the public interest and then attempts to decide which kind of loss is the least severe. Instead of only serving the interests of the economic actors, the balance of power also serves the interests of the nation. Additionally, he made note of how labor is becoming more powerful, which ought to help market participants understand its legal rights. In an institutional sense, a power struggle might be described as taking place between the principles of labor and the prerogatives of capitalism and the industries. Employers and their own labor managers have the ability to take over the restraining effects that employees have on free competition. It is possible for organized labor to achieve participation with management in the protection of their jobs, just as the barons and capitalists were able to achieve participation with the King in the protection of their property and businesses. Therefore, a common law of labor should be founded on the principle of maintaining a balance of power while also maintaining a separation of powers. The working class ought to be managed by selecting behaviors that are reasonable, rejecting the harmful practices of labor, and depriving both labor unions and management of their arbitrary influence over the market.

Commons outlines in great detail the proper economic relationship that should exist between the working class, the government, and the industry. In any scenario, the industries should also not give the impression that they have the authority to restrict the free will of the labor, and the workforce itself should avoid producing harm that is in conflict with the public interest. General sentiment needs to play a deciding role, but it should not invest solely in one side to gain popularity. There should not be any authority that may be used arbitrarily over the market. It ought to choose the course of action that inflicts the least amount of harm on society. All of these processes are rejected by populism. It provides prominence to the working class while simultaneously reducing the influence of industries by either nationalizing them or restricting the activity of production facilities. If a populist party is successful in gaining power across the working class for the sake of its own interests, then the public interest will be the option that is considered to be the last resort. The function of the court can be to disregard common sense when necessary. It is possible to exclude some industries. The working class has access to a significant amount of power, which might lead to a decision-making process that is unreasonable. Given that there is no decision that is devoid of options, it is necessary to make a selection.

The concept of elitism is intricately linked to Veblen's evolutionary perspective, wherein he posited that the government functions as a mechanism to uphold the interests of industries and enterprises. Elites, who are regarded as the most admirable people in the nation, are the ones who determine how the industry operates. The American government and rising property prices provide cover for the predatory business elites who run the country. Institutional forms that are grounded on business values provide an atmosphere that is consistent and secure. This leisure class kept its hold on the society by imposing its conservative beliefs on it. This is bolstered by the influence that this class has a wide range of business operations (Stabile, 1987). The business elites believe that the only objective worth pursuing is capital growth. Productivity is thus of little significance. Veblen argues that this circumstance results in a confrontation between the business elites and the working class. Despite this, he also proposed the establishment of an industrial structure that would exercise authority over the working class and the nation as a government. Engineers are the appropriate professionals to develop this structure (Stabile, 1986). Veblen was critical of the business elites of his day because they were unable to effectively manage the industries they controlled and instead devoted their time, energy, and expertise to nonproductive endeavors. Veblen posited the emergence of a novel form of elitism that undermines traditional institutions of business elites, despite the people being affected by these elites and their activities being supported by the government. Consequently, an alternative trajectory for evolution may be initiated. He prioritized the capacity of engineers with a robust educational foundation and valuable technical expertise to advance and foster diverse industries. To be more precise, he was clearly suggesting a technocratic kind of elitism, which is capable of playing a significant part in the decision-making process. The industrial sector of the economy is an example of the kind of elitism described by Veblen, which is founded on a new business class or technocrats. These industrial elites have a position of dominating control over the workforce. The industrial and technical republic is the society that Veblen envisioned as the ideal human civilization. The requirements of the populace should be prioritized by the republic in terms of economic policy. For businesses to operate effectively, there has to be a stratum of technocrats comprised of professionals such as economists, engineers, technicians, and trained employees who are able to wield authority and organize the labor in service of new goals. He did not provide any details on the methods that could be required to ascertain the perspectives of the labor force (Tilman, 1972). The assertion that Veblen's idea was founded on technocratic elitism can be still controversial, and there is room for debate regarding this point. However, so long as there is no pluralism and no institutional forms to establish a balance of power and separation of power, it will not be simple to remark that the concept does not belong to an elite ruling class. In addition, a system that lacks institutional reform based on pluralism is more likely to become either elitist or populist over time. The labor force is the foundation upon which Veblen built his utopian system, often known as scientific collectivism. It is likely that a policy that aims to give disproportionate power to the working class to attract the mass constituencies for revolution will, in its initial stage, fall into populism. A new elite class will be likely to emerge to control the people as long as there is no institutional form that can minimize the probability of this phenomenon. Instead of industrial engineering, the term institutional engineering more accurately describes this issue.

Populism is not compatible with extreme political philosophies such as fascism or Marxism. This is the reason why it does not have a particularly strong ideological base. Thus, when populist governments lose elections, it is not difficult to understand that society is going to quickly forget about their political parties. This is just transitory because of a lack of commitment and philosophy. Nonetheless, radical ideologies have remained in existence for longer than populist parties have throughout the course of many decades. This situation suggests that the regulating function of the relationships in the infrastructure is generated in a rigorous way in the superstructure. Several eras may be distinguished from one another based on socioeconomic factors. The social structure and kind of accumulation that a country is in will define the type of economic system. Altering the growth model does not in and of itself signify a shift in the mode of production. It is possible to maintain outdated and inflexible institutional structures. The characteristics may be found within the framework of the macroeconomic configuration. If the institutional changes that are taking place in the systematic structure are not an economic revolution, and if the changes that are taking place within the currently dominant production system themselves resuscitate it and help it reproduce itself, then this demonstrates that that mode of production is still in existence.

Three approaches are evolving as a result of institutional reforms in various countries. Figure 3.1 presents these approaches and their characteristics. These ideas can be applied to explicitly classify political structures. Each category has its own unique characteristics, which could be capable of explaining subsequent political developments in economic systems. The number of categorizations may be raised by going deeper into the characteristics. Nonetheless, taking into consideration these three headlines is one way to assess the political status of a country. The philosophy of Commons is mirrored in pluralism. This is a democratic approach to how social and economic activities ought to be perceived. It accomplishes this without taking into account the economic actors' individual levels of power inside the economy, and as a result, maintains the delicate balance of power that exists between those actors. This strategy does not allow for consolidated authority to be held in one place. In other words, it is necessary to ensure that there is not only a balance of power but also a separation of power between strong actors and weak actors in the scenario. The approach is adaptable and can be utilized to lessen path dependency. Finding innovative solutions to conflicts requires more of a revolutionary approach when applied to institutional forms. In addition, it is the foundation

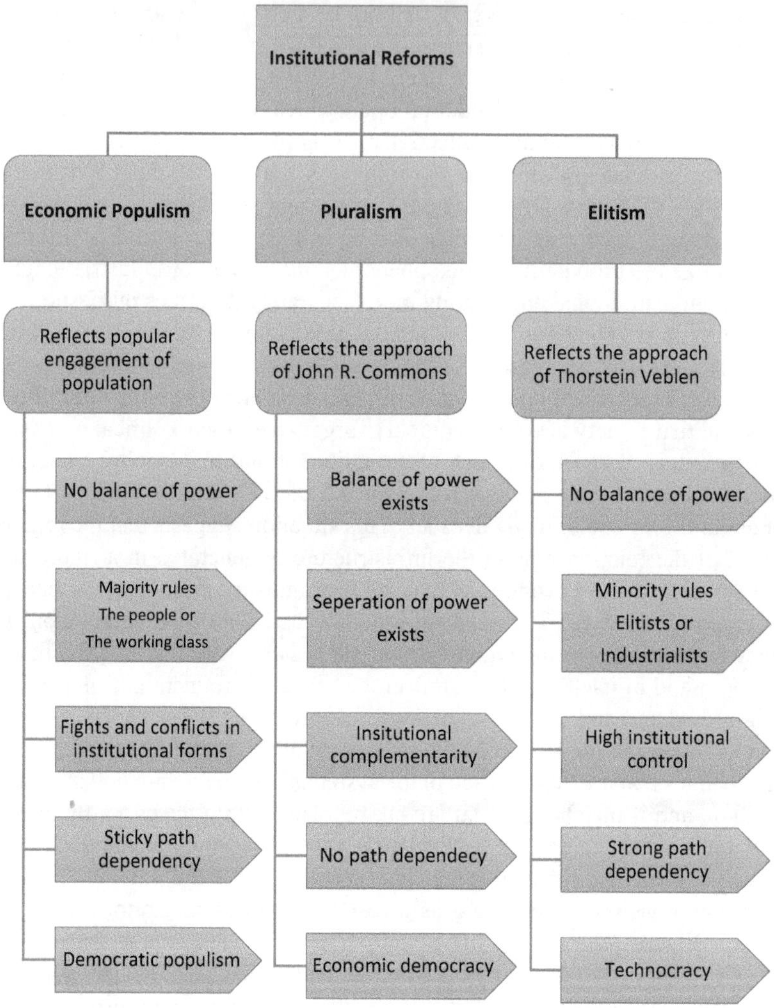

Figure 3.1 Trajectory of institutional reforms in political systems

upon which economic democracy is built. It lends credence to the concept that economic power ought to be redistributed from powerful actors to those with less power. As a consequence, there is the potential for economic actors to achieve a balance. The concept of Commons is one of the conditions that is very challenging to realize in a social setting. In spite of this, the door is left open for institutional adjustments to be made to lessen the number of tensions. Because of this, the approach is both novel and fundamental. The countries that adhere to democratic principles are the ones that deserve consideration under this category. Commons exhibit both institutional complementarity and economic democracy. Essentially, any economic uncertainty may work to the detriment of a nation. According to

Commons (1925b), high production costs, economic cycles, and organized labor are essential factors that have to be taken into consideration for the purpose of maintaining continuous output in industries. Classical economics, which focused on the liberty of labor, did not previously take these aspects into account. For him, organized labor is more likely to enhance daily wages quicker and higher during periods of inflation and to attempt to keep them up even if there is a collapse in the prices of goods and services. In the event that the cost of production is high, business owners and workers alike might pass the increased expense on to customers to maintain high levels of profitability and salary levels. Nonetheless, each individual has the potential to act both as a producer and a consumer in the end. The high cost of products bought results in losses for both the customer and the manufacturer, particularly in terms of business and employment. If the economic turmoil that is brought on by uncertainty could be removed, the cost of manufacturing for consumers may be decreased. Producers would witness a rise in industrial production and employment. In a market in which all dynamics are related to one another and have a part in maintaining economic stability.

When implementing institutional reforms and pursuing consensus within the framework of pluralism, it is essential to consider not just power dynamics and interests but also ethical standards to progress toward an appropriate outcome. There should be an established framework for consensus building that can effectively encourage economic participants to freely adhere to the requirements. Institutional economics aims to provide a set of acceptable standards as an ethical framework for the process of reforming institutions in a democratic nation that is based on the presence of multiple values and ideologies. The implementation and elucidation of institutional change should be undertaken to convince individuals with divergent interests and values, therefore fostering a comprehensive consensus. Ethical frameworks acquire significance when they may be applied universally in any culture or economic context. Hence, institutional reforms have to be grounded on ethical principles that provide the rationale for the validity of arguments, which are validated by scientific methodologies. To clarify, it is necessary to establish a structured consensus among the actors. The term for this is the reasonableness criterion, and it constitutes a fundamental characteristic of democratic societies (Fujita et al., 2023). Institutional economics must identify the prominent barrier behind economic turbulence to create a profound transformation via the use of a robust scientific foundation. One conceivable method to democratic institutional changes that could assist in reducing the potential hazards of political interests is the establishment of an observatory commission and the implementation of consensus-building tactics. This strategy could substantially convince and establish credibility for developing plans for institutional reforms.

The methodology of Veblen is more evolutionary in nature, focusing on the advancement of technology. On the other hand, the delicate balance of power is disregarded. There is no check and balance on authority. In other words, there is no separation of powers. The technocrats and the working class need to collaborate in a manner that is compatible with one another. In spite of this, those with higher social status and more expertise would hold positions of authority.

This would lend an air of elitism to the concept that Veblen developed. When a society has been established via a revolutionary process, it is able to establish its own elite class, which is able to subdue the strength of the working class and the functional organs of government. In this circumstance, the individuals who make up the minority would control the majority of the population. Those with lower levels of education and who are not held in as high regard cannot hold positions of authority. It is possible to alter the institutional structures such that they favor elitists. In addition, it may be used to prevent other organizations from participating in the decision-making process. Institutions are exposed to an extensive amount of control to ensure the safety of society's upper crust, which is at the forefront of technological advances. As a result, there would be a significant degree of path dependency on the revolutionary ideology and principles. This political arrangement is more characteristic of a technocracy than a democracy. There are nations throughout the world that were founded by revolutions and thus have a minority elite that dominates the system. Maybe not every nation in the world satisfies the political definition of Veblen, but many countries come close. This may occur due to either ideological movements or military interventions. Moreover, elitism is antagonistic toward pluralism (Hawkins, 2010). Hence, elitists are of the opinion that high-ranking organizations, such as the military, intellectuals, property and company owners, educated individuals, and aristocrats, should have the power to control the common people and the economic connections inside the nation. It undermines the theoretical basis of institutional economics, which is based on the decision-making process and the distribution of power. It also rejects the ideals that are held by the ordinary individual. This runs completely against democratic principles and the will of the people.

A new political strategy, which I refer to as economic populism, has the potential to be developed via the modification of institutional forms. Because of the essential institutional reforms that, if they are driven by the popular participation of the people, have the potential to create a new political structure, the system fails to adequately acknowledge the concerns of industrialists and elites. Instead of being invested in the modernization of the economy, a significant amount of benefits is retained for the working class by the government. Both the government and the working class have the ability to participate in the political arena on issues that are of particular interest to the general population. Thus, there is an absence of division of powers. The bilateral interaction is fueled by the demands of the working class and the supplies of the government. As a consequence, the government addresses the demands of the working class based on the prevailing public demand. In other words, the individuals comprising the majority wield influence over the system. Political objectives are pursued via the exercise of control over institutions. Hence, there is no systematic approach to dealing with the economic challenges in a way that is reasonable. This will lead to conflicts in various institutional forms. When the fiscal policy is expansionary, but the central bank is required to conduct a contractionary monetary policy, this is a scenario that may be witnessed, such as a case in populist economies. A nation has the option to choose a development strategy focused on export-driven growth while simultaneously having institutions that can effectively handle growth fueled by domestic consumption. This reveals a deficiency in the compatibility between institutions. There would be a persistent path dependency. Even if the administration was to announce future plans for additional institutional reforms, the degree of advancement would not significantly improve. In this system, the government's stance and its actions would be justified via periodic elections and referendums. Therefore, democracy is not discarded but utilized to accomplish the objectives of populism. Populism may harbor a dominant power structure that might hinder the intellectual identities and pursuits of scholars. This is in direct opposition to the principles of pluralistic activities and the harmony of power. It is effective in dismantling the institutions that are responsible for maintaining the separation of power. It disrupts every social and economic equilibrium, and then, it uses this disruption as a source of legitimacy in its efforts to gather people and rescue the nation. If this does not change, there is a very real risk that the economy would completely crumble. For populist politicians, if there is no such government, then other groups and old institutions will have the ability to split the nation apart and encourage adversaries to invade, transform society, and control the markets and resources of the region. Populism hinders the establishment of any form of economic equilibrium within an institutional framework. Only individuals who adhere to government policies are eligible to receive benefits distributed by the government. Political affiliations serve as the primary motivator for all economic endeavors, and it is imperative that these affiliations remain aligned with power.

4 What is populism?

It is difficult to provide a clear definition of populism. It lacks any specific characteristics that may be identified. It is possible for its meaning to change depending on the political atmosphere at the time, making it a slippery concept overall. It is fruitless and disappointing to search for a definition of populism that perfectly captures its essence (Taggart, 2000). Nevertheless, this can at most apply to populism in politics. In the context of politics, the term populism refers to an ideology that glorifies the rule of the people as the ultimate authority. It is possible for homogeneous groups of people to mobilize against elites like politicians, intellectuals, and the media as well as against perceived dangers like immigrants or other marginalized groups. Legitimacy is a strategy that populism uses to demonstrate that it represents the people. In certain nations, populism is fashioned in a way that helps to promote a liberal economy, but in other nations, populism works against a free-market economy. It does not only arise as a reaction against existing power structures but is also a method of defending an authority that is already established. It has deep roots in both elitism and antielitism as ideologies. A wide definition of elitism might include political elites, the state, intellectuals, and economic forces like production centers and unions. It is generally recognized that populism is a legitimate strategy for winning support, and its foundations might lie either in right- or left-wing ideology (Jagers and Walgrave, 2007). Its objective is to convince the vast majority of the people to mobilize behind a certain political party, social movement, or ideological stance. To organize the masses, it uses strategies based on capitalizing on popular topics (Canovan, 1999; Lyrintzis, 1987). The populist power that works to abolish the dominant power is strengthened by social mobilization, which is a critical part in the process. People get a boost of inspiration from populism, which encourages them to become involved in politics and provides them with an alternative way to exercise their will. Thus, a new government is established in which the people want to reject the practices of the previous ones. The people have strong aspirations that the system can either be reevaluated or radical institutional reforms can be created. Populist governments are masters at manipulating the expectations of their supporters. It is possible for the mass constituents of a nation to be lured to support their political leader by a utopian vision of the country. Populism may be disconnected from reality, making it difficult to assess and implement essential reforms. In such a scenario, progressive populism comes to an end, and political

DOI: 10.4324/9781003438090-4

populism takes its place, with the latter working to further its own interests rather than that of the people to whom it makes promises.

Institutional issues are another aspect of populism. These elements arose as a result of the postwar party system and other economic coalitions, such as employers' associations and trade unions. The contributions of average citizens were given more weight in the political system. Thus, it is up to the government to demonstrate that it serves the needs of ordinary people (Zaslove, 2008). By appealing to 'the will of the people' and placing an emphasis on the preferences of the majority, populism is a political ideology that supports the principles shared by the majority (Boxill, 1997). Agrarian classes and peasant movements in the United States and Europe, as well as intellectual middle-class movements in Russia, were the driving forces behind the rise of populism in those regions (Mudde and Kaltwasser, 2012). Movements in Russia are regarded as an early indicator of populism. The transition away from feudalism in economic systems made it possible for farmers to develop organized movements, which led to the rise of the peasant class. The demand of the peasants was closely tied to economic concerns. Rural workers made endeavors to enhance their economic position and secure the right to choose the market value of their products in the United States. In this scenario, economic populism actually originates as a reaction to free markets and the pricing mechanism of the dynamic interaction between demand and supply. These movements were also directed against the authority that was possessed by established institutions, elites, and politicians. Intellectuals were the driving force behind antiimperial uprisings in certain other parts of the globe, which were led by protest movements. To establish Marxist movements geared against the tsarist political structure, these intellectuals focused their strategies on the peasantry. The intellectuals who came from the aristocratic and bourgeois classes collaborated with those from lower strata to spread the socialist doctrine. Russia was not a participant in the industrialization and economic revolutions that occurred in Europe. Peasants were deemed to be of the same social status as proletarians. Hence, there was a possibility for a revolution by the working class in Russia (Wortman, 1967). Under the flag of communism, the concept of people who longed for equality began to take shape. Increasing tensions among peasants and slaves gave momentum for the tsarist authorities to distribute lands and outlaw slavery to maintain their control on the population. This was a limited reform intended to decrease the speed of mass movements. In the end, this sparked revolutionary movements directed against established institutions. To keep the military class pleased in the Ottoman Empire, sultans provided them both social and economic privileges. Alternatively, such a situation might have resulted in discontentment among the elite class, prompting them to demand a new sultan and further privileges. After the empire had the ability to lessen the influence of the military class, the foundations of democracy began to take shape. Within the realm of the empire, intellectuals made use of their abilities to establish a parliament with the purpose of constraining the authority of sultans. In other words, by the time of the constitutional monarchies, the very first step toward creating pluralism had already been taken. This also suggests that populism can be a dynamic force under various sorts of regimes as long as a popular sovereignty can form to claim equality, justice, and economic rights. With the end of the First World War, the culture of rudimentary democracy had the opportunity to maintain its existence. It was eventually determined that the only legitimate power to govern the nation was the parliament. Due to the people's allegiance to the empire, it was easier to maintain control over large groups of constituents, in contrast to other regions of the globe. Nevertheless, the war provided an opportunity to overthrow this structure. In the decades after the Great Depression and the collapse of the world's great empires, the rise of populism coincided with the emergence of modern political parties and their subsequent ascent to power. A vital component of both pluralism and competition is populism. Emerging in direct opposition to one another were a plethora of conflicting philosophies. Furthermore, other definitions of political populism have emerged, including populist democracy, populist dictatorship, authoritarian populism, constitutional populism, and others.

Populism refers to a wide notion that is often used by political scholars. However, depending on the area of research interest, populism may have a variety of meanings. The possibility that populism may be concretely defined in social, economic, and other fields is still an open topic. Since scholars disagree on how to conceptualize populism, a wide variety of political parties, governments, institutions, and individuals could be classified as populists (Weyland, 2001). Despite the fact that populism is difficult to describe, it is possible to classify this idea under a few different headings. According to Mudde (2004), there are two primary interpretations that can be taken on the concept of populism. The first is that populism is heavily reliant on rhetoric that is both emotionally charged and overly simplified. It makes advantage of the feelings and pains of people. Something sentimental and straightforward is far more appealing to it than something intellectual and serious. Slogans are the backbone of campaign politics. The second argument is that populism is regarded as a method for analyzing exploitative policymaking. Appeasing people and earning their support take precedence over finding the solution that makes the most reasonable sense. The populist movement is often viewed to be a struggle between the people and the elites. The movement against more powerful classes in politics is paid by the common people. To clarify the defining characteristic of populism is that it strives to represent and unite the people under shared interests against the antagonists of the people, such as wealthy minorities, international organizations, and elites (Rodrik, 2018b). This political strategy has the potential to be risky if employed against entities that are regarded as the established order. In particular, there will not be a separation of powers, free media, or an independent judicial system in emerging countries since these nations have not yet established robust democratic structures. Populist regimes that attempt to manipulate the people via the judiciary and the media have the potential to erode democracy. This allows populists to retain control for longer. Populists engage in the practice of politicizing state institutions such as the courts, security forces, tax agencies, and electoral authorities to undermine their opponents (Levitsky and Loxton, 2013). A clear separation between the common people and the ruling elites is essential to populism. There are good people and bad ones on both sides of a political fight. In this context, good refers to the people on whose behalf populist governments strive for their advantage, whereas bad refers to the elites with whom ordinary people should confront. People are portrayed as being truthful and virtuous, but elites are characterized as being fraudulent and corrupt. There is a stark divide between political factions and governments that adhere to populist ideologies (Kaltwasser, 2018). A national divide is established in populism, with 'us' on one side and 'them' on the other. Others that are a part of them may be considered elites. Populists are the saviors, defenders, and real guarantors of the people, and they are also the avengers of the people against them. No matter what it is, political groups or elites have to show respect for the sovereignty of the people. Liberal democracies often exhibit the pattern of holding elections that are free and fair. Thus, populist authorities are antagonistic against liberal democracy and the free market economy. This is due to the fact that liberal democracy is an institutional system that was specifically designed to sever the nexus between populists and mass constituencies. There would be a strong emphasis on individual liberty and free enterprise. Institutions such as the central bank would be free-standing and self-governing, and they would not be subject to the sway of votes cast or the size of the population. Populists believe that elites and minorities can benefit from autonomous organizations. In this way, they would justify the use of power over formerly independent bodies. The desire of the people for a more populist administration is also an important driving force for the rise of these parties. If mass constituencies have the perception that elites and established institutions are working for the benefit of the system rather than for the will of the people, populist governments could gain more support to work against these structures.

Populism can be described by the personalities of national leaders and their political philosophies. There is no one coherent theory that can be applied to populism. According to Mudde (2004), populism is a thin-centered ideology, which means that it can easily be coupled with quite diverse ideologies such as communism, socialism, liberalism, nationalism, and ecologism. To promote political goals in a way that is attractive to the people, ideological components are required. De la Torre (2000) makes the observation that populist policies are founded on the actions of crowds. Occupations of public areas are carried out by groups of individuals with the intention of becoming politically active and voicing their demands for integration. These people are employed by the leaders to instill fear in their opponents. Mass constituencies begin to have the impression that they are genuine and honest participants. Working in the name of a leader has the potential to become more essential than respect for pluralism. Barr (2009) argues that the concept of populism is murky since its meaning changes depending on aspects such as culture, political movements, political styles, and regions. Populism can be characterized as a mass movement that is headed by outsiders or dominant leaders who strive to achieve and maintain power by antielite appeals and plebiscitary links. In this regard, a movement or party cannot be considered populist if it adheres to policies that are advantageous to insiders and does not provide policies that are hostile to the establishment. The conventional understanding of populism is to provide an alternative to the practices of preexisting institutions. To some scholars, the importance of a populist leader's personalism cannot be overstated when attempting to identify that politician as a populist. To define populism, it might be vital to have charismatic leaders who desire to battle against established elites and the ideologies they defend (Barr, 2009). Individual aspirations have the potential to mobilize large groups of people depending on their loyalty. Personalistic leadership is not based on ideologies, communities, organizations, or other variables of any kind; rather, it is focused on the allegiance of people. People are free to disapprove of politics and need not necessarily belong to any particular ideology. They have the ability to look for certain characteristics in those who would rule the nation. Nevertheless, it is important to be aware that there have been populist leaders in the past who lacked charisma and had a less personalistic approach to leadership. A leader's charisma is an advantageous source for gaining support and instilling trust in both politicians' ability to perform and the population's belief. Because of this quality, it would be much simpler to direct the public toward achieving political goals. It is not enough to describe a government as populist, as Müller (2016) noted, since populism might rely on the criticism of elites. Otherwise, it would be sufficient to label a charismatic party leader as populist only by speaking out against the status quo. If this was the case, then any leader who follows campaigns against an existing organization would be considered a populist. However, focusing just on criticism of elites would not be sufficient to investigate populist behavior. Although populists seem to be in conflict with antipluralists, they assert that they represent the vast majority of the general population. When governments are unable to live up to people's expectations, it can lead to a severe loss of support. Some of the people can be represented by a single party, but there are no remainders when it comes to populist parties. Even though they do not make up the majority of society, populists believe them to be genuine people. The only thing that matters is that the genuine individuals be together, and everyone else is irrelevant. Only these people should be eligible for the legal protection, but those who do not share the same political perspective need to be dealt with in a different manner. Therefore, when they are in power, they can take considerable action against opponents. This results in a significant increase in the degree of polarization in society. Individuals or organizations that are opposed to the policies of a populist administration are likewise antagonistic against the legitimate people. Government actions that deviate from established norms or standards should not be regarded unethical, as long as they are undertaken to benefit genuine individuals and achieve their objectives. This may also be employed to generate individuals with homogenous characteristics. Nevertheless, it may be defined as government policies that are formulated based on the welfare of the public. Populism is contingent upon a dedication to implementing policies that are advantageous to the people. The market conditions may potentially foster the emergence of populism. It has the capacity to focus on social concerns or political crises. There is no one explanation that can be provided. Each academic area has the capacity to examine populism from a distinct perspective.

The origins of populism might differ significantly across diverse nations. Right-wing political parties across Europe are often opposed to immigration. Latin American countries exhibit a distinct political landscape, with the left-wing ideology firmly entrenched in positions of power. The concept of populism is explained as a method for the process of policy formation. The populist movement is a political philosophy that encourages people to have optimistic expectations for the future. Targeting ordinary people is one of the primary characteristics of populism. A political party or movement that combines the philosophies of the left and the right can govern populism. Formation of policy might include opposition to multinational corporations, wealthy families, and other financial interests. The circumstances of a nation might cause shifts in political movements. If socialism is the prevailing ideology in a system that is in the process of crumbling, then populism might be structured to combat this ideology and become the dominant system. Liberals, conservatives, nationalists, and socialists can all appeal to different parts of the population. Populism is capable of making criticisms of existing institutions by using a democratic system. It opposes the ideology of powerful elites and rejects formal institutions as the embodiment of the people. Leaders of populist organizations often attempt to innovate new methods of population control or to undermine existing institutional procedures. The use of speech in the process of enacting changes is the most essential component of populism. The ordinary people who live in challenging political, economic, or social situations find this expression to be highly appealing. When leaders possess the capacity to manipulate institutions, laws, or norms, populism may transform into a distinct kind of policy development referred to as authoritarian populism. Even if populism is a form of tempting people, this occurs when it is applied inside a democratic system. The notion that the silent majority plays a crucial role in democracy is fundamental to populist political movements. Under populist administrations, elections are the time and place for the majority of people to break their silence and speak out against the ruling elite. Political regimes frequently utilize elections as a platform for democratic engagement. Nevertheless, it is evident that their policies primarily aim to enhance their degree of popularity. According to Müller (2016), populists do not oppose elites when they themselves are the ones leading the people, and they do not oppose representation when they themselves are the ones representing the people. Policymakers are implementing actions that align with the preferences of the majority of people. Hence, the responsibility for the outcomes will not fall solely on a single governmental entity but rather on the people.

As was highlighted by Müller (2016), there is also the noninstitutionalized notion of people to consider while discussing the political process. An influential leader has the ability to guide a disorganized group of individuals to achieve success via their strategic campaign endeavors. There is a silent majority or majority population, but they are not institutionalized. It is reasonable to presume that his notion precisely mirrors political perspectives. While acknowledging that populists tend to prioritize institutions that serve their own political goals, it is important to recognize that this does not invalidate the existence of populism via institutional reform, suggesting that it is institutionalized. The notion that established institutions may be the driving force for populism is overlooked. In the field of economics, there is a lack of consensus over the definition of populism, similar to the lack of consensus in the realm of politics. The term is subject to interpretation and might be construed differently by researchers. A populist movement may be characterized by the implementation of expansionary economic policies and the widespread distribution of incentives to the public. Expansionary policies are crucial tools for maintaining the support of the general population. However, Weyland (2001) pointed out that the political investigation of economic populism might be ambiguous. This is due to the fact that expansionary economic policies are able to be developed by the option of the government, whether it be parliament refusing to raise taxes to fund extra expenditure or other authorities working for the benefit of the masses. He points out that all of the ways are identical and that these approaches might be regarded as examples of economic populism. Thus, he argues that the political definition of populism is superior because it situates populism as a specific way of competing for and exerting political power. When economic populism is taken into consideration, concerns over the budget and expenditure are greatly decreased. In this work, populism can be interpreted in terms of economics, and it is institutionalized by means of regulations, norms, and rules. Thus, the debate of economic populism is different in perception from the discussion of political populism. Institutions may indeed yield unexpected consequences, and it is not just populist regimes that bear responsibility for such outcomes. Therefore, despite a change in government via political elections, the new administration may still be subject to control by the prior institutions. The dysfunctionality of a government is an unavoidable outcome, and populists lack the inclination to tackle economic concerns. This phenomenon occurs because the institutions in which a significant majority of people participate are the primary catalysts for failures.

There are primarily two approaches that are antithetical to populism. The first one is elitism. Within the framework of this idea, there are two polar opposites: Good and evil. The situation is the same, but with just an opposing viewpoint, when it comes to populism. Elitists have the view that people are dangerous because they are dishonest, vulgar, and have less education. They are not culturally developed, they lack intellectual capacity, and they do not have strong moral values. Elitists hold superior positions to the majority of the norms and values in society. For this reason, they do not want the nation to be ruled by ordinary people who are not superior in terms of their morals. According to Taggart (2000), populism is both harmful and potentially disastrous. Therefore, the political participation of the people should be controlled. Elitists aim to have a predominant influence on politics. There is a democracy, but it is limited and weak. Elitism is quite anti-democratic. It is completely against the will of the people. Elitists are those who believe that the lower classes and economic activity should be governed by intellectuals, military leaders, aristocrats, and wealthy classes. The second principle is pluralism. Additionally, the antithesis of this is elitism. Pluralism is an ideology that opposes radicalism and does not support the fragmentation of society based on beliefs or interests. People are allowed to have a variety of ideas under the umbrella of pluralism. For Mudde and Kaltwasser (2017), this is considered to be a strength rather than a weakness. There should be a wide variety of organizations, and authority should be distributed among them. Consequently, it might provide a challenge for a single party to accumulate all the powers, thereby promoting both power harmony and the division of power. The economic democracy that exists in the market serves as a mirror of pluralism. No economic group has the ability to exert complete control over all other economic groups since there is no one entity that governs the price, demand, and supply.

Populism can be categorized as classical populism or neopopulism in the evolution of global economies. Technological advancements lead to the emergence of more inventive political aspects. Classical populism is often regarded as the early phase of populism, arising from the emergence of democratic institutions headed by determined political leaders in governments. While democratic systems began to take form in some nations, others, like Türkiye, continued to struggle to develop their democracies in the face of intense political rivalry and the presence of a diverse array of competing political parties. This is also the case with nations located in Latin America, such as Argentina. The traditional form of populism is primarily concerned with the dynamics that exist inside a nation. Ideologies such as nationalism, Marxism, anarchism, fascism, and communism all play a significant role in its implementation. Sometimes, the achievement of goals is contingent upon the leader's charm. A charismatic leader is someone who has exceptional talents, exhibits a divine nature, and demonstrates unwavering determination. According to Hawkins (2010), the populist leader behaves in a way that leads toward making dramatic reforms. A bond that is not conditional exists between the leader and the people. The emphasis should be placed on the leader's personality rather than the substance of the discussions. The populist leader is regarded as a messianic figure who defends the best interests of the people. However, a new ideology known as neopopulism has emerged by globalization and technological advancement. They exhibit a nonradical approach in their actions and have a tendency to collaborate with others to establish communities. This phenomenon might arise when the democratic system is conspicuously and firmly entrenched in countries. The new global developments have altered individuals' understanding of political authority. It is common practice for the policies to be formulated within the framework of globalization as well as the progression of technological, social, and economic life. The old populist policies give way to the new policies that are molded by globalization, which means that the policies that are only applicable to one nation gradually lose their significance. In this kind of populism, political parties have a greater tendency toward chameleon and do not necessarily adhere to policies that are in line with radical ideologies. They have the potential to convey the image of nationalism, conservatism, and liberalism. They possess soft power and have an inclination to join with other parties. Hence, the ideological pillars of populist governments are malleable. Even when governments make an effort to give the impression that they are socialist or nationalist, neopopulism is still the dominant ideology. The new populist policies that are gaining notoriety prioritize xenophobia, environmental concerns, feminism, multiculturalism, gender equality, and homosexuality. Prior to the establishment of the EU, the majority of states were governed by extremist ideologies, and their governments implemented policies that catered to popular sentiment. Nevertheless, these countries are now capable of uniting inside the EU to pursue common objectives. Their internal concerns mostly stem from an economic populism that revolves around tax policy, retirement policy, employment policy, energy policy, and trade conflict.

Populist regimes have a detrimental attitude toward existing institutions. To sustain their attraction, it is essential for them to preserve their religious and traditional elements. They have a nostalgic point of view. Due to the secularization process, older establishments were initially unfavorable because they did not support a particular ideology. It is based on the premise that individuals have the freedom to exercise their ideologies while also benefiting from a prosperous community. The administration capitalized on this reality by asserting that under Ottoman Empire authority, the country thrived and existed in a more utopian state. Various national and international contributions were provided, all with the objective of convincing the people that life under the empire was more desirable than the current age. Therefore, these measures may persuade the people that the government will endeavor to recreate such a society once again. Following the assumption of power by the left wing in Türkiye, this approach transformed into a populist program. During the era of Atatürk, there was a period of economic prosperity characterized by diligent labor and the production of commodities. Individuals must once again inhabit such a world. Another instance of nostalgia could be observed when Trump adopted the phrase Make America Great Again. He was asserting that the United States was far more prosperous in the past when it manufactured items domestically and hired its own citizens. A significant number of individuals in the former Soviet Union have the conviction that Putin has the capability to reinstate the country to the same degree of power it had throughout its initial decades. Governments have the capacity to highlight that existing institutions may be the cause of issues and misery. Although this may be true in some instances, it does not obscure the unfavorable policies of present-day populist authorities, who deliberately utilize formerly successful techniques. Nevertheless, these political perspectives are based not on historical or scientific evidence but rather on the imaginative thoughts of the people. Nostalgic perspectives are in opposition to pluralism and aim to unify the people behind a single ideology to advocate for certain policies. The concept of pluralism is devoid of any mystical or romantic connotations associated with political personalities. It does not provide a rosy or glorified depiction of the past or its achievements. It attempts to address current and global issues by using advanced and evidence-based approaches while also embracing both supportive and opposing perspectives.

Populism and democracy

The concepts of populism and democracy are intricately intertwined with one another. The idea of democracy is often used as a fundamental goal by political parties, particularly in industrialized nations. In spite of this, developing a genuine democracy can be a challenging endeavor. The reason for this is that democracy is fundamentally connected to pluralism. Populism is a reaction against both pluralism and elitism. The repeated use of phrases such as the people rule the country by populist regimes, whose ultimate aims are to build or maintain democracy as a political system, can be a method for consolidating the large constituencies of their supporters. A political party in a democratic society or parliamentary system has the ability to depict itself as a savior of democracy and the people by opposing and diminishing all other political ideologies and parties. Populism can be founded on a wide variety of ideologies, while democracy is predicated on liberalism, a power balance, and the separation of powers. Moreover, populism can be subdivided into concepts that lean to the left, right, or conservative viewpoints. Marxist philosophy is the foundation of leftist populism. Under this strain of populism, governments pursue measures with the goal of winning over the working class. The status of the working class all across the globe evolved because of this strategy. The assumption that the implementation of reforms may minimize the potential hazards of communism was accepted by governments as an alternative to reforming the economic structure itself. The pressure of populism is often grounded on issues pertaining to wage-setting policies, collective bargaining, and the general working conditions of workers. The ideology of nationalism is at the core of right-wing populism. These forms of politics are prevalent in developing nations since such countries need an ideology to follow and that can unify the country as a whole in opposition to globalization and multinational companies. Otherwise, living conditions can be challenging, and having a job is especially important under difficult circumstances. Religion, morals, traditions, and cultural concerns form the foundation of the conservative populist ideology. However, it might be difficult to grasp the distinctions between democracy and populism. The populism of one person might be the democracy of another. This state can be referred to as a populist democracy so long, as all populist parties are able to participate in elections, have political participation in parliament, and have thoughts about the future of the people. Although adherents of different ideologies may not consistently have equal opportunities to articulate their ideas, it is feasible to assert that democracy and populism can coexist.

Pluralism, which is necessary for democracy, paves the path for finding the optimal balance in terms of freedom, equality, and representation of all different kinds of individuals living in a nation. Democratic governments recognize that society is comprised of diverse individuals who are free to have a variety of opinions, aspirations, and points of view. Democracy is in opposition to both populism and elitism since both of these ideologies support the dominance of homogeneous groups, individuals, communities, and people. Müller (2016) argues that populism presents a danger to democratic systems. An inherent weakness of democracy is its potential to facilitate the rise of populist leaders. Hence, Müller (2016) asserts that the danger to democratic systems does not come from left-wing or right-wing ideologies, Islamism, or Soviet-style communism. Instead, the threat arises from populism, which seizes upon the fundamental principles and ideals of democracy, namely the empowerment of the people to govern. Hence, democracy inherently carries the risk of collapse, therefore creating the possibility for the succeeding party to assume power. Democratic policies are based on empirical research and are better aligned with reality. Democratic parties recognize their deficiencies. The soundness of their policies can be presented via political studies. Unfortunately, this option is not available during populist administrations. It is presumed that their policies achieve success consistently. Even if their policies are ineffectual, it is impossible to disprove them. Pappas (2014) did a study to investigate the events that occur when a populist party assumes office. There are two separate results. Populism would either undergo a power transition and transform into an opposition force or would consolidate its control on power. Populist democracy occurs when a populist party comes into power and other parties attempt to replicate its policies and techniques. Populist opposition parties may gain power. Ultimately, prominent opposition parties can embrace populist measures. The evolution of populist democracy may be characterized by clearly identifiable phases. It has its origins in a nascent form of political liberalism. Right-wing populists often harbor animosity toward both elites and marginal groups, viewing them as unrepresentative of the real people. Left-wing populists advocate for measures that target a substantial majority of those who are in opposition to right-wing ideology. The political perspective is shaped by the prevailing conditions inside a country.

Democracy does not remove the possibility of populism. Populism is a strategy utilized to undermine democratic systems. Nevertheless, it is still necessary for it to rely on democratic systems to legitimately protect its position. While democracy and populism are distinct concepts, populists nonetheless want to employ democracy to expand their influence. It is conceivable to ask why populists do not fully eliminate democracy and make it simple to execute their agendas. They would have significant challenges in creating it. Populists favor exploring flexible methods for achieving their objectives. Otherwise, they could anticipate encountering significant resistance from communities, governments, and international organizations. It is possible that relationships on a global scale may become more challenging, and individuals in their ordinary lives should anticipate encountering new problems. While elections take place, there is no assurance that new norms and regulations can be adhered to. The concentration of authority might facilitate the emergence of a populist administration to create a new constitution. This new development can be witnessed as a novel regulation aimed against entrenched elites. In certain nations, the remains of communism, left-wing or right-wing movements, conservatism, and other political ideologies can be found among elite individuals. These individuals are referred to as Kemalists in Türkiye. However, when these groups are on the verge of obtaining power, they describe elites as imperialists or proponents of the Ottoman Empires. Every group attempts to legitimate itself by portraying the conflict as one against the established elites. If populists are successful in seizing power, they will be in a position to amend constitutions and other regulations to minimize the influence of nonpopulist parties and the methods in which they may one day dominate the government. For populists, there is no such thing as alternative representations, and all competing parties are the same, even if their ideologies are distinct. The reason populism emerges is because it aims to fill the role of democracy, which could not accomplish its promises. This means that populist regimes have the potential to affect change in society and attract the attention of ordinary people. Nevertheless, populism weakens democratic institutions to the advantage of the prevailing political party.

Democracy engenders a side effect of populism. Pluralism emphasizes the significance of vote counting in the process of establishing the legitimacy of a government. It does not suggest that the majority should have absolute authority over all matters, nor does it advocate for the suppression or dismissal of competing perspectives. Populism has the capacity to steer society and divert it from the established principles of democratic and liberal political systems. This is a harmful condition. If used with malicious intent, it has the capacity to propagate among all the entities inside the institutions. Furthermore, it creates a distinct division inside the nation between the good people and the evil elites. Hence, it is imperative to either render democratic procedures impervious to this inadvertent consequence or to rectify it. Populist parties will use not only electoral strategies but also sociological and economic methods to establish long-lasting administrations and govern the country, disregarding the actual circumstances. The discontent that arises under the rule of populist governments is not caused by the incompetent policies of the ruling parties. These are the result of invisible adversaries originating both outside and within. Policies are designed to address conspiracy theories and fictions, both of which may be difficult to understand owing to their complex nature. Due to the hypnotic sway exerted by the media and supporters on the general populace, it is not difficult to perceive the problem as being orchestrated by other nations or enigmatic factions.

A strong and interdependent connection exists between democratic principles and populism. Populism is closely related to the fundamental ideals that form the basis of democratic political systems. It is not an easy effort to assume that a democratic society can thrive apart from populism and political parties that appeal to the populist ideology. The presence of populism poses a perpetual threat to democratic institutions that recognize and appreciate pluralism. The reorganization of democracy and the adoption of new institutional changes both prepare the way for a new sort of populism. It is a parasitic organism that sustains itself by consuming pluralism. It might be advantageous or dangerous. It depends on how it is employed to impact individuals and society. Institutional economics relies on the presence of a proficient judiciary and democratic governance as its essential components. A significant association exists between adherence to the rule of law and achieving remarkable economic prosperity. Countries that have achieved significant progress in modernization and the establishment of democratic systems are more likely to attract major investments, skilled workforce, and financial resources.

Ensuring the protection of property rights, as well as the rights of diverse cultural groups, minorities, and communities, via a democratic and autonomous judiciary, would enable these individuals to remain in the country, make investments, and pursue employment there. Institutional complementarity may facilitate efficient economic operations. However, the institutional dimension of democracy must not be disregarded. A country that has both institutional complementarity and democracy can appear more attractive for economic endeavors in a world that is becoming more global. In the absence of an autonomous justice system, a country may more easily employ its economic tools in an undemocratic approach compared to a highly democratized economy. Countries with populist economies and vulnerable democracies are at a higher risk of having their monetary and fiscal policies manipulated to further the goals of a political party. Populism enables the coordination of collective activities among groups who share similar ideologies and have little differences within their communities. It is commonly acknowledged that populists may weaken the credibility of current institutional structures and dominant wealthy and influential classes to develop new foundations that emphasize the interests of the general population.

Populist regimes heavily depend on the media as a powerful tool in shaping their policies. The occurrence of media populism is not limited to a certain geographical area. It may be connected to any digital and technical devices that are accessible to the people. It is infeasible to have various political voices or a platform for diverse ideologies. Media outlets that contravene this criterion or fail to prioritize the welfare of the public should be cautioned or penalized. Media populism undermines the presence of diverse viewpoints. This exemplifies a recurring pattern observed in nascent democratic institutions. It obscures the truth and has a significant manipulating capacity. It fails to inform people on the reality of the issue. Uncovering the underlying cause of the problem is a challenging task. The populist movement aims to achieve consensus by using the media. Its purpose is to exert influence on people in alignment with political objectives. Hence, it is difficult to locate a space for democratic expressions within the prevailing atmosphere of populism. It utilizes prominent individuals because of their effective communication skills to exert influence on others. Moreover, it hinders academics who are capable of offering more constructive insights and expertise on matters. Therefore, the efficacy of freedom of speech is compromised within the context of populism. The democratic institutions lack efficacy and are fragile. The internet poses significant risks to political strategies. Televisions served as a potent medium for the general public's expression of ideas and opinions until the year 2000. Since then, internet technology has expanded to become an increasingly vital element of everyday existence. The importance of social media has escalated. Political parties have to use these venues to get support from the people. By adopting this approach, they may gain popularity and build a strong presence in the society, enabling them to have more influence on a larger number of individuals. Establishing polls in this area has become vital for obtaining an accurate understanding of the perspectives held by the working class. Political leaders often enhance their own public image by highlighting their robust leadership qualities. These forums eventually transformed into a platform where legislative candidates might be located. The conventional mode of populism viewed on television has a digital equivalent via the use of social media. Emerging nations are considered to be leading consumers of social media. However, the lack of regulations in this emerging industry may prompt governments to take a more authoritarian stance. Nations such as China and Russia, which want to retain control over social media platforms, have created their own alternative possibilities and are actively promoting their use among their own populations. Social media may serve as a potent platform for critiquing economic shortcomings. The main focus of emerging countries largely revolves on their economic conditions, poverty, and inequality. Hence, it serves as a platform for populist leaders to disseminate economic news while capturing with people's interests. Furthermore, it serves as a forum for the people to engage in conflict with media organizations that are controlled by the elite class.

Populism also encompasses a response to the emerging global version of liberalism. A movement has emerged as a reaction to the new demands of social tolerance toward beliefs, cultures, religions, human rights, secularization, migrants, refugees, same-sex marriage, gender equality, and democratic values. This movement is driven by the people who need to preserve their tradition, culture, and religion. Technological advancements have the potential to cause a change in the values of society. Nevertheless, it is also possible for a counteracting tendency to emerge that hinders the pace of the transformation (Inglehart, 1977). An alternative explanation for this phenomenon is that it signifies a cultural transformation that facilitates the rise of cultural populism and increases people's inclination to adopt populist policies. A revolution can be defined as an evolution in a society characterized by the adoption of libertarian principles, the embrace of multiculturalism, and the cultivation of environmental consciousness. The emergence of a new global culture is impacting several aspects of life and diverse cultural practices. The increased availability of educational resources and technological progress have led to a generational transition characterized by less extremism and a decline in antipolitical ideologies. However, people from traditional cultures and value systems start to respond negatively to modern advancements and progressive ideas. They could perceive the current developments as a dilution of their deeply held convictions, which have been essential in unifying them as a nation. The people may look for a leader who has the ability to halt this transformation and safeguard their entrenched principles as they evolve into widespread constituencies inside the country. There is the possibility for a cultural movement to emerge as a response to these concepts. This kind of transition is regarded as a menace by the population. This exemplifies the concept of path dependency in the realm of politics. The contemporary zeitgeist is tainted by antiquated habits, customs, preferences, and ideologies.

Populist regimes often direct their animosity at the fundamentals of democracy, such as constitutions, institutions, human rights, and free market economy. The populist movement is against the concept of power being distributed among several entities. It strives to implement drastic institutional changes to dissolve the connection between the regulations and the population. By doing this, it is feasible to build a direct connection between the populist leader and the people. Populists want to enhance their sovereign power by attempting to modify both the principles of democracy and the foundational structure of the country. Upon assuming power, a populist administration often endeavors to dismantle any preexisting constitutions to formulate its own set of regulations and principles. Populists have the capacity to modify constitutions if they can substantiate that such amendments align with the primary interests of the sovereign will. In countries with established democracies, it is customary to impose term limits on leaders, restricting the number of times they may be elected before transferring power to the following administration. In countries where populism dominates as the prevailing political philosophy, it is reasonable to amend the constitution to allow multiple reelections of a leader. The event took place in Russia under the leadership of Putin. As a result of the modifications he made to the constitution to prioritize the well-being of the people, an authoritarian populism gained more influence. Xi Jinping used a similar strategy to bypass the restriction imposed by the communist party, which imposed a two-term limit on a leader. This was also witnessed in Venezuela under the leadership of Hugo Chávez, who advocated for a change in the country's constitution to do away with term limits for the presidency. His activities had their start as a backlash against the government, which at the time was attempting to carry out so-called neoliberal policies. His attempted coup failed, but his movement gained momentum, and he became widely recognized as the people's leader. His democratic actions were referred to as the democratic revolution in elections. His charismatic stance and populist attitude to the democratic process contributed to his election as president. He aspired to extend his authority by disdaining the institutions that were in place, much like other populist presidents. In the past, political and economic institutions had a certain degree of autonomy, which at the very least ensured that diverse parties were given an opportunity to be represented in proportionate form. Institutions were transformed into mechanisms that functioned to reflect Chávez's political actions, which governed the nation to the disadvantage of other political factions. People were motivated and controlled by institutions, but not all democratic principles were eradicated. Chávez's Bolivar administration was thus considered a hybrid kind of democracy. His government devoted the first year of its term to the drafting of a new constitution. One more of the government's goals was to exert control even over significant businesses. Chávez made an effort to reorganize the state-owned oil corporation by mentioning that it was under the influence of corrupt technocrats of the old institutions; nevertheless, this resulted in a huge rally against his administration. He exercised a significant amount of authority over the judicial system by establishing a majority of individuals who were able to work favorably for him (Hawkins, 2010). The goal of populism is to expand its influence such that it encompasses all institutions. The amendment to the constitution does away with the institutionalized forms of liberal democracy, paving the way for politics and economics to be influenced directly by the relationship between the leader and the people. Constitutional amendments would restrict the activities of competing organizations and ideas. The amendment to the constitution garners momentum due to the support of the people, making it the most noteworthy advancement. Since populist leaders do not take into account the viewpoints of other groups, they will legalize constitutional changes as long as the mass constituents are in agreement with them. A referendum or an overwhelming vote in parliament is needed to verify this.

In hyperpresentialist regimes, the rules and regulations that exist between the government and its constituents are dramatically reduced. This is because these governments dismiss liberal democracy. The implementation of the principle of separation of powers has been shown to be a crucial factor in promoting growth and development within the nation. Liberal democracies prohibit the government from making simple modifications to the constitution. The government will be able to simply execute its policies to the benefit of the people without experiencing any opposition if there are no intermediaries. This will allow the government to achieve its objectives. If the government is unable to implement necessary policies and achieve certain goals, it is probable that enduring institutions and liberal democracy persistently hinder populist advancement and growth. Once this approach garners the endorsement of the majority, there will be a complete absence of resistance for amending the constitution. In conclusion, populism establishes a robust institutional form based on constitutional modifications that will prove resistant to updates or repairs in the long run. This constitutes a drawback of populism. The introduction of institutional modifications in legislation can result in path dependency, a lack of institutional complementarity, and an asymmetry of power between actors in the realms of economics and politics.

A robust connection exists between democracy and the equitable allocation of authority as well as the establishment of mechanisms to maintain a state of equilibrium in power dynamics. In accordance with Commons's viewpoint, institutional economics is an aspect of pluralism that advocates for the equitable distribution of rights and opportunities among participants, regardless of whatever disproportional power they may possess. Economic democracy is the pluralistic manifestation in the economic domain. This concept is antithetical to populism as well as elitism. While economic actors can possess a disproportionate amount of influence, economic democracy promotes equitable opportunities for these actors to establish a power equilibrium. It ensures that all individuals involved in the economy have a fair opportunity to make choices. In the absence of economic democracy, both elites and populists retain the capacity to jeopardize the economy via their specific influences. Populism undermines economic democracy and exploits economic instruments for the advantage of the people and the populist movement. Institutional forms have the potential to preserve the traditional principles of economic democracy. Furthermore, pluralism is an important component of institutional reform. Populism aims to consolidate all authority under a single faction by establishing an exclusive economic party. Every country has its own distinct political system and faces a unique array of issues. This implies that there is enough space for a diverse range of populisms and democracies. Various subcategories of elitists exist, each exhibiting a predilection for wealth, luxury, and commerce. Individuals belonging to the privileged social strata have the capacity to undertake many positions, including global political figures, corporate executives, experts in technology, autocrats and their relatives, monarchs, military strategists, or those from other social classes. The concept differs based on the prevailing conditions in each country. It is important to distinguish between the populist tendencies demonstrated by emerging nations and those displayed by industrialized ones. A significant proportion of revenue is allocated toward essential needs in low-income nations. Therefore, populism that prioritizes improving living circumstances or providing benefits can appear to be a more enticing option to pursue. People in developed countries often prioritize strategies for increasing their financial resources and designate a part of their earnings toward activities that provide them satisfaction and comfort.

Populism in the modern world

Populism has emerged various times and in various places throughout history. Thus, the definition of populism and the forms it takes have been influenced by the conditions of nations. Although populism experiences periodic decline, it has the capacity to make a comeback in the mid of political, economic, and social crises all over the world (Moffitt, 2016). In Latin America, populism can be interpreted to refer to left-wing movements, whereas in Europe, it refers to right-wing parties. In certain nations, such as the United States and Türkiye, it is possible for political parties to form on both the right and the left. Populism takes shape in response to economic setbacks or ideologies (Mudde and Kaltwasser, 2017). Political parties begin their campaigns on the basis of an underlying ideology. Political ideals become irrelevant when economic populism comes to power. As long as a party adheres to policies that aim to appease mass constituencies, it can be very difficult to categorize the political orientation of the party as either left wing or right wing. There is room for a wide variety of political populisms to compete for the support of the people. However, it would not be incorrect to classify populism as a chameleon that changes to the colors of its environment in classically populist economies.

In recent years, European countries have witnessed the emergence of antiimmigration politics as a manifestation of populism. The quite xenophobic nature of the society gives rise to the rise of the right-wing populist movement. Immigration is regarded as a potential danger to the identity of the native population. There is a perception that multiculturalism is imposed by elites against the will of the people. Therefore, modern populism is characterized by a significant anti-EU reaction. European integration is often considered as an elite authoritarian project (Mouffe, 2005). In France, populism has long been used as a rhetorical device. The nation is home to a wide variety of political perspectives. Jean-Marie Le Pen was considered a populist as he voiced opposition to the previous government (Surel, 2002). Rassemblement National is regarded as a right-wing movement. Jean-Luc Mélenchon continues to lead La France Insoumise in his role as a populist left-wing party leader. The electoral votes for the two ideologies are quite close. Both parties are working to create populist strategies that can be deployed against existing forces and elite politicians with the goal of providing an alternative to neoliberalism and offering an alternative choice. Right-wing populist movements frequently engage in an effort to advance authoritarianism and nativism. They take a position that is antagonistic against immigration as well as the multicultural policies of the EU. Their approach to economic policy is influenced by xenophobia and nostalgia. The national priority should take precedence over every other factor. The strategy adopted by movements assumes that active participation by the government in the economy is required. Left-wing movements in France are considerably closer to the economic populist policies in Latin America than right-wing movements are. They are opposed to measures that adhere to both neoliberalism and austerity. They hold a socialist economic ideology in high regard. They encourage public expenditure as well as interference by the government in the economy. The reduction of unemployment, poverty, and taxation as well as an earlier retirement age is the primary objective of the movement. They also make an effort to raise the tax burden placed on the actions of the business class. They are opposed the idea of flexible labor markets and want to achieve a rise in real wages. People are demanding that public services be expanded to better serve them. A significant focus of the movement is directed on augmenting the rights of workers. Both parties are more inclined to disregard neoliberal approaches and embrace heterodox measures. They are opposed to the liberal laws of the EU, multiculturalism, free trade agreements, and globalization. Distrust in pluralism and the institutions of representative democracy, international law, constitutional law, and mediating forces have been a hallmark of the far-right parties (Ivaldi, 2019). Their economic populism is more polished with protectionism and isolation from the principles held by other industrialized and liberal nations. They prioritize France's national sovereignty above its relationship with the EU and advocate for an adjustment in the country's stance toward the EU. Nevertheless, it was clear to observe that the right-wing party makes pledges that are consistent with left-wing ideas or vice versa. They maintain policies and methods that are comparable to one another. This phenomenon demonstrates that populist policies of all ideologies have a similar characteristic, in that they are based on the same general direction to attract voters. Macron did not back down in the face of extremist populist forces. In spite of this, the demands of the populists slowed down his policymaking. The Yellow Vest Movement in France, which involved demonstrations against the living circumstances of the working class, had put major pressure on the administration of Macron. The administration was forced to concede certain economic conditions to end the demonstrations. The Yellow Vest Movement organized protests, some of which escalated into acts of violence, to express their objection to high taxes and insufficient purchasing power (Ricci, 2020). Without taking into account the economic realities of the nation, the French administration had to eliminate resentments due to the populist demands of the working class. France is a country that is located close to Germany. However, it was unable to develop an economy that could compete with that of its neighbor. Germany had the potential to produce a large surplus in their current account, in contrast to France, which faced a deficit. The rhetoric of Silvio Berlusconi was an illustration of populism inside the EU. The style in which he communicated with mass constituencies was a key factor in his government's rise to power in Italy. The movement of his administration was not governed by any particular set of rules. Technology, television, social networks, and other forms of mass communication had given rise to a new wave of political populism (Anselmi, 2018). In a society where new innovations were an integral element of politics, this phenomenon was viewed as a populist component of cultural transformation. He was also a populist leader who polarized political ideologies. Nevertheless, there were no radical ideologies that might be regarded as characteristic of wartime governments. In this nation, the influence of neopopulism has resulted in the creation of activities rather than ideological militants.

The United Kingdom, a well-established developed country, opted to withdraw from the EU as a result of economic challenges. Populism was built around a political discussion that opposed globalization and the formation of unions between nations. The enactment of populist regulations was primarily motivated by anti-European and antiimmigrant sentiments. The United Kingdom intended to conduct a referendum for the general electorates. Due to the weak side of democracy that is propelled by populism, the country obtained an outcome that went against the progressive objectives of diversity and globalization. Nevertheless, economic considerations played a pivotal role in fueling populism. In comparison to Germany, the country's economic power remained much lower, which contributed to the country's lack of competitiveness. The country's currency rate was overvalued, and the pace of increase in productivity remained stagnant (Ünal, 2017). If the nation were to join the EU's Economic and Monetary Union, the country's level of political and economic competitiveness versus Germany might drop even lower. The combination of a large trade imbalance and a lack of political strength gave rise to populist movements. The decision to leave the EU was met with widespread approval from the people. The global surge of populist nationalism is strongly connected to the fundamental reasons of Brexit. It also indicates significant geopolitical divisions that are emerging within the global system. The Brexit campaign slogan of 'take back control' appealed to the people who were dissatisfied with the EU's internationalism, particularly on trade laws and immigration. Trump's popularity in the United States stemmed from his ability to connect with the widespread dissatisfaction and anxiety toward internationalism and globalization (Dent, 2020). Brexit and Trump's policies caused economists to be concerned about the economic effects of populism.

In the United States, the working class is frustrated by the decline of the manufacturing sector, and the slogan 'Make America Great Again' has the potential to mobilize people in Trump's favor. Furthermore, the slogan implies that everyone who opposes Trump is equally against the greatness of the United States. Populist slogans can be crafted to show that governments work for what ordinary people want even in most industrialized countries. The populist pattern was evident in the results of the presidential election in the United States in 2016. Elites and intellectuals had a difficult time comprehending how someone like Trump who targeted members of society's lower and middle classes could ascend to the position of power in the United States. Conservatives, left-wing groups, academics, and the media, among others, launched attacks on him. He was skilled at employing xenophobic scare tactics primarily against immigrants of Hispanic and Muslim descent, China and its economic policies, and conspiracy theories (Inglehart and Norris, 2016). He made a campaign pledge to build a massive wall close to the border with Mexico and to prevent radical Muslims from entering the United States. His strategy was predicated on the notion that he was the only person who could place America first and save regular Americans from foreign foes, corrupt institutions and the old political dominance of elites and intellectuals to liberate the United States and enable its citizens to live in prosperity. He was a nativist who battled against multiculturalism, arguing that it degrades American ideals, and he leveraged the nostalgia of previous triumphs from nationalist and protectionist eras to support his position. Formerly, the United States was living in prosperous times; however, the country was experiencing a decline in its strength as a result of both foreign adversaries like China and domestic adversaries like elites. The industrial elites are exclusively concerned with commercial operations, even those taking place in other nations, but they never take into consideration the interests of the white working class. They are making it more difficult for people in their native nation to get employment and achieve the American dream for themselves. He presented himself in a manner that suggested he was the representation of the true American people. He was critical of wars and of the US's role as a protector of other countries across the world. He declared battle on free trade, neoliberalism, and globalization. He intimidated companies by threatening to impose more taxes on their operations if they refused to conduct business in the United States. His policies were geared at the implementation of protectionist measures, in particular, with regard to China. This was a moderate strategy to attract the people, in contrast to the drastic decisions that were pushed on the people of Latin American economies by more authoritarian governments. The election of Trump showed that populism can exist even in industrialized economies and that it has the potential to become prevalent across the world, leading to the establishment of protectionist policies and antineoliberalism. His rhetorics were very different from the policies that the United States has constructed up until now, such as the Washington Consensus, neoliberalism, free trade, and globalization. It became a common theme in political campaigns to emphasize the need of providing assistance for domestic companies and giving priority to the welfare of American workers. He implemented counterproductive measures directed toward left-wing movements while making statements that were more heterodox than orthodox. He was a true populist who did not have any strong ideology, but instead appealed to the people via charismatic leadership and heterodox economic speech. Bernie Sanders, a populist politician who adhered to a left-wing worldview, was yet another example. His political philosophy was much more aligned with that which is practiced in places such as Türkiye and Latin American nations. The masses were supposed to be attracted by the left-wing movement with the promise of improved access to medical care. He brought attention to democratic socialism by starting a struggle against industrial elites and the inheritors of the capitalist system in the United States.

In the United States, a populist uprising known as the Occupy Wall Street Movement gained traction. This uprising emerged in response to the capitalist system's role in causing widespread poverty and inequality in the wake of the 2008 financial crisis. The movement maintains that the financial industry's elites have a significant amount of wealth in their hands. Only a little fraction is distributed to the general population of the most powerful economy in the world. Consequently, there should be widespread hardship due to economic disparity and poverty. This movement embraced heterodox economic policies and opposed neoliberalism. The global financial crisis served as a catalyst for the movement. On the other side, a movement known as the Tea Party formed with an opposing viewpoint asserting that the government should stay out of the economy entirely. This movement aimed to reduce the size and scope of the government as well as reduce the taxes placed on economic activities. The Japanese society became more unified as a result of the perceived danger posed by North Korea. According to what can be seen in the media, North Korea has been portrayed as a big foreign opponent that is capable of dropping missiles on the Japanese island at any moment. Nevertheless, these populist movements were not the same as the populist phenomena that are witnessed in Argentina and Türkiye. The populist movements in the two nations were more radical and aggressive. Even if the economy was not very developed, the people would still be able to demand greater government involvement, better wages, and transfer payments.

The world's long-standing institutions are being shaken by globalization. Demands for civil rights and the rights of marginalized groups and immigrants are growing in many parts of the globe. The majority of individuals, many of whom are traditionalists and attached to established institutions, are concerned about this development. Therefore, there is a current upward tendency in the popularity of populists. They are considered to be the last line of defense against globalization. For instance, the growing number of immigrants throughout the world, animal rights for pets, the rights of homosexuals, and the green movements are all subjects that are gaining relevance and keeping the media busy. Despite this, the vast majority of individuals refuse to confront these issues. Because of this, nationalist and conservative administrations are forced to act in the interests of their constituents. The United States makes an effort to do this to China. It has been said that China is home to the majority of the world's businesses. As a result, genuine individuals can no longer enjoy economic success. Because of this, communism, the United States's primary opponent, can be harder to defeat. Depending on the degree of development in a nation, the concept of populism may be interpreted in a variety of ways. The various forms of populism should be analyzed together to fully grasp its economic effects. Populists are able to establish their policies by taking into account these categories to appeal to a broad segment of the population and provide answers to their concerns while operating under the guise of an ideology. The growth of various populisms politicizes issues that affect particular segments of the people. There are two main varieties of populism that are practiced in today's politics. The first kind of populism is exclusionary populism. This kind of populism often arises in wealthy nations when society is worried about the effects that immigration will have on the nation. Because of increased immigration rates, native employees with low to medium levels of education may feel as if they are not receiving enough advantages from the government. In addition, they may be concerned that their salaries would decrease or remain the same as a result of immigrants who are able to work for a cheaper rate and who may even be able to find work that is not documented as official employment. There is a risk that people can feel negatively toward the languages spoken by immigrants as well as their growing population, religion, and culture. Because of this scenario, extreme and right-wing organizations are more likely to push their political objectives. These groups, such as immigrants, are supported by the existing system, which, on the other hand, penalizes hard-working native people with high taxes and rules that are not essential. The inclusionary populist movement is the second. This kind of populism is typical of developing or underdeveloped nations, which are characterized by pervasive issues such as poverty and rampant corruption. Under these circumstances, ideologies such as socialism and radical leftism gain popularity. A political perspective arises that condemns existing institutions for unfair socioeconomic policies (Kaltwasser, 2018).

The new generation has been the driving force behind a silent revolution throughout Europe. Policies that were more tolerant resulted in significant gains for underrepresented groups, immigration, and gender equality. There was also a rise in the popularity of green and progressive parties as a result of the increasing detrimental impacts of climate change and global warming. The growing population as well as the use of genetically modified crops have brought to the forefront the need for alternative policies that will lead to a more environmentally conscious and compassionate society. These movements are opposed to the construction of nuclear power facilities and intend to establish alternate sources of energy instead. These parties are attempting to form a coalition to better reflect their newly developed ideologies. However, the policies of the silent revolution also generated a negative influence among the individuals who represented the old-fashioned populist views that were molded by traditional, nationalist, religious, and extremist values. The charismatic leadership or extremist principles that formerly fueled populism are no longer the motivations behind the movement. It is reasonable to anticipate that this populism or political tactic will continue to proliferate in different parts of the world. In Russia, ideas that are populist in nature have gained momentum in opposition to Western style multiculturalism, democracy, and capitalism. He gave the impression of being a charismatic leader. He made an effort to sway large constituencies in opposition to the policies of the United States and Europe. His ideas served as a typical illustration of populism, which became popular throughout Europe in the decades after the First World War. However, populism can be risky if it is not channeled toward the achievement of productive goals. A conflict broke out between Russia and Ukraine as a direct result of Russian authoritarianism and populism, which had unimaginable consequences for the rest of the globe in the 2020s. In addition, there are a few nations, such as Canada and the countries of Scandinavia, in which the influence of populism has remained remarkably limited.

Societies that have experienced authoritarian regimes like fascism, nationalism, or populism may be more equipped to make the leap from a traditional to a contemporary way of life (Anselmi, 2018). Nations that were unable to finish their development stage to achieve technological frontiers can choose to slow down their social and economic transformation. Hence, developed countries have far more thoroughly evolved societies, daily lives, and democracies. Countries that are plagued by populism and have a populist government tend to be similar to Türkiye and Argentina in that they are stuck in a middle-income trap and have a mediocre standard of living. Nevertheless, throughout the history of these two nations, when authoritarian governments originated by defeating old colonial or imperial structures, they were able to lead their society to at least the beginning levels of democracy and a parliamentary system. As a consequence, secularization and a greater degree of freedom are incorporated into society. In other words, the modifications that were made to institutions resulted in the elimination of older institutions that were founded on traditions and religions. In most cases, the new authoritarian governments that came to power after the fall of older authoritarian regimes adhered to political ideologies connected to fascism, nationalism, or Marxism in their approach to governance. Each ideology favored adopting populist measures in accordance with their own perceptions of the world. These ideologies developed their own foundations of loyalty and doctrines to reach the more evolved societies of the advanced capitalist nations that had accomplished the first stage of democracy. In today's globalized world, the influence of populism is no longer confined to the economy of individual nations or even domestic economies. Globalization and technological advancements both have an impact on the political and economic climate of other nations throughout the world. It will be completely challenging to conceive of a scenario in which populism in the United States would be confined to the borders of that nation alone. In addition, populist regimes have the potential to alter a nation's competitiveness, economic performance, and development, all of which may have an effect, either directly or indirectly, on the economies of other nations.

Populist movements in the contemporary world do not prioritize institutional factors, which may be more effectively exploited to solve economic difficulties. Each political movement consistently maintained its position against the division of powers and the complex equilibrium of authority. They tried to attract the working class by offering economic incentives. They endeavored to secure the support of the majority to forward their own agenda. Despite its origins in industrialized and democratic economies, pluralism was dismissed. The task of acquiring influence on the support of the people in emerging nations is not limited to the governments of such countries alone. There are several countries, each with the capacity to influence socioeconomic class, inequality, religion, immigration, poverty, and human rights. These countries may include either the United States or economies in Europe. The populism witnessed in emerging economies, such as Argentina and Türkiye, differs from the populism observed in developed countries. This is because governments in emerging countries are prepared to assume the risk of creating economically unfavorable circumstances to attract people. The policies that focused on income and the exchange rate had disastrous consequences in these countries. The propensity of these countries to consistently find themselves in a state of crisis is a significant characteristic. The institutional framework plays a crucial role in incentivizing a charismatic leader to implement policies, even if such policies have an adverse impact on economic performance.

There are a multitude of options that attract people. Globalization, immigration, unemployment, liberalization, human rights, cultural change, deindustrialization, radical ideologies, digital life, and other emerging developments in social and economic spheres exemplify some of these contemporary themes. Even if populist leaders are displaced, these or other problems may persist, allowing populist politicians to capitalize on their positions for individual advantage. The leaders would always be motivated to acquire power due to the prevailing inclinations in society. The form of institutions is crucial in minimizing the threat presented by semidemocratic regimes. Even if the contemporary world lacked a regulatory mechanism, institutions and their form would still need to operate effectively. The EU has made significant progress toward this goal. It is impossible for any populist movement to embrace people without recognizing the rights of minorities and other groups because of the difficulty in establishing a union under a flag and a currency without any borders. This might show the significance of institutional change for a unified area. As a consequence, populist movements need to criticize this kind of institutional structure to solidify their authority.

Populism in Latin America

Latin American nations have a history of being home to dictators and other types of extremist leaders, military coups, persistent inflation, currency problems, inequality, and poverty. The continent is the place of many extraordinary political movements, internal conflicts, and crimes that constitute the core elements for many political and economic works. In particular, populism has been a defining characteristic of the region. Even though there are nations in Latin America that are vast in terms of both population and size, the region's economic development has lagged behind that of many other industrialized economies. During the time of colonization, the living conditions in North and South America were considerably more comparable to one another. The South fell further into poverty and witnessed an increase in the frequency of civil wars, military coups, and economic upheaval. Despite having a larger population, more area, and important raw minerals such as oil, South America's GDP per capita has remained far lower than that of the United States or Canada. The disparity in economic status continues to have an impact on the lives of millions. Many people in Latin America want to improve their quality of life by migrating to more prosperous countries. People who are unable to leave their country and enter a developed economy are more likely to blame globalization and capitalism for their own poverty and inequality. Political parties are tasked with filling this need. This indicates that there could be government control and regulations that lean toward protectionism. These nations have all been subject to authoritarian governments and dictatorships in the past. As a result of the collapse of the free market economy, developing nations can be involved in the black market. Drug smuggling, acts of terrorism, and an increase in the trafficking of people may all become entrenched in culture. The outcomes are comparable to well-known examples in Latin American nations. In instance, it is widely known that Mexico has a problem with drug cartels that it has to confront. In spite of the fact that some nations practice what is referred to as democracy, populism continues to have a greater influence on political life. Some of these nations had economic crises, which led to attempts on their part to enact free market economic policies based on the Washington Consensus (Goldfajn et al., 2021). It could be hypothesized that improving people's standard of living might be accomplished by establishing a market economy that is comparable to that of wealthy countries. The free market might provide a chance to build more equitable societies. Even though neoliberal reformation is a contentious topic, the failure of economic reforms is often attributed to the implementation of free market principles. These nations' shift toward left-wing ideas may be attributed to the failure of institutional changes.

A sustainable fiscal policy, a stable currency rate, low inflation, balanced foreign trade, and a favorable environment for firms are the essential components of a free market economy. In contrast to these characteristics, the nations of Latin America suffered from high tariffs on international trade, high and persistent inflation, overvalued and unstable currency rates, massive public enterprises, and defaults. In the 1990s, it was widely believed that neoliberal policies could help produce investment, employment, and prosperity. Nevertheless, it became clear that these nations were unable to successfully implement deregulatory policies. The extent of institutional changes remained limited. Moreover, the nations do not have significant advances in productivity, which are necessary for maintaining economic development. Austerity policies that did not include high taxes and low spending continued to produce enormous deficits in the budget. Finally, most of the nations in Latin America fell into severe economic slump. The most important information here is that populist economies still face the challenges of classical economic instability. It is unusual for advanced countries to have traditional economic issues in today's global economy. The Latin American nations had achieved substantial progress between the years 1940 and 1980 owing to protectionism designed under the strategies of their own governments. The transformation from agricultural to manufacturing industries is the most reasonable trajectory for developing nations to undertake. When it comes to the development of domestic industries, import substitution industrialization becomes a primary approach. The transformation was characterized by the replacement of agricultural growth with a rise in populist politics and industrial production (Roberts, 2007). Thus, countries became more protectionist and less open to international trade. This was a significant change in the institutional structure of the nations in Latin America. Even factories that manufacture items of poor quality have the potential to become even better. Because the global economy develops connections between nations, exporters run the risk of becoming the ones to lose in this scenario. Since each country needs to focus on a certain aspect of the product, this can inevitably lead to cooperation between nations. It may be possible to raise the cost of export industries and thereby discourage their involvement in global trade by imposing high tariffs, quotations, and indirect restrictions. If the fixed exchange rate is put into place, an overvalued currency might be an extra kind of economic punishment for export industries. The high cost of manufacturing is a direct outcome of protectionist policies implemented by governments. The significance of exporting declined, and instead, a new way of production formed in the nations of Latin America. This implies that the role of government in the market increased significantly. The process underscored the critical relationship between import substitution industrialization and charismatic populist presidents like Juan Domingo Perón in Argentina, Getulio Vargas in Brazil, and Lazaro Cardenas in Mexico (Panizza, 2005). A new industrial society emerged, and trade unions achieved greater levels of influence. It was for the reason that governments attempted to foster industrialization. Although this growth plan had the ability to increase wages in the manufacturing sector and strengthen core industries to some extent, it did not ultimately alter the fortunes of the Latin American countries. During the 1980s, most industrialized nations completely reformed their economic systems, moving away from protectionism and toward an open trading environment by increasing exports. The economies of Latin America were forced to adopt the same approach, which consisted of pursuing deregulation policies. The progress was slowed down. Moreover, path dependency has become a reality for nations, and the institutional characteristics of this reliance, which are based on poor property rights, safety, the judicial system, government intervention, and weak democracy and inefficiency, have become increasingly vital behind growth. The primary objective of economic changes enacted throughout the 1990s was to improve export performance while simultaneously mitigating the negative impacts of protectionism on the economy. It was essential to lessen the number of limitations and tariffs placed on imports. It is generally accepted that more trade liberalization is positively correlated with accelerated economic expansion. Therefore, lowering trade barriers becomes crucial for nations that want to get integrated into the global economy. It was brought out that the import taxes in Latin American nations were much higher even in comparison to those in East Asian countries.

When compared to East Asian countries, Latin American nations had substantially slower economic development. The recession both reduced the possibility for growth and destroyed hopes of reducing poverty. This provided governments with the opportunity to place responsibility for economic problems such as persistent inflation, currency crises, a lack of investment, unemployment, and poverty on international organizations. Particularly Argentina, Brazil, and Chile, along with a number of other nations, suffered extremely high chronic inflation rates, which contributed to a rise in the average inflation rate throughout the continent. Therefore, the government attempted to enhance its political standing by providing a justifiable argument opposing liberal initiatives. A political party appealed to the masses by using jargon associated with socialist ideology and nationalist rhetoric. The characteristics of populist regimes have been developed in opposition to the norms of their own nations. They employed populist measures to compete with their existing political systems and liberal democracy. If a nation is enthusiastic about implementing change, it must first possess a strong will to perform and then ensure that its government is capable of meeting the demands of the market. Liberal economic policies are often blamed for the corruption and collapse of nations, although this is difficult to prove. In most cases, the populist framework has been disregarded. When there is economic populism, it is irrational to expect these emerging nations to function like established capitalist economies. Protectionism, a lack of a free market economy, corruption, drug use, and ineffective institutions are all issues that still need to be addressed by the nations of Latin America. These outcomes may have been brought about by ineffective economic policy. Economic populism manifests itself via institutions that are dysfunctional, hence reducing prosperity, which ultimately leads to an increase in the number of people emigrating to other nations. Populist policies remain prevalent in contemporary Latin America even after certain reforms were implemented (Levitsky and Loxton, 2013). Hugo Chávez's government in Venezuela, Evo Morales's government in Bolivia, Rafael Correa's government in Ecuador, Luiz Inácio da Silva's government in Brazil, and Néstor Kirchner and Cristina Fernández de Kirchner's government in Argentina are some of the most well-known examples of populist regimes (Muno, 2019). Elections in these emerging economies are often met with a lot of heated rivalry. They have been subjected to a number of military coups, economic crises, and social upheavals, but each instance has had its own unique characteristics. These nations are ruled by populist ideologies that lean to the left and right. Nationalism served as the primary motivating factor for populism in Bolivia. It is possible to trace the origins of the institutional framework of the nations that constitute Latin America all the way back to the colonial eras. Since that time, Latin American nations have been noted for significant currency devaluations, moratoria, and relatively high levels of inflation (Edwards, 2010). It was speculated that the organizational structures of the institutions were different from those observed in North America. However, the majority of Latin American nations have a comparable economic history.

Varguism was a significant factor in the development of populism in the Brazilian economy and played a leading role in this regard. It was formed by members of the working class who gained an awareness throughout the process of economic development. This resulted in a popular foundation of support. The populist strategy was developed by generating a threat (Groppo, 2009). Under the leadership of Luiz Inácio da Silva, economic populism in the modern era gravitated toward socialism as the dominant political ideology. The government of the nation had the goal of agricultural reform and the nationalization of significant banks and companies. The socialist rhetoric has a certain allure for nations that live in impoverished circumstances. In light of the fact that the population as a whole is vulnerable to significant social and economic disparities, it can be an important strategy to appeal to the people by making assurances of more equality. Therefore, the free market economy is presented as the root of all the problems that exist in these nations. The decades between the 1960s and the 1980s are sometimes referred to as the era of military influence in developing countries. For many decades, Brazil was under the rule of militarism. In this view, the only way to bring people around for the working class who are suffering under the burden of militarism is to propose a revolutionary approach. Although each nation has pursued a distinct strategy, their stance toward the United States has remained consistent. If this is the case, then the campaigns they are running against neoliberalism have grown greater support, as these nations have moved toward more leftist policies. In this regard, Türkiye may also be characterized as one that is antagonistic against neoliberal economic policies. Political campaigns in this nation are also often framed negatively against the United States. In this context, the heterodox economic approach is more widely accepted than the orthodox one. This is because heterodox philosophies facilitate political manipulation and control over the country.

Hugo Chávez is often cited as an example of a famous figure who ignored the fundamental characteristics of the economy and embraced policies that are classified as heterodox. Venezuela's president often made anti-American statements, and the country's government aggressively opposed the development of a free market economy. Chávez mobilized broad-based support to challenge privileged authorities. The organization of mass constituencies has the potential to lead to a more robust confrontation against elites (Roberts, 2006). This does not indicate that the government is making the proper decisions for the nation, but it is a method for gathering people by setting a goal. In this respect, the nation wishes to demonstrate that its problems are not inherent but rather the result of external adversaries. It can be easy for these nations to formulate populist economic policies when confronted with an environment dominated by free markets. If there is a failure in the economy, it is due to the tensions or penalties that are imposed from the outside. Latin American nations have engaged in rhetorical criticisms directed against globalization and the industrialized nations. Hence, the justifiable grounds might be shown to impose that governments should participate in the economy to safeguard the well-being of their own citizens. Chávez was able to gain greater personalized influence over the institutions and government with the support of new and radical followers. Populist leaders are easily recognizable by their use of catchy slogans in the style of marketing. Socialism of the twenty-first century was the term used to describe the new period (Hawkins, 2010). The governing administration began promoted by the state economic activities and made efforts to gain major influence over critical sectors of the economy, including the oil and telecommunications industries. The populist regime was opposed to the economic activity of free markets, the independence of institutions such as the central bank, and the liberal market. To create the conditions necessary for the establishment of a socialist society, it is necessary to prohibit both foreign investments and the operation of private businesses. Nevertheless, this course of action has the potential to transform the nation into a more authoritarian state. In other words, the constitution can be amended to provide the governing party the ability to remain in power for a long time. After consolidating his power, he continued to dominate the nation until his death. In 2009, a referendum was held to create this requirement. This is a tendency that emerges consistently throughout all populist governments. After the 2012 elections, Chávez decided to move in that direction. They feel that if they had more authority, then their positions would be more deserving of respect. This is one method to lessen the impact of political risks. Even if populism is often an unintended outcome of democracy, political parties only have a certain amount of time to remain in power. Hence, they might be susceptible to increased political risks. Chávez was able to maintain his position as president for an extended period of time of any other leader. The attitude of the leader with no deadline was increasingly radicalized against the United States and the environment of free markets. It is vital for left-wing populists in Latin America to interfere in the market economy because regulations are an absolute must in the context of the predominance of policies that lean toward socialism. Nationalism is another issue that might influence the market. Nationalist sentiment has been a cornerstone of populism in Bolivia (Levitsky and Loxton, 2013). The mining and agricultural activities were nationalized in the 1950s. Mexico also followed a pattern quite similar to this one. At the end of the 1930s, it nationalized the oil industry. Currency crises plagued each of these nations to varying degrees. During the 1800s, when Argentina first gained its independence, it was faced with the challenge of macroeconomic instability.

Throughout its history, it had significant depreciations of its currency. Chile was another country that was affected by the issue. Both countries expanded their money supply without regard for a functional monetary system. The initiative received widespread support from politicians.

In spite of all the unfavorable reports that circulate about the countries of Latin America, it is not possible to assert that these nations would never have developed economies. The landmass of Latin America is enormous, and its coastlines provide opportunities for trade and tourism. Copper, iron, and oil are only few of the economic resources that are abundant in this region. As demonstrated in Venezuela, these massive resources can be deployed for populist ends (Müller, 2016). However, without implementing changes to the institutional forms that regulate economic activity, it will be unattainable for these countries to transform into dominant economies and establish themselves as technological and industrial giants. Moreover, the agricultural industry, the mining and quarrying industry, the petroleum industry, and the service industry are not sufficient on their own to establish enduring prosperity. The growth of the manufacturing sector was the primary impetus behind both the modernization and the globalization of the world. Additionally, this sector is a key driver of both productivity and continuous economic expansion. Natural resources can assist a country in overcoming obstacles. Nevertheless, it may also be at risk of contracting the Dutch disease. This indicates a high level of dependency on natural resources, which may be affected by changes in the global price of commodities as well as other economic factors. Productivity necessitates innovation, skilled workers, and a favorable market, all of which rely on well-established institutions. Without the ability to compete in export markets, achieving prosperity in today's global economy may be a challenge.

Following a model of development driven by exports is one way for East Asian nations to raise their GDP per capita. They might eventually catch up to the majority of developed economies. However, for a nation to have a production strategy, it is necessary to have an accumulation regime. The establishment of the working class and the mode of production are required. A robust industrial sector is essential for this to occur. The competitive automobile sector in East Asian nations like Japan and South Korea has resulted in a culture that is more involved in manufacturing and technology. The nations of Latin America do not have a system that allows for accumulation. In this way, they are reliant on outside funding to develop manufacturing facilities. To accomplish this goal, industrialized nations must provide technological and organizational assistance. China could complete this task. Despite the fact that the nation did not have its own accumulation system, it made efforts to adopt the process used in industrialized nations. Technology could be transferred to China, allowing the country to generate more electronic goods with a medium and high level of sophistication. It had a huge growth in its GDP per capita. The phenomenon, which aims to elucidate the disparity between productive and unproductive nations, is profoundly influenced by the institutional forms present in these countries. It is important that the forms be developed according to the objectives of economic activity. If a nation wants to boost its economy, it must provide an environment in which businesses can set up operations without facing interference from the government or threats to their ownership. To achieve this, it is essential to have stable macroeconomic conditions. In other words, there should not be significant inflation, large fluctuations in currency, trade imbalances, and other chronic difficulties. In this way, industries could be better to protect themselves against potential economic risks. It is essential to be aware of the fact that nations that do not have sufficient macroeconomic stability are unable to stimulate investments in the nation. The first step is to make structural adjustments to the institutions to achieve macroeconomic stability. Then, the remaining institutional reforms have to be geared toward protection and the rights associated with property. These goals should not be restricted to the elites; rather, they should include all citizens as well as businesses run by individuals from other countries. There is a strong correlation between increased equality and increased levels of both efficiency and production. For this reason, the judicial system is essential to the process of resolving conflicts without discouraging potential investors.

These nations need to address institutional issues. Eliminating economic populism is one approach that may be implemented. If this pattern is permitted to persist, every administration may continue to employ diverse institutional forms as a means of manipulating power. To develop more functional market economies with stable structures and efficient production, it is required to make fundamental modifications to existing institutions. Nevertheless, it is essential to be aware that to build a stable economy, a democratic form of government is not required. There must be a willingness to take all possible political risks. Otherwise, neoliberalism will be portrayed as the reason for the collapse of these states. Macroeconomic strategies are essential to the process of building a robust economy. China has a history of being ruled by the communist regime. However, it initiated significant alterations to its institutional forms in the early 1990s. The expansion of exports was the primary focus of this approach. It intended to employ a large quantity of labor in its production objectives. The nation was able to improve its GDP per capita, living conditions, and production. Therefore, for people in Latin American nations to become a part of the production process and globalization, it is necessary for governments to develop macroeconomic structures that perform better via institutional reform. This would lead to a rise in the country's GDP per capita, living standards, and productivity. Therefore, for Latin American nations, the implementation of institutional reforms to create more effective macroeconomic frameworks may enable people to actively participate in the production process and globalization.

Even if communism does not serve as the foundation for their economic systems, it is utilized as the inspiration for the rhetoric employed to promote the ideology. The economic and political climate of Latin America has pushed its nations toward the political left. In particular, the failure of neoliberalism has transformed the perception of nations toward alternative approaches, which was hidden in heterodox economics. There is a wide variety of political parties, all of which engage in fierce competition and make ineffective use of economic means. Then, it is necessary to make people aware that the danger is not posed by ideology but rather by populism. The nations of Latin America were unable to bring about the significant institutional changes that would have been necessary to produce a market economy that was more inventive, efficient, and well-functioning. The Mexican economic crisis in the early 1980s acted as a cautionary signal for other Latin American countries, indicating that their efforts to implement import substitution industrialization had been unsuccessful. Ultimately, Mexico failed to meet its financial commitments due to declining revenues. The currency experienced a substantial depreciation. Latin American countries had significant challenges with currency crises and enduring inflation. Ultimately, the macroeconomic volatility compelled these governments to request financial assistance from the IMF. In the 1990s and 2000s, the reforms remained incomplete. They continue to be vulnerable to the populist movement. The high cost of manufacturing was disastrous for the expansion of the economy. The rise in wages is far higher than the growth in productivity, and poor productivity has a negative impact on the ability to compete in international trade. Depreciation of the currency rate is essential to compete with other nations under conditions of high-cost manufacturing. Although there was low productivity and a high cost of production, the exchange rate was intentionally maintained overvalued. The majority of the nations suffered from significant trade imbalances, stagnant export growth, and high unemployment rates. Consequently, the nations failed to establish competitive industries that could compete on a global scale. It is necessary to have a fundamental understanding of economics to comprehend the fact that, in the context of a currency that is linked to the US dollar, governments should have only a little amount of space to pursue expansionary policies, which might lead to a rise in inflation and, in the end, cause the currency to fail. Because of this, expansionary policy should take into consideration an increase in productivity. For whatever reason, these governments have ignored that fundamental knowledge. There should not be significant wage growth to cause persistent inflation if productivity is insufficient. Furthermore, poor productivity suggests the nations would struggle to compete in the global market. These nations are unable to experience a significant rise in productivity for a number of critical reasons, the most important of which are path dependency, restricted institutional change, and a lack of institutional complementarity. A high production cost precludes the establishment of a fixed exchange rate regime. These two policies were implemented in China in an approach that was consistent with each other. During the 1990s, it adopted a fixed exchange rate system while managing to maintain a very competitive production cost. Hence, its strategy had a prospect of achieving success. The absence of populist initiatives may be attributed to the underlying presence of communism as the fundamental basis of the system. Nevertheless, the nation's government implemented policies aimed at promoting free market activity. It facilitated access to previously unavailable markets and enticed a substantial number of multinational firms. Although China is governed by a communist party, the nation has labeled this transformation as the adoption of a socialist market economy.

The currency rate was blamed as a contributing factor to inflation in Latin American nations (Edwards, 2010). Therefore, they reasoned that maintaining a constant exchange rate would shield them from this issue. The fact that economic populism, and not exchange rates, is the primary source of inflation is a point that is not often acknowledged. In other words, measures that encouraged economic development led to an increase in inflation, and it was only natural for the currency to reach out its level of equilibrium. To perform this, it was necessary for the central banks to depreciate or devalue the currency. The way in which the economy was characterized made it possible for speculation to occur, which in turn led to currency crises. To temporarily mitigate the consequences of widespread economic issues is the goal of the economic populist policy. It is generally accepted that exercising control over the exchange rate by either manipulation or pegging may at the very least halt the ascent of inflation, which has the potential to quickly affect market prices. Therefore, political parties made advantage of this situation to achieve gains for support. Thus, Latin American economies failed to perform as expected. In general, they were not capable of producing sustainable growth, low inflation, or a policy that maintained a stable currency rate. Both a lack of openness to international trade and an absence of a free market economy, which might contribute to a reduction in inflation, have been features shared by the nations. Because of their growing levels of debt, the governments were forced to finance their expenses. This led to an increase in inflation as well as a loss of competitiveness among export sectors, which ultimately resulted in significant reductions in the reserves held by central banks. It is expected that their status would not improve in the future as it has in the past without institutional reforms that might generate favorable macroeconomic variables, develop innovation to compete in international trade by attracting multinational corporations, and increase productivity.

The disparities between the United States and the Latin American states may be ascribed to inherent dissimilarities in their institutional frameworks. In the United States, institutions have been established to encourage the protection of property rights and the fostering of competition. The free market economy facilitated the growth and prosperity of banking institutions and stock exchanges. Nevertheless, in Latin American nations, the absence of robust democracy and a free market system benefited some industrial and financial factions while impeding the entry of others into the market. On the contrary, the institutions were designed to promote the interests of small investors in the United States. In Latin America, the development of the banking sector and stock exchange was sluggish, and investors were deprived of a chance for secure and unrestricted competition. Developing successful economic strategies to accomplish objectives in populist economies has proven to be a difficult task. Both the privileged and the working class possess the capacity to resist the alterations. Therefore, the government may be reluctant to adopt steps that would build an effective market economy characterized by limited inflation and stable pricing. Due to the possibility of a significant change in power dynamics, the governing elite, who own businesses and properties and still support the government, would be resistant to the proposed changes. This group might perhaps protect itself from competition by implementing stringent trade barriers and maintaining a limited degree of industrialization. They possess the capacity to exert monopolistic control. If there is a shift in the growth policy, the working class may choose to abstain from making sacrifices. The main goal of trade unions is to provide more stable and rewarding working conditions. Members are public sector workers who are not accountable to a management that is responsible for promoting innovation and increasing profits. The working class faces the potential of losing its state of ease, which motivates them to react adversely to changes. The government may use the working class as a means to create the illusion of actively addressing unemployment and enhancing the people's quality of life. The utilization of specialized terminology is an effective tool in countering deregulation initiatives aimed at appealing to the general public's economic interests. The privatization of public services in this situation presents a risk to the working class if they are unable of adjusting to new markets via competition or education.

To begin on changes that would promote production, there must be a political will to accept all of the associated political risks. Nevertheless, this alone is not sufficient. To encourage changes beyond their current scope, these nations must build institutional complementarity and lessen path dependency. In other words, a rise in productivity cannot be sustainable if there are not already established institutional mechanisms that are operating effectively. Economic populism should be removed from institutions. They have to be founded on economic policies that are more reasonable in accordance with the realities of the market. In the case that this does not occur, inflation will remain a significant issue. The currency will continue to be an obstacle to the maintenance of economic order. People will continue to struggle to find work, which will drive them to participate in black market. There will be a widespread presence of poverty, and the general standard of living will be significantly diminished. In addition, uncertainty will persist, which will have a detrimental effect on businesses, multinational companies, and entrepreneurship. Finally, insufficient institutions may reduce the government's ability to combat crime, the mafia, and terrorism. Only those nations that have the political will to follow through with significant institutional reforms in spite of the political risks involved will be able to move their societies into the next stage. Due to a lack of initiative and courage, political uncertainty makes it difficult for politicians to implement necessary institutional reforms.

5 Forms of economic populism

Economic populism manifests in several ways as a reaction to the unique challenges encountered by different countries. The working class may be drawn to a range of economic prospects. Various economic strategies may be formulated to serve this objective, depending upon the requirements of the people. The labor demand and supply in a country with a free market economy are primarily influenced by economic dynamics. Tax strategies might be used to attract the people in this particular kind of country. Xenophobia may have an impact on economic populism, and the disposition of the working class may change in response to a significant influx of immigrants in a country. It may be deduced from this that right-wing populism has the potential to locate a place in society where it can cultivate its ideologies (Mouffe, 2005). The disparity in earnings between immigrants and native workers may result in elevated levels of unemployment. A political party can attempt to appeal to individuals by advocating for increased employment opportunities via the implementation of immigration policies. In addition, if a country has lower competitiveness in international trade, it results in less employment possibilities and diminished wealth creation. A government may use economic mechanisms to establish boundaries for a market-driven economy. The United States employed this strategy in its relationship with China. The Trump administration expressed disapproval toward US multinational corporations operating in China, and this received significant media attention. To protect American workers from loss of employment and maintain the country's high standard of living, the administration suggested imposing trade restrictions specifically targeting the Chinese economy. The approach to economic populism varies across industrialized and developed countries. Economic populism in developed countries mostly focuses on preserving the private wealth of people and the employment sector. The main objective of economic populism in developing countries is to maintain the purchasing power of the working class. These countries possess economies that are classified within the medium-income bracket. People's earnings are significantly consumed by daily necessities, such as housing and food. Thus, wages play a crucial role in economic populism. Insufficient incomes provide more challenges in life, therefore making the achievement of financial stability a primary objective. The working class is continuously worried about the decrease in their ability to purchase things, which brings the exchange rate into the framework of economic populism. Substantial decrease in the currency's value function as a catalyst for

DOI: 10.4324/9781003438090-5

inflation, thereby further eroding the living standards of the working class. This might potentially compel governments to employ price control techniques, notwithstanding the limited long-term effectiveness of such applications. There is a potential for similar outcomes when populist policies are forced into action. The impact of wages, currency rates, and pricing controls may be succinctly described as a catalyst for populism in developing countries. It should not come as a surprise that economists have a negative opinion of populist politicians (Rodrik, 2018b). In the field of economics, populism is often associated with irresponsibility, inadequate policies, and unintentional consequences. The last phase of populism can give rise to circumstances that are unfavorable for the general populace. Politics in the modern era is a crucial component of global economic concerns. Certain circumstances attribute issues to cultural factors, such as immigration, which significantly fuels populism. However, this also has a direct relationship to the field of economics (Ricci, 2020). This phenomenon occurs as a consequence of economic difficulties in certain countries, which compel citizens to relocate to other nations in pursuit of employment prospects. Concerns arise among individuals that immigrants are displacing them from employment opportunities, leaving them devoid of other career options. The issue may have a more economic dimension rather than being simply a social matter.

As a distinguishing feature of economic populism, the lack of quantitative procedures for determining wage and exchange rate dynamics can be regarded the defining characteristic. This populism is a clear indication of a lack of a well-defined wage plan and an excessively overvalued currency. It is a strategy that employs economic instruments to attract people's interest. It fails to consider both the problem of excessive inflation and the possible danger of substantial depreciation in the currency rate. Hence, economic populism exhibits antagonism against both capitalist and communist economic principles. The basis of any of these two economic systems is on the use of quantitative procedures or the adoption of robust concepts. Communist economies are fundamentally based on the principles of centrally planned production and consumption. The expenditures must be adjusted to meet the needs of the community. Policies of austerity are implemented to ensure that people have access to the essentials of life. The free market economy is an important need for capitalist economies. Hence, it is highly discouraged for the government to engage in any kind of intervention. Both firms and consumers would like to witness their interaction inside a market that is governed by natural forces. In essence, it must function within the confines of a liberal democratic structure. The government enacts numerous initiatives to enhance the market's position, both inside the country and in the realm of global trade. The basic objective of international institutions is to provide favorable circumstances for the functioning of free markets. Economic populism lacks a foundation in established economic systems. An appeal to the public is presented using the economic instruments made accessible by the government and the central bank. It contradicts the fundamental principle of a free market economy. It may potentially disrupt the functioning of the pricing system. Populist regimes may manipulate taxes by disregarding the necessity of austerity measures. Disregarding productivity, they have the potential to stimulate an increase in wages, which might result in elevated consumer expenditure and an expansion of the money supply. They possess the capacity to exert influence on central banks, enabling them to lower interest rates and expand the money supply to fulfill monetary needs. The government may persist in providing assistance to sectors with poor productivity to ensure that people have access to public sector opportunities that provide more stable employment and social prestige compared to those available in the private sector. Central banks can influence exchange rates to generate an overvalued currency and a misleading perception of prosperity. Assuming that the economy can sustain these burdens indefinitely by continuously circulating money and collecting an infinite quantity of debt is an exceedingly irrational assumption. As a consequence, populist governments tend to attribute the failure of their economic policies on external factors outside their own boundaries. Ultimately, the working class may endure the brunt of escalating impoverishment and declining purchasing power. Nevertheless, the narrative of economic populism starts with pledges to enhance the financial status of impoverished and middle-class individuals, thereby expanding their purchasing power. It is rational to recognize that it is impractical to expect these people to resist economic populism. These countries may suffer from a pervasive lack of publicly acknowledged economic literacy. Enhancing the general understanding of populism would lead to a decrease in its detrimental impact on the economy. Individuals lack knowledge about the functions of the market and fail to comprehend the connection between expansionary policies and elevated levels of inflation. Hence, given the potential occurrence of hyperinflation, their only recourse is to find ways to satisfy their essential requirements.

Müller (2016) argues that populist governments undermine the integrity of existing institutions. They are opponents of the system that determines representation. In remaining with this concept, it is clear that populist regimes are the opponents of economic institutions. They possess the capacity to exert influence on mechanisms as well as the capacity to critique economic institutions for failing to fulfill their requirements. Statistical organizations and central banks are typical instances of such institutions. The central bank of the country lacks full authority. The media identifies it as a catalyst for escalating inflation. This occurs when the central bank utilizes interest rates, leading to inflation as a consequence. Conversely, based on a conventional economic theory, the connection between inflation and interest rates should be inverted. Heads of economic institutions often experience turnover under populist regimes. Administrations in democratic states are allowed to remain in office until the last day of their tenure. Populist governments evaluate these institutions in the framework of economic populism, considering their compliance with policy requirements. Assistance is only available to those who adhere to the norms considered acceptable by populists.

The term populism is subject to several interpretations in politics, primarily because it is difficult to categorize this notion under a single framework. Common populist economic solutions often include measures such as raising wages, implementing expansionary fiscal policies, using monetary instruments, providing benefits, and promoting government-led industrialization (Roberts, 2007). This strategy can be employed to both large populations and specific privileged groups, such as elite classes, communities, media, political, or cultural organizations. Hence, economic mechanisms may be applied to achieve the intended outcome of garnering popular support. Economic populism refers to the adoption of policies that eventually harm the economic welfare of the majority. These measures often disregard inflation and concerns over economic disparities (Kaltwasser, 2018). Economic institutions have the capacity to counteract populist regimes by curbing their political power. Populist governments in the realm of economics have the ability to disregard limitations placed on the implementation of economic policy. They are against self-governing regulatory entities that aim to meet the demands imposed by both internal and external limitations. The populist policies encounter a restricted range of options. Thus, it is crucial to regulate them (Rodrik, 2018b). To provide a clear and short explanation of what is meant by the phrase 'economic populism' in the context of this book, the following is provided: Economic populism refers to a set of government policies that are born by institutional reforms for the mass constituency. Ultimately, these policies will lead to a decline in the purchasing power of the working class and can be damaging to the overall welfare of both the people and the nation. Economic populism has its origins hidden deep into the foundations of institutional forms. Hence, even in the event of a new political party assuming power, there is a potential danger of succumbing to the obstacles imposed by outdated institutional forms that were formulated in the distant past. Therefore, the next government will have no difficulty in effectively governing the country via economic populism, or it should adopt the institutional form to formulate policies for the majority of the population. Populist governments can employ economic strategies to cultivate a substantial support base and provide short-term economic and social gratification.

Economic populism, as noted by Dornbusch and Edwards (1991), makes expansionary policies seem appealing but ultimately leads to failures. It is certain that inflation will continue to grow, that budget deficits will widen, and that economic crises are inevitable. Inflation and fluctuating currency rates will worsen economic conditions, hurting the poor the most. Exclusionary populism and inclusionary populism are two forms of economic populism that can both have an impact on the pattern of economic populism. The second kind is widespread in Latin America as well as in Türkiye. When governments have influence over the circulation of money, it has the potential to produce inflation in the economy. This may have a negative impact on low-income people and contribute to inequality. The fiscal and monetary policies of the populist administration are not constrained in any way. There is a noteworthy exception to this rule. It is permissible in the eyes of liberal economists for the government to utilize the authority and economic instruments at its disposal to protect democracy and the market economy. During the time of the Great Depression, this circumstance came about. In response to the risk posed by communism, governments attempted to formulate more demand-side measures, which were hailed as the only way to save the capitalist economy. The government should utilize its authority to prevent mass constituencies from hurting themselves. It is generally acknowledged that populism that undermines democratic principles and norms is a dangerous scenario. Rodrik (2018b) mentioned that economic populism is the one and only method that can be used to prevent the much more threatening kind of populism that is its cousin, political populism. Despite the fact that this assertion is accurate, economic populism has the potential to serve as a driving factor behind political populism, specifically, if economic populism is founded on institutions that are controlled by populist administrations. Before elections, these activities might include things like decreasing taxes or raising salaries as well as delivering financial incentives to mass constituencies.

Latin America is characterized by notable examples of economic populism. The Venezuelan administration is mostly influenced by economic populism due to the country's status as a major oil producer (Sagarzazu and Thies, 2019). Initially, the implementation of liberal economic policies was attempted, but due to their failure, there was a significant rise in government intervention in the market. This intervention gained the approval of the people (Davila, 2000). A national populist movement emerged in Bolivia with the aim of offering an alternative solution to the economic issues faced by the country, distinct from both socialism and capitalism. To achieve this objective, nationalist populism directed its critique against imperialism, which was viewed as the primary catalyst for the exploitation of the working class (Burke and Malloy, 1974). The financial well-being of the working class is intrinsically linked to government policies since this demographic represents a significant proportion of the population. Hence, the degree to which economic populism is evident differs between nations as a result of the impact of diverse institutional circumstances. Economic populism often targets the socioeconomic group that has gained the most from institutional reforms. Emerging populist parties, which gain pace from economic factors such as trade shocks, financial globalization, or migration, will exert pressure on a government, and the government will conform to these policies to appease populist parties. Populism in Western European states is often driven by immigration policy. The electoral performance of political parties may be impacted by migration, which can be perceived as an institution needs control. Political parties may increase their chances of gaining the support of the working class and the lower middle class by adopting migration policies that are more restrictive. The declining economic supremacy of the United States compared to China is a significant factor in the emergence of populism in the nation. Enhancing the nation's capacity to rival China and promoting its industries are strategies that obtain widespread favor.

When economic considerations began to shape populism, it also led to the emergence of economic populism, which may be defined as the implementation of excessively expansive macroeconomic policies. In other words, economic populism arises as a consequence of the expansion of populism, which is influenced by economic elements. Both fiscal and monetary policy have the potential to result in an expansionary macroeconomic stance. Government involvement in the market, whether via direct or indirect ways, aims to promote wage growth to stimulate consumption and preserve the purchasing power of the working class. Given the ongoing growth of the economy and its reliance on imported commodities, one way to stimulate demand is by boosting the value of the currency. Sachs (1989) highlighted the political pressure for macroeconomic measures aimed at enhancing the living standards of lower-income segments, resulting in poor economic performance. The problem is exacerbated by excessively expansionary macroeconomic policies driven by populist directives, resulting in elevated inflation and substantial imbalances in the balance of payments. Additionally, it has been asserted that Latin American countries intentionally kept their currencies at an artificially high value to prevent currency devaluations, which would result in a decrease in real wages. Economic populism can be defined as the deliberate manipulation of economic factors, such as wages and currency rates, to garner support from a substantial segment of the people. A connection exists between economic populism and a consistent occurrence of elevated inflation, volatile currency rates, and frequently unbalanced macroeconomic situations.

Policies on the macroeconomic front that are excessively expansionary cannot be maintained. Therefore, modifications to existing institutions are required to build an economy with less problems. In most cases, governments cannot pursue significant institutional reforms because they are afraid of the potential political backlash. They also have a general resistance to imposing restrictions on their freedom of action by establishing new institutions (Weyland, 1999). A government may lose control of the economy and power to another political party if it enforces institutional reforms that are detrimental to the working class. Two different characteristics of wage–labor relations are accountable for this situation. In the first place, salaries are an essential aspect of economic populism. Implementing a strategy that is flexible while also undermining the power of the working class might, therefore, culminate in an unfavorable response against the government. Second, given the importance of wages in influencing the election outcome of the working class, governments might be inclined to avoid making institutional reforms in favor of economic populism. This is due to the fact that wages are a significant factor in swaying the vote of the working class. Additionally, economic populism may pave the way for rivalry between political parties, regardless of the ideology of those parties whether they are on the left or the right, which can lead to the weakening of institutions. The form of the political system in existence is inconsequential; the crucial factor is the government's willingness to undertake the required institutional modifications, regardless of the risks involved. However, regarding the global dimension of economic revolutions, both left-wing and right-wing factions exhibit a notable similarity: They often hold identical viewpoints. Neoliberalism and deregulatory economics are ideas that can be countered by economic populism, and these concepts can give rise to a populist discourse. The populism attempts to explore unorthodox methodologies, maybe including the adoption of unprecedented policies that lack prior documentation or experimentation.

Dornbusch and Edwards (1991) researched macroeconomic populism in Latin American countries, while Kaufman and Stallings (1991) defined its hallmarks. The idea that real wages were utilized as a foundation for populist policies adopted by governments was the most significant conclusion included in both of these works. In the end, this contributed to excessive inflation as well as a decline in real wages. In other words, populism leads to economically inappropriate policies.

These are characterized by excessive expenditure, external debt, sky-high inflation, and, ultimately, dramatic economic reforms to bring stability back to the economy (Mudde and Kaltwasser, 2017). It is necessary for populists to use economics as a tool to affect political outcomes and satisfy the demands of mass constituencies. Economic populism has its origins in Latin America, where the scholars provided one of the first instances. Despite this, their approach remained quite constrained in terms of finding a solution to lessen the influence of economic populism. They failed to provide significant insights on the institutional characteristics of economic populism or its operational mechanisms inside an economy. They just focused on neoliberal policies and disregarded the interdependence that occurs among various institutional aspects. The suggestion was made that Latin American countries may enhance their export capabilities by adopting a more open approach. Nevertheless, it was disregarded that neoliberalism, which proposes an idealized economic model, should highlight the importance of an appropriate distribution of power. Furthermore, they conveyed the notion that a fixed exchange rate system may potentially expose an economy to substantial risks, although they neglected to underscore the importance of economic growth models in ensuring the preservation of macroeconomic stability. The economic progress of China would be unattainable under the existing system if the maintenance of a stable exchange rate presented a substantial danger. The crucial inquiry to be addressed is whether the present exchange rate is undervalued or overvalued. An overvalued currency might pose a threat to macroeconomic stability, even in a system with a flexible exchange rate. In addition, they failed to prioritize wage-setting policies and institutional reforms, which are essential components of industrialization. This process created a reliance on established practices and contributed to the emergence of economic populism.

In the 1970s, Western European nations experienced rising inflation, which required new institutional adjustments to reorient their economies toward growth in exports (Ünal, 2018). This meant giving up protectionism for export and consequently global trade. In the United Kingdom, which was experiencing issues with rising inflation and prevalent strikes, the government led by Thatcher attempted to decrease inflation and create a more flexible labor market with policies that were considered to be a form of authoritarian populism. These policies included operations on trade union power and existing welfare policies (Jessop, 1990; Jessop and Sum, 2006). Ünal (2016b, 2017, 2018) analyzed the institutional change of the Turkish economy and demonstrated that it still lacks institutional complementarity when inflation is taken into consideration. The concept of complementarity refers to the coexistence of multiple institutions that collaborate to steer an economy in a direction that is more favorable. The institutions collaborate to improve the desired outcome, which indicates that the confluence of their efforts produces higher performance (Amable, 2016; Glückler, 2020; Jackson and Deeg, 2008). When an economy is trying to reduce excessive inflation, depreciations in the currency rate, and other macroeconomic difficulties, pursuing expansionary fiscal policy while simultaneously conducting contractionary monetary policy produces conflict. The economy needs complementarity to function and to solve issues and provide stability. Path dependency, and thus economic populism, are reasons why complementarity cannot be generated. It is important to investigate how economic populism has played a part in the institutionalization of wage–labor relations. When an entity acquires negotiating power, it may lead to the emergence of economic populism. The alterations in the institutional forms that govern wage–labor relations, the tendency to follow established paths, and the imbalances in the overall economy can be served as indicators of economic populism.

The prevalence of economic populism in a given nation can be attributed to a variety of reasons. These factors change according to whether the nation is developed or developing. Economic populism builds momentum via a range of concerns that are distinct from those that are prevalent in populist nations such as Argentina and Türkiye. In industrialized nations, free market economics, flexibility of labor, and extreme neoliberal policies have prevailed because economic uncertainties have stoked public resentment of political elites. Particularly, neoliberalism is blamed for inspiring populism (Ricci, 2020). Neoliberalism is a system that calls for ongoing changes in both the economy and the social structure. As resentment levels rise, it might pave the way for the rise of populism as well as a backlash against required and unrestricted economic development in the country's production system. Low wages for unskilled employees, flexible and part-time jobs without social security, long-term unemployment, low social benefits, expensive education and health care, high taxation, and increased immigration are some of the factors that have driven people in industrialized nations to search for a populist leader. Populist parties have alleged that the elites have appropriated the wealth, job prospects, and public services of the people via their immigration and control strategies (Inglehart and Norris, 2016). Collective activities that attempted to organize and communicate the concerns faced by the working class were marginalized in industrialized nations. The bargaining power of employees was diminished. Their rights were restricted due to the requirements of international markets and multinational corporations. They are required to compete with other workers in terms of the global values and talents they possess. However, populism in emerging countries takes a very different form than it does in developed ones. There is a high rate of unemployment, vast social benefits, tax reductions, repressed prices, cheaper imported products, significantly high wage growth, public employment policies, an inflexible labor market, low part-time jobs, early retirement, bonuses, almost free education, and the low cost of health care service. The rights are not taken away from the people by their respective governments. Instead, the government needs to raise the amount of revenue it spends on public projects for the benefit of the working class. Populist parties in emerging nations adhere to economic policies that are antagonistic toward liberalism. People are concerned that they will lose their employment in the public sector if the economy is allowed to become more free-market oriented. Under the conditions of low internal competition, there is no required prerequisite for the labor force to enhance its level of expertise. Institutionalized wage–labor relations still cover a large portion of society due to minimum wage policy, negotiations, and wage-setting policies in private companies and public sectors despite the weakness of formal unionization and the decline of industrial workers due to technological advances. Both developed and developing countries are susceptible to the rise of economic populism. Despite this, it is still abundantly evident that populist policies in wealthy nations are far less harmful than those in poor countries. The presence of populism cannot be overcome by economic advancement and general prosperity. Populist actions are implemented in the short term, but the consequences eventually manifest in the long term. As a government increases its level of control over a country, there is a higher likelihood that support for the government can diminish.

The working class and populism

When assessing institutional forms, it is essential to regard wage as the most critical factor. The wage form, workforce structure, labor lifestyle, payment system, and the impact of the welfare state all play a crucial role in ensuring the reproduction of labor. In relation to this issue, many distinguishable components may be obtained from prior iterations. These include various methods of production: The distinctions between technical and social aspects of labor, the processes of hiring and employing workers, the variables that directly or indirectly affect income, and the ways in which commodities and social services are obtained outside of traditional market transactions (Boyer, 1990; Boyer and Yamada, 2000). The institutionalization of the wage–labor relation is an unavoidable prerequisite for the creation of a wage form. Over the course of history, countries have employed various strategies when it comes to determining how wages are structured. Wage–labor relations manifest in diverse and distinctive ways within the economic structures of different countries. The wage form has a significant place among the institutional forms in contemporary economies. There are several conceivable wage relationships. In countries characterized by free markets, a connection may arise between the working class and various industries. In economies characterized by regulated markets, however, it might emerge between the working class and administrative institutions. Economic populism entails the wage form, which denotes the interaction between the working class and political parties. The wage structure is defined as a distinguishing feature of economic populism, representing the antithesis of the dynamics observed in both free market and communist economies.

Commons (1925a) asserted that the working class lacks the ability to choose their own boss, but an individual worker has the potential to transition out of the class and into a leadership position within the capitalist system. Wage earners must unite as a collective group to progress inside a socialist system and assume control over their own work. The working class includes people from diverse religious, ethnic, racial, communal, organizational, ideological, gender, age, and intellectual backgrounds. Nevertheless, all competing values and ideologies emphasize their own importance in relation to work and compensation. The level of incompetence presented is reduced due to the influence of populism. It diminishes the conflicting ideologies on work and salaries. It has the capacity to unite all individuals on a common trajectory. Essentially, it gives the working class the ability to wield influence in representation on comparable with that of an employer. Society is incentivized via the use of economic instruments. The working class ultimately recognized that they might potentially acquire more advantages from capitalism by participating in collective bargaining and using the state's authority over industries.

The institutionalization of wage–labor relations and two primary elements of macroeconomic dynamics can provide an explanation for the pattern of economic populism. The first concern is the escalating wages that are surpassing both the increasing productivity and inflation rate. This political phenomenon can be defined as wage populism. When it comes to economics, this kind of populism requires a significant degree of involvement from the government, and it also calls for wages to be standardized throughout the country. The populist administration is able to exert a greater level of control over the working class throughout the whole of the nation if it implements a national wage policy that is uniform. This indicates that the government has the authority to make decisions on wages throughout the entire economy. The goal of wage populism is often to provide benefits to employees, those earning the minimum wage, and public servants. When evaluating wage dynamics in economic populism, it is not crucial to give much importance to characteristics such as productivity, inflation, and competitiveness. The lack of consideration for inflation in the market, as well as macroeconomic imbalances, is quite evident. Within the framework of economic populism, the labor movement can be regarded as a left-wing populist movement that opposes the influence of existing institutions or right-wing ideologies. This kind of activism is in direct opposition to liberal economic policies such as privatization, foreign intervention, and open economies (Panizza and Miorelli, 2009).

In developing countries, throughout the 1960s, the institutional changes that were brought about for the benefit of the working class rendered the labor movement increasingly reliant on the policies of the government. In particular, salaries became a way of protecting and attracting employees, and each political change aimed to emphasize the interests of the majority of people in society (Richardson, 2009). This led to the formation of an interdependent relationship between the working class and the government. The government transformed into a populist power structure with the goal of preserving its position. This was accomplished by giving priority to the concerns of the working class and defending its interests against open economic policies, privatizations, and free-market economic reforms. Naturally, liberal economic policies that reduce inflation and promote competitiveness and productivity are not in the immediate interests of the working class. However, these policies may be favorable for the economy overall. The working class has shown throughout history that it is capable of self-organization for the purpose of defending its purchasing power, improving working conditions, and ensuring continual employment. Wages are the primary means by which economic populist nations satisfy the demands of their working classes. This is the simplest approach to give the impression that a rise in earnings results in an increase in purchasing power. Inflation may be spurred by excessive wage growth that is not connected with economic growth, which can cancel out any actual improvement in purchasing power. In these nations, higher wage demands are often prompted by the persistently rising cost of living. Wage rises have the potential to exacerbate existing inequalities if not all workers get the same degree of raise. Wages in countries that do not suffer from persistent inflation are often left up to the forces of the market or are managed to remain in line with overall economic expansion. The purpose of this fiscal strategy is to maintain a stable level of prices in the market. During election periods, wage growth has the potential to exceed the inflation rate. Nevertheless, this leads to higher levels of inflation in the subsequent years. Upon examining economic populist regimes, it becomes evident that the working class often experiences a significant increase in their wages, either before or after an election. Regardless of whether the government is populist in nature, whether it be economic or political. When governments attempt to garner support among the working class, they often concentrate their efforts on three specific categories: Civil officials, those receiving the minimum wage, and employees of private enterprises. Furthermore, governments may also endeavor to entice those who are already retired or get benefits via transfer programs.

Labor populism provides a notion that closely approximates the definition of populism as a perspective focused on the working class. According to Roberts (2006), labor populism was defined as a significant element influencing the policies enacted by Peronists. The formation of labor unions is intrinsically connected to the ideology of labor populism. Hence, labor unions have the capacity to function as the primary mechanism for implementing populist ideas. Peron proactively undertook the task of mobilizing workers to secure their support on a political scale. Consequently, there was a significant surge in union membership among workers under his leadership. Peronists constructed their movement on the labor force, which served as its foundation. Moreover, these workers who were part of a labor union orchestrated powerful protests that prevented Peron from getting imprisoned in 1945. The workforce has since become a vital element of national political campaigns and activities. Roberts (2007) noted that following the 1980s, economic crises as well as reforms led to the weakening of labor unions and parties that were founded on a mass base of support. Although this may be more accurate for nations that were able to effectively create their new economic systems via the implementation of neoliberal policies and free market economies, it is possible that this is not the case for certain nations. The connection between governments and mass organizations is inevitably disrupted as a natural consequence of privatization and other neoliberal economic policies. The institutional structure could still be functioning. In particular, rules and norms for the working class might not be abandoned even if governments strive to follow deregulation procedures. After the 1980s, most nations experienced a drop in their level of unionization. This also provided antielitists and political actors with opportunities to directly contact with unorganized mass constituencies. The policies of the government may be utilized to put into effect the regulations and norms that are applicable to workers who earn the minimum wage, workers who are working in the public sector, and workers who are employed in private enterprises. In such a situation, it would be pointless to consider the rates of unionization in countries since it would be irrelevant. This is due to the fact that there is still a strong connection between the government and the working class. The minimum wage as well as other sorts of wages that are appealing to the mass constituency may be easily determined by populist regimes. Considering the growth rate of productivity is necessary if wage growth is to be sustainable in the economy. Raising wages that outpace the growth of both domestic and export productivity are an indication of unjustified wage growth. This may lead to high inflation as well as high interest rates, particularly in the case when the rate of wage increase is much greater than the rate of growth in domestic productivity. Additionally, an unstable exchange rate is the result of a situation in which the pace of rise in wages is larger than the growth rate in export productivity. Measuring the impact of the labor force on wages is important for understanding the factors driving wage cost and their underlying dynamics (Ünal and Köse, 2018). A wage growth rate that is above the rate of inflation is what the trade unions demand. A high rate of wage growth may be needed as long as inflation remains high. When it comes to collective bargaining, trade unions often point to the rate of inflation as a legitimate reason for significant wage increases. The real pace of economic growth is a crucial factor that is determined via collective agreements to ensure that the labor force gets a large share of benefits from the expanding economy. This is particularly true in developed countries. Over time, a substantial increase in real economic growth is expected to result in a significant surge in wages. Trade unions may use this information to advocate for proportional wage increase in line with real economic expansion. In countries that are still in the process of developing, the situation may be rather different. In these nations, the inflation rate often surpasses real economic growth. In the context of collective agreements, the major emphasis is given to the rate of inflation rather than economic progress.

The exchange rate system and populism

An essential instrument for adjusting the purchasing ability of the working class is a modification in the currency rate. Populist economic policies are extensively connected to the exchange rate since it serves as a means of regulating prices and purchasing power (Dornbusch and Edwards, 1991; Szusterman, 2000). Governments recognize that preserving an artificially overvalued currency rate is crucial for sustaining political support. Despite the significant inflation in the economy, real wages are being increased without considering this factor. Additionally, the exchange rate is being artificially kept at a stronger value to counteract the price hikes caused by imports. It is conceivable to consider it a mechanism that is accountable for the growth of real wages that is the driving force behind prices and exchange rates (Checchi, 1996). Therefore, an overvalued currency rate is a fundamental weapon in populist economic strategies. Through the implementation of such policies, governments might attempt to gain the support of the working class by manipulating wages and currency values. If these populist policies remain unchanged, any increments in nominal wages may be nullified by the devaluation of a currency. In the event of a substantial depreciation of the national currency, there may arise demands for fresh elections and the establishment of a new government. Having an exchange rate that is higher than its actual worth might potentially reduce the political risk connected with elections for a government that strongly opposes a devaluation in the exchange rate. Consequently, the working class is able to maintain their purchasing power unaffected by imported goods, hence preventing cost increase and subsequent inflation. Failure to take into account the rate of production growth while raising wages may result in substantial inflation and an unstable exchange rate. At the end, this results in a rise in the trade deficit and has the potential to produce a considerable depreciation in the value of the currency, which in turn has an effect on the purchasing power of the working class.

Developing economies are considerably far from the technological frontier, which is under the dominance of industrialized economies. They have an obligation to import both the intermediate and final goods, which might vary in terms of technological sophistication from moderate to advanced. Their economy is mainly dependent on imports. Hence, when an economy relies on an overvalued currency, there is an increased likelihood of encountering trade balance problems. An excessively maintained currency is crucial for obtaining imported goods at reduced rates. Conversely, the working class could experience a decrease in their purchasing power due to a devalued currency rate. The economies may experience panic and financial crises as a result of abrupt devaluation of their currency. It is common practice to suppress the exchange rate, which may ultimately lead to an overvaluation of the currency. There are three different approaches that countries might choose to determine their currency exchange rates: Fixed, managed, or flexible. It is a significant issue to consider whether or not it is permissible for a currency to be overvalued. Political concerns are associated with currencies that are not permitted to depreciate. However, it is inevitable that this will happen as a direct result of continuing price increases. Currencies in economically populist states often experience volatility and persistent devaluation. The occurrence of a currency crisis has the potential for a government to hand over power to an alternative political faction.

Price control is a widely used approach across all types of economies and is not exclusive to populist governments. However, populist governments specifically use expansionary policies to assert dominance over the working class and thereby reduce the amount of political vulnerability. Specifically, individuals may become dissatisfied with these policies when the price of essential daily necessities increases. The obligation is on the market, rather than the government, in such circumstances. The media often attributes the responsibility of increasing prices and stockpiling in anticipation of future demand on markets and companies. In general, governments would assert that this constitutes an exogenous threat to the market, deliberately orchestrated by corporations to augment their profits. While it may be advantageous for businesses to maintain their manufacturing operations, the working class often regards this as unbearable. Hence, governments are occasionally compelled to participate in the market to demonstrate their ability to regulate price levels. Furthermore, sometimes, with governmental assistance, novel enterprises are founded, capable of providing commodities at rates that are more affordable than those of established competitors. These factors contribute to the overall perception among the general public that governments serve as protectors of the working class against the avarice of companies. While governments possess the capacity to manipulate prices temporarily, according to general equilibrium theory, prices will ultimately stabilize at their natural market levels.

6 Rising economic populism in Argentina and Türkiye

The institutionalization of the wage–labor relation in Argentina and Türkiye contributed to the rise of economic populism in both countries. Due to the concurrent institutional changes, both countries underwent the process of industrialization, resulting in a transition of the population from the agricultural industry to the manufacturing industry. Prior to this, the working class had a less organized and more widespread distribution throughout the nation, residing in small towns that were often situated in rural regions. According to Finchelstein (2017), there is a strong historical connection between populism and fascism. The current state of our globe is characterized by factors such as economic instability, xenophobia, and populism, which continue to shape its development. However, it should be noted that none of these issues are novel. They had previously existed. He asserts that fascism marked the inception of history, whereas populism currently reigns as the prevailing political philosophy. The acceptance of a nondemocratic administration served as the catalyst for the emergence of populism in Argentina. The embrace of democratic values is a crucial requirement for the rise of populism in this context. Roberts (2006) asserts that the transitional periods in Latin American countries provided favorable conditions for the emergence and growth of populism. During this period, there was an extensive adoption of import substitution as part of the industrialization process. Amid periods of change, devoted factions often disassociate themselves from well-established political organizations. This is a favorable chance for populist leaders to take advantage of the situation. With each political change, new classes of people who have previously had no involvement in politics come to the forefront. The emergence of mass politics is a direct outcome of the era of industrialization. Emerging economies underwent the process of import substitution industrialization. During this period, collaborative alliances were established between workers and their affiliated labor organizations. This presented populist parties with a chance to capitalize on this trend as a means to administer a large constituency, distribute rewards among various constituencies, and harness the political involvement of their supporters. Previously, it was difficult to get a consensus on economic issues. In other words, there were no labor unions advocating for the interests of the working class throughout that period. Following the institutionalization of the working class as an official part of society in these nations, the practice of bargaining for wages and engaging in strikes became the norm. The governments tried to preserve a fragile equilibrium of power, despite

DOI: 10.4324/9781003438090-6

the considerable strength of the left wing or, particularly, the influence exerted by the Soviet Union. Conversely, this institutional transformation also contributed to the emergence of economic populism. Prior to 1946, Türkiye was under the rule of a single party–controlled government. After the Second World War, the people expressed discontentment with the limited democratic alternatives at their disposal. Society's ability to choose a ruling party from a diverse range of possibilities had become crucial. The implementation of this institutional change resulted in fierce competition among political parties. Wage dynamics had become an essential instrument in the policymaking process. The events that occurred in Argentina have a striking resemblance to those that transpired in other nations. The process of making a society more democratic and the competition among several political parties made way for the acceptance of utilizing economic instruments to influence societal behavior. Antagonism becomes a feasible option when political parties start to compete, challenging preexisting political ideologies and the coalitions that support them. At this juncture, the formation of the populist movement begins. In the context of elections and political decision-making, economic populism is frequently employed as an approach to attract the general public and garner widespread support. Hence, economic populism is not founded on doctrines but rather on aspirations, passions, and potential risks. At the start, it was established to satisfy the needs of the socioeconomically disadvantaged segments of the society. After the end of the Second World War, the Argentinian government turned its attention to import substitution industrialization as a strategy to revive the nation's domestic market. First, local industries should be developed, and then, those sectors should be opened up to trade with other countries. The new approach signified substantial institutional changes not just in Argentina but also in Türkiye. These changes had place in the mode of production, leading to the government ultimately being the dominant participant in the market. Furthermore, the working class acquired more influence. The bond between the working class and the government became even more robust.

When employed efficiently, import substitution industrialization can function as an advantageous strategy that promotes domestic industries in enhancing their organizational structure and infrastructure to effectively compete in the global market. This mode of production must be extensively scrutinized. Attempting to stimulate growth in every area of the economy is not practical. Identifying certain industries with the capacity to impact other industries, both directly and indirectly, is essential. For instance, the automobile industry has the potential to have an impact on a diverse range of other sectors, including the textiles, furniture, steel and iron, plastic, energy, machinery, and electronics industries, among others. Indirect industries have room for improvement in terms of productivity. Therefore, the approach needs to be centered on potentially applicable sectors. In addition, this strategy needs to only be used temporarily. Unfortunately, it is not simple to update institutions as new developments arise. It is especially difficult to reduce the influence that the government has. When the working class assumed control over the economy, any efforts to revitalize production would be futile due to the extremely inflexible nature of the institutional forms, making them resistant to modification. This is a side effect of import substitution industrialization to prepare industries for international trade. A strong working class is essential to the success of this approach. If we go back to the Great Depression of 1929, we may attribute the decline in output to the low effective demand that existed at the time. Conditions for overproduction were developed before the 1929 crisis, and production had begun to rise with the advent of Ford's moving assembly lines. However, even if output was enhanced by using more recent technological advances, it would not be possible to adopt novel types of institutional forms. The most important factor in this was the absence of power to regulate the establishment of appropriate institutional forms, despite the fact that a new model for economic growth had been developed. In other words, the time period in consideration was incapable of providing a sufficient response to the innovations that took place. To adjust to these modifications, novel regulations had to be created and implemented. Following the crisis, sectors underwent extensive redesigns as a result of new institutional reforms in an effort to maintain demand. The working class was able to gain power via mass production, which prevented employers from suppressing salaries, which would have been detrimental to demand.

Consolidating the influence of the working class poses a significant political risk for the government, thus granting rights could be a more straightforward approach than implementing institutional changes. Both of these countries employed import substitution industrialization as an innovative approach, which, however, became problematic due to its association with increased levels of inflation. The presence of the working class, along with the reliance on the market and government intervention, created significant obstacles in confronting the persisted issue of inflation. When a government sets restrictions on its borders and enforces high tariffs, there is a greater need to satisfy domestic demand. The process of industrialization can fail due to a lack of demand. The government should naturally have a role in setting salaries for public employees, those earning the minimum wage, and others to drive demand for the primary industries. Extensive and robust protection may develop in all economic activities without the selection of essential sectors. It is possible that this may promote industries that have a low level of impact or connections to other industries. If institutional reforms cannot be performed rigorously and sensitively, lobbyists would be able to promote their facilities as the most influential activities. As a result, they can have an enhanced capacity to exploit the advantages of imposing high taxes, restrictions, and quotas. Policymakers can be influenced by persuasive arguments that advocate for the elimination of certain sectors, even if such industries have the potential to make a substantial contribution to the economy. Although both countries implemented import substitution industrialization, their industrial growth remained modest. Although the strategy has not been successful, its institutional forms continue to operate in the present day. Evidence indicates the existence of a significant trade deficit, low productivity, extensive government involvement, and a deceleration in economic advancement. The strategy of industrialization should be built upon the basis of cost-effective production. The working class may exert substantial pressure on the industrial process. The convergence of substantial benefits and unrestrained authority may have catastrophic consequences for enterprises. The working class endured coercion to expedite the development of cost-effective manufacturing, while domestic industries were protected by import restrictions. East Asian countries could employ substantial pressure by actively attempting to boost their exports. The plan exhibited both similarities and differences between two areas. Despite substantial government intervention in the economies of East Asian countries, they managed to sustain low manufacturing costs. This arose as a direct outcome of the strategy to enhance the volume of exports. The requirement for demand was relatively unfulfilled in the domestic market, but instead, it was satisfied in overseas markets.

Import substitution industrialization resulted in a substantial increase in government investments in essential sectors such as mining, oil, and chemical industries, as well as telecommunications and other large monopolistic firms. Given the perception that these are critical sectors, it became very challenging to operate them according to the principles of a free market economy. A large portion of production and employment was kept by public corporations.[1] Nevertheless, as the government pursued protectionist economic policies, these businesses became a significant financial burden on the state. The process of making regulations turned into a political risk, and to make manufacturing more efficient, the majority of the people employed by the government had to be fired. As a result, this became a significant obstacle in the way of deregulation initiatives. When political parties first attempted to win the support of the people, they advocated for nationalization as an alternative to privatization. Adopting populist economic measures does not enhance the purchasing power of the working class. Conversely, their earnings witness a substantial decline due to significant currency devaluations and escalating inflation. The currency rate of Argentina exhibited significant volatility on several occasions. This serves as a terrific instance of examining the economic conditions in Latin American nations. Shortly after the country achieved independence in the 1800s, indications of economic instability began to emerge. Subsequently, the economy had many instances of currency devaluation.

After significant events, such as a financial crisis, Argentina began the process of implementing structural changes. The situation in Türkiye was the same. However, neither nation was able to successfully complete the economic reforms. New power structures are likely to evolve along the evolutionary path of economies, modifying the distribution of power. In each of these nations, authoritarian governments came to power in an effort to dismantle legacy colonial or imperial institutions. As a consequence, two nations were able to get closer to democracy. Traditions and religious beliefs were the primary foundation for many of the older institutional structures. On the other hand, this shift, which was being driven by national populism, could result in societies that are more secular and contemporary. The authoritarian governments made efforts to create modern, democratic, and progressive societies founded on shared principles of morality. Because of this, national populism may be distinguished from both left-wing and right-wing factions due to its primary objective, which is to reach the middle-class society. It was the urbanization of the masses that gave rise to the national populist movement (Anselmi, 2018). Massive migration from rural regions to the cities and industries of nascent authoritarian regimes has the potential to define new social and political strata. This urbanized society served as the primary inspiration for both the Perón populism of Argentina and the national populism of Türkiye, both of which were mostly influenced by coalition administrations that are similar to one another or by traditional ideologies on the left.

In Argentina, the Peronist movement has been a populist phenomenon. It has been an antiparty movement since the charismatic leader was responsible for making the majority of the choices. Populist rhetoric is distinguished by its focus on the working class (Barros, 2005). The rise of Peronism served as a turning point in the process of defining democratic and political identities in Argentina. Not only did Perón play a significant role in the institutionalization of wage–labor relations, but he also played a significant role in the establishment of polarization and antagonism in Argentina. Antagonism became a more important tool in political strategy than the creation of political consent (Groppo, 2009). Perón had the potential to introduce a new style of leadership, an attractive ideological sensation, appealing masses, and rhetoric that interested the people. He did not have a clear philosophy or an extreme political perspective that he could use to appeal to the people. The strategy of Peronism was a political maneuver that institutionalized the wage–labor relationship as a means of bringing together previously disparate groups of people. The populist policies centered mostly on the viewpoints and demands of ordinary individuals as their primary constituents. The policies of the Peronist party are often characterized as a struggle between the ordinary people and the ruling elite. A new form of policy that is molded according to the working class and its components emerged as a result of the rapid industrialization that took place in the nation. This led to a cohesive and homogeneous class that, from an institutional standpoint, brought together people of varying beliefs, genders, and expectations. Political parties have used this practice to gain support from the people even after Perón's death. This political approach is founded on the opinions of the general population. It opposes policies that are favorable to the nation as well as policies that are reasonable and might be important for the interests of the country. As a result, it is not difficult to apply economic strategies to this political phenomenon. Following the end of the Second World War, personal power and public agreement came to be considered as more important, which led to the continuation of what was perceived as the fascist ideology of Peronism (Finchelstein, 2018; Kenworthy, 1973). However, Perón can also be considered as a political leader who pulled the working class away from the concept of socialism by offering a pragmatic package to promote contentment. In other words, he satisfied their need for pragmatism.

The policy agendas of left-leaning parties in Türkiye were built around the principles and objectives of Atatürk. Following the first establishment of democracy, a multitude of political parties arose. During the 1950s, liberal economic policies were far more widespread compared to the present. Although Türkiye did not actively participate in the Second World War, it was included in the development initiatives of the Marshall Plan. This had an advantageous effect on the Turkish economy via liberal policies. This era came into existence as a response to the restricted economic policies that Türkiye imposed during that time period.

Following its victory in democratic elections, the newly established government endeavored to cultivate more amicable ties with the United States. Turkish military forces also participated in the Korean War. The country received financing to enhance the agriculture and automotive industry in the nation. In the 1960s, the Turkish economy increasingly relied on protectionist policies. Since the 1960s, Türkiye has been plagued by chronic macroeconomic imbalances resulting from excessive money supply, which has become a detrimental condition. During the 2000s, conservatism had a significant increase in popularity. This ideology is rooted on long-standing structures and imperial concepts that have been present for centuries. This was acknowledged as a right-wing movement. This was in contrast to the newly created left-wing institutions in Türkiye. Nevertheless, economic populism remained prevalent in each of these situations. Argentina encounters a situation that is fairly similar to this one. The beginning of this tendency in Argentina occurred throughout the 1940s. Although populism in this country is sometimes referred to as Peronism, it is important to note that economic populism is the exclusive manifestation detached from any specific political ideology and instead rooted in institutional reforms. The success of populist governments in these countries hinges on their capacity to construct a cohesive social group that brings together the majority, despite their diverse ideology and economic differences. Although the government of Argentina was formed by more populist and closed economic policies, liberalism was always there as an option. Through the process of rewarding them, Peronism effectively established its own working class. The hitherto individual hopes of the working class became a subject of extensive public concern. Urban workers converged with a collective demand. Political leaders who can discern the needs of the working class and implement policies that respond to their demands emerge as significant actors in elections.

The process of industrialization in Argentina started much earlier than in Türkiye. Following the First World War, Türkiye made an effort to mitigate the damage caused by the war. It struggled to maintain its position while having significant war debts. The pace of industrial growth was remarkable, but progress toward becoming a developed nation was moderate and required an extended period of time in Türkiye. Migrants from Argentina's rural regions made their way to the country's newly industrialized cities in the 1930s, marking the beginning of the country's transition to a new growth model. Both Buenos Aires and Rosario evolved into cities that were home to the country's working class. Therefore, Peronism rose to prominence in these urban centers throughout the 1940s (Panizza, 2005). In the decades spanning the 1940s and 1970s, Perón rose to authority as a political figure. In the early 1940s, he was a part of the militarist movement that led a coup that ousted the administration of Castillo and took power for themselves. He became a key member of this movement among political organizations. Policies regarding the national economy were enacted by the militarist regime. It positioned itself as both a governing body and a protector of democratic principles in the country where it was put into effect. It was mentioned that the real goal of military rule was to restore institutions and provide freedom to the people. The military government legitimized its position by stating that its goals were to organize the nation, decrease the number of corrupt acts of government, clean up the administration, and restore the country to its original principles. Once the tasks have been completed, the government intends to hand over control of its position to the general political environment. Attracting the working class, which was growing in influence as the economy transformed from agriculture to manufacture, was a crucial part of Perón's strategy throughout the period. This represented a fundamental shift in the way the nation would proceed with its economic paradigm. Antagonism and political conflict were increased as an outcome of the labor rights problem, which became an important concern. The political approach was geared on recognizing the working class. Perón's charismatic leadership and his ability to manage the mass constituencies via rhetoric won over the new social class (Groppo, 2009). The desire of the government to have supporters, as well as the economic instruments it had, were essential considerations in populist policy. Significant changes were made to institutional forms to enhance social security, provide greater salary, and increase the minimum wage. In addition, he made the first steps toward legalizing labor unions by outlawing competing unions. The working class and the elites were engaged in power battles, and the government was a prominent player in those conflicts. The distribution of the wealth was determined with the use of economic instruments. The idea of class alliances and antagonisms came into existence. The class struggle focused on getting higher salary increase rather than concentrating on how the nation may become more efficient and productive to meet its demands. There was no external force that had a part in protecting lobbyists, and the function of government was not one of them. The government and its policies were regarded as economic intermediary that aided the working class by fostering antagonism. In 1946, he had a good chance of winning the election. He was victorious in elections once again in 1948, 1951, and 1954. Notwithstanding this, his leadership was unable to continue because the economic issues that had been plaguing the country became worse, and he was unable to garner support from the church or the military. As a consequence, after he was sent to exile, he was required to leave the chair. After a significant amount of time had passed, he was finally elected, but upon taking office, he was met with further economic turmoil and chaos (Muno, 2019). Although the populist ideas were successful in getting the candidate elected, they were not enough to stabilize the economy.

In the 1980s, significant institutional reforms were necessary and were accomplished via liberal and deregulatory policies. Although governments had vowed to implement these policies, they remained hesitant and unsuccessful. The liberalization of the economy was pushed forward after a military coup in Argentina in 1976 (Pion-Berlin, 1985; Jordan, 1977). The situation was similar in Türkiye in 1980. Nevertheless, the adoption of open economic policies, intended to reduce inflation and minimize government interference, proved to be an ineffective approach. Although all the major political parties promised to address the macroeconomic imbalances, none of them were able to provide a robust and precise solution. What strategies may a government employ to decrease inflation while simultaneously boosting wage growth by over 50%? Moreover, what specific measures might a government utilize to mitigate inflation while implementing continuous expansionary policies? An exchange rate system that remains fixed is not the solution. The populist regimes that were elected often made inconsistent promises. The one factor that masked economic difficulties is the growing openness. The outcome of the fixed exchange rate and artificially low costs was to alleviate the dissatisfaction among the people. Both of these nations exhibit the characteristic of possessing a weak democracy, and the reforms that were implemented subsequent to import substitution industrialization were futile in their endeavors to construct export-oriented and internationally competitive countries. It was still possible to find remnants of the previous rules and regulations.

The institutionalization of wage–labor relations

The institutionalization of wage–labor relations marked a significant turning point for both nations. The labor movement became structured to protect its own interests. This took place in Türkiye throughout the 1960s and 1970s. In 1960, when Türkiye made the decision to continue with its planned economic programs, policies shifted, and as a result, the laws were modified in favor of the working class. In 1963, workers obtained the right to organize strikes. During this period, trade unions achieved the newfound capacity to engage in collective bargaining, marking a significant milestone in the realm of institutional economics. In 1963, Türkiye first began officially experiencing the total number of working days that were lost due to the strike. A new piece of law that was enacted in 1965 laid the groundwork for the organization of public servants. In 1974, a regulation that required employers to pay a certain minimum wage went into effect. The issue that attracted the most interest was the year in which a national minimum wage was instituted across all sectors of employment. The 1960s were a pivotal decade for Türkiye since it was at this time that the country began its transition to an industrial economy and workers began migrating from rural to urban regions. During these years, it became easier for trade unions to attract new members and organize strikes that were more successful. In Türkiye, the growth of trade unions had the purpose of encouraging domestic consumption, much as in developed nations. As a necessary result of this, Türkiye implemented a strategy of import substitution industrialization. The primary objective of this policy is to provide assistance to native industries, and one method of doing so is to place restrictions on imports. Because of this, labor was a significant component of not just production but also household consumption. The labor force, which acquired legal rights throughout the course of time, became a significant element of state policy and developed the capacity to impact wage rises and inflation. The number of working days that were lost as a result of strikes reached an all-time high in the 1990s, and the number of strikes that were organized by trade unions remained high in general until the 2000–2001 economic crisis.

The early 1900s witnessed the beginning of efforts in Argentina to create a legally mandated minimum wage for its workforce. Joaquin V. Gonzalez, minister of the interior, presented a proposal for labor that included provisions for a minimum wage in both the public and private sectors. There were legislative proposals in various years. However, Argentina passed legislation that created a minimum wage for workers throughout the country in 1964 (Campano, 1966). The government of this nation gave its approval to a minimum wage policy that was designed to attract support from a wider cross-section of the population. During the 1940s, Perón was a significant player in the process of increasing the pressure that trade unions exerted on the political environment. This presented a chance to legitimate his rule with the widespread support of the working class, who had hitherto fought to obtain rights and participate in political processes. The populist leadership was able to pay attention to the demands of the common people who had congregated in large numbers in the manufacturing facilities of the main cities. The working class was not repressed by the government; rather, the populist regime began an endeavor to harness the political power of workers. This resulted in the working class giving their consent and legitimacy to the policies. In particular, Perón was effective in responding to the aspirations of ordinary people. He was able to effectively apply populist strategies to interact with the working class, which has evolved into a massive support constituency for populist policies even in the present day. The enduring implementation of new reforms continues to be hindered by the considerable institutional changes established during the era of import substitution industrialization. Governments have undertaken endeavors at different times in their past to establish stronger relationship with the working class via the establishment of labor organizations. The working class and the government forged robust connections due to certain institutional modifications. The workers' rights functioned as a conduit through which the government could directly engage with the people. The government would be motivated to sustain these connections in the next years irrespective of the economic trajectory.

Following the end of the Second World War, a significant number of industrialized nations adopted a development strategy that prioritized domestic consumption, as noted by Ünal (2018). One of the primary dynamics inherent in this model is to the working force, which constitutes the foremost component that supports domestic consumption. Given that domestic consumption serves as the primary driver of economic development, several policies are enacted to bolster the labor force and maintain their ability to make purchases inside the domestic market. One of the most significant initiatives among these was the provision of formal union rights to the workers. Another significant policy implemented during this time was the consideration of the inflation rate while implementing wage increase, with the aim of protecting the purchasing power of the workers. Constitutional amendments provide the concrete framework for institutional reforms. This development contradicts the fundamental principles of liberal democracy such as free market economy, checks and balances, and the idea of separation of powers. After the institutional changes that occurred in wage–labor relations in both countries, the working class was able to build a more solid and formal structure. As a result, the institutional revisions in the laws concerning trade unions and labor rights undermined the division of powers and stability in the market, both of which are essential for the efficient functioning of a free market and a liberal economy. The working class rose to prominence and gained power throughout this time period. Therefore, it will be far more difficult to alter and rearrange this robust structure.

The collective will of the people exercised a dominant and unambiguous impact. The elites, who had influence over the industries and businesses, were disregarded. The negotiation process led to a reduction in the influence of industry, ultimately establishing direct contact between the government and the working class.

Agricultural output serves as the first foundation for nations as they embark on their path toward economic growth. Work is conducted without any regulations, and remuneration is received via the informal sector. A substantial proportion of the workforce is employed in the agricultural sector of the economy. The growth of urban populations relies on the development of agricultural businesses and the adoption of new technological equipment. In other words, agricultural production stimulates industrial output. The agricultural sector has a gradual decrease in production, while the manufacturing sector lures workers away from rural areas and unproductive agricultural fields due to new government regulations. This suggests that workers are integrated with modern culture. Both extensive government intervention in the economy and protectionism may create different labor markets. The working class has access to employment opportunities both in the governmental sector and in privately managed companies. Labor is incorporated into the activities of the industrial sector. During the period when agriculture was the dominant economic activity, people lived in rural areas throughout the nation. Workers were unable to effectively organize and assert their rights. Conversely, the expansion of industrial sectors could employ individuals who shared similar ideas. Workers performing for public corporations had the chance to enjoy increased wages, enhanced employment stability, retirement, and improved healthcare benefits. Due to technological advancements, people in industrial enterprises may face unemployment and subsequently shift their careers into the newly developing industries. It is possible that workers can be employed in a manner that is more flexible at this stage. Nonetheless, the implementation of a minimum wage policy within the framework of import substitution industrialization for urban workers results in significant dependence of the service sector on government involvement. The expansion of trade unions was driven by the need to regulate wage dynamics.

Previously, there was apprehension over precarious employment that may be terminated abruptly. Nevertheless, to prevent a decrease in real demand and maintain the market's vitality, assurances were given to the employees to prevent layoffs. Given the possible risks associated with pay reductions and arbitrary layoffs, it is crucial for employees to possess the capacity to establish labor organizations. This enables them to defend against a decrease in demand and maintain the stability of domestic industries. To fulfill the requirements associated with the growth model and wage–labor relations, institutional reforms were adopted. Employment prospects were given high priority in multiple aspects of large-scale and mass manufacturing. During this period, manufacturing areas included industrial hubs that prioritized employment and emphasized the government's role in maintaining a substantial purchasing power. The concept of governmental intervention in the market gained popularity, while the conviction in allowing the market to operate freely remained unpopular. Certain rising countries have benefited in particular ways by deemphasizing free trade. Due to their emphasis on domestic industries, these nations were unable to rival the more dominant economies, namely the East Asian countries known as the Asian Tigers. The industries in these countries had advanced to the extent that they were able to engage in global market competition. This might be achieved via the implementation of import substitution programs.

The nature of the regulatory system for monopolies required the government to take action in the market. Because of this, the concept of the free market was completely disregarded, and restricted economic policies became the focus of attention. The widespread perception that the government had a significant role in regulating process led to increasing governmental involvement in the economy. The expansion of free trade was constrained by the adoption of regulatory measures. Policies were implemented with an awareness of the welfare state and with the aim of achieving social goals. Due to the fact that such a structure would make it possible for monopolies to raise their profit rates while maintaining effective demand. At the national level, governments made use of their monetary and fiscal power to maintain long-term demand stable. The expansion of industries and their rising output were encouraged. People were covered by national social welfare and unemployment insurance programs, and more critically, it was feasible to avoid the loss of stability in demand by preventing the drop in purchasing power. Nonetheless, the purpose of these regulations was not to assist industries in completing the necessary growth processes so that they might participate in international trade. The working class amassed an incredible amount of power, which resulted in an imbalanced relationship with the industrial sector. The government had the ability to exercise control over significant public industries, such as those in which the working class was directly affected by policy. Over time, severing the relationship between two actors became more difficult. The government and the working class emerged as powerful entities, while industries progressively diminished in prominence and accumulated substantial debt. However, this situation would be short-lived. If the economy were to reach its constraints again, this would indicate the start of an evolution toward a new growth paradigm. Institutional forms of the growth model would be unable to adapt to the emerging circumstances resulting from the advancement of novel methods of production and enhancements in technology. This signifies the onset of societal discontentment and the commencement of economic downturns. In general, populists, democrats, and organizations with left- or right-wing ideologies, all claim that they possess the ability to safeguard democracy. Scholars have shown enduring interest in deliberating on the economic condition. Although this concept is straightforward, it might be challenging to comprehend. Despite the limited investigation conducted, the Soviet Union had a substantial influence on developing economies, namely by offering assistance to left-wing groups and the dissemination of communist ideology. It is noteworthy that the military coups in both countries led to a change in the ideological orientation of their respective administrations. Coups were distinguished by their utilization of rhetoric that targeted imperialism and capitalism. Although these events effectively discouraged the working class from endorsing command economies, they also weakened the balance of power and further solidified the government's control over the working class by excluding the industrial elites. Perón and the military dictatorship executed the national economic plans. In particular, proponents of militarism supported the establishment of trade unions and emphasized matters pertaining to the minimum wage and social security. Perón's entry into the system was widely regarded as a pivotal milestone that signaled a transition from a political and institutional struggle to a transformative social revolution.

It was in 1943 that Perón was first assigned to a position inside the National Department of Labor. After that, he was appointed to the position of Secretary of Labor and Welfare. He was able to observe the demand of the employees, who were engaged in production despite the difficult working conditions. The politician was motivated by the social justice movement to gather support for his objectives. Even in the most rural parts of the nation, President Perón instituted a minimum wage and offered higher compensation to employees as part of his efforts to protect them. It was hypothesized that the issue was caused by a mediocre level of consumer spending in the economy. The nation produced twice as much as it might have used up. The implementation of a minimum wage and a general increase in wages throughout the country would increase aggregate demand, which in turn would encourage consumer spending and contribute to the expansion of the country's overall economy. It was asserted that despite the negative impact of increasing wages and domestic consumption on exports, industrialists should nonetheless maintain regular profits and provide benefits to the working class (Groppo, 2009). By prioritizing the principles of equality and fair distribution of resources, involvement in the labor organization facilitated the attraction of trade unions. It is possible to make the argument that the beginning of social politics occurred at the same time as the establishment of this organization. The intimate relationship that existed between the government and the working class became very obvious. As a direct consequence of the formation of labor organizations, the government started its involvement in the economy. A move was made by the administration to develop a connection with the working class, which was a departure from the prior way in which it had portrayed itself. The people had a greater awareness of their social status. The working class evolved into a unified structural form that was established on the basis of rules, norms, or laws. It began to acquire momentum in both culture and society. After a military coup in Türkiye in 1960, the government implemented measures that were strikingly comparable to those implemented in Argentina. The government adopted further policies that were considered to be leftist in nature. In Türkiye, a left-wing public servant structure developed over time. The labor market evolved into a very rigid environment. Productivity was not a primary consideration. During the course of the era, this rendered the two nations uncompetitive. The working class and various trade unions served as the basis for a populist government. The inclusion of the working class in the Peronist movement and party, as well as social reforms aimed at improving the lives of workers, were vital and a breakpoint for creating new institutional change. This facilitated the endorsement and validation of government policies. Similarly, this was also the case in Türkiye. The working class had the ability to provide their support to populist parties, a phenomenon that was justified due to institutional changes. Not only is the income significantly important, but the social security system is also an important factor in ensuring the financial security and well-being of the working class. The social reforms implemented by Perón during his term as secretary of labor were embraced by the general population. The pension system was extended to include workers, along with their other entitlements, such as vacation time and access to healthcare services, among additional benefits. During Perón's presidency in Argentina, a substantial segment of the working class became part of the social security system. To ensure discipline among the working class, it was essential to observe loyal officials as constituents of labor organizations. Therefore, a direct connection was established. Türkiye had the same dilemma throughout the 1960s. Unlike the scenario in Argentina, where the head of the Peronist movement had complete control, the leadership in Türkiye was entrusted to the government rather than a specific political party. Notwithstanding this, the policies of the two countries exhibited a high degree of similarity. Peronism empowered the working class, giving them more influence and enabling them to attain the long-desired benefits and substantial earnings. Perón's objective was to convert individual aspirations into the collective necessities of organized masses. His ability to foresee the requirements of the working class and give the necessary resources for the growth of manufacturing industries, widespread consumption, and large-scale support allowed him to attain significant accomplishments (Groppo, 2009). During that era, there was a noticeable emergence of class awareness.

In the 2000s, the governments in Türkiye and Argentina adopted policies that were very comparable to one another, particularly with regard to how they took advantage of trade unions and mass constituencies. It has been difficult to describe the Argentinian government as left wing. Nonetheless, policies that tended to be more left wing were implemented by both of the regimes. Argentina may be categorized as a country that has not undergone significant reforms and has a lack of responsibility in its populist policies (Etchemendy and Garay, 2011). It is also possible that this is appropriate for Türkiye. Policies that were implemented by Argentinian governments were directed against international creditors and large international corporations. One of the slogans that the Turkish government has used is opposition to international organizations and financial institutions like the IMF and the World Bank. As both nations adopted antimilitarist policies, they became more comparable to one another. They provided assistance to traditional trade unions to influence wage-setting policies and formed alliances with social movements and organizations that are considerably closer to the government. An intriguing aspect of the relationship between the two administrations is the fact that they slowed down the process of deregulation when the two nations had minimized the crisis impact that had occurred in the early 2000s. As soon as there is an institutionalization of the wage–labor relationship, various types of clientelism might begin to enter into the realm of politics. Populist regimes put out their best effort to maintain control over the population. This institutional transformation can serve as the foundation for populist policies, which will help acquire support and credibility. The perception that the market should provide this dynamic is changed. Instead, it fosters a conducive atmosphere for direct government intervention on specific matters that pertain to the working class.

In Türkiye, the rise of economic populism was not attributed to the emergence of a specific political figure, unlike the situation in Argentina. In Türkiye, the roots of economic populism can be attributed more to communal endeavors rather than individual ones. During the 1960s, the adoption of import substitution industrialization was regarded as a deliberate policy by the government. For the successful implementation of the desired economic policies, it was essential for every political party to participate in a cohesive state strategy aimed at fostering industrialization. It is imperative to persist in the pursuit of industrializing the nation's economy, regardless of any changes in political leadership. Therefore, adopting a certain political figure as the starting point for economic populism would be an exceedingly unfeasible approach. The structural changes that took place in the country served as the foundation for the collective measures that were implemented by political parties. Economic planning has always played a crucial role in shaping economic activity throughout history. During the 1930s, the Soviet Union was considered as a prospective ally for Türkiye in its endeavor to enhance its heavy manufacturing industry. During the 1960s, it became more autonomous in exposing the economic imperatives. However, a shared characteristic of populism was the significant emphasis focused on raising wages. This action was undertaken with the aim of bolstering demand and increasing consumer expenditure in the economy. As a consequence, the importance of the export became much less significant. As a novel kind of industrialization, this is advocated for the concept of national self-sufficiency by minimizing dependence on foreign suppliers. This strategy constituted a governmental directive that political parties must embrace and actively pursue. These policies promoted widespread consumption, large-scale production, and extensive employment. The establishment of wage-labor power was laid as a fundamental governmental policy. In other words, it is imperative for all political parties to focus their efforts on overcoming political disputes that revolve around matters of social justice, inequality, inadequate salaries, and insufficient benefits.

Growth models and the high cost of production

Designing a new growth model and implementing appropriate institutional reforms both have a role in shaping the distinctive development style of a certain era. Each age is defined by a unique developmental pattern and style of advancement. This idea clarifies the boundaries in which countries reach their intended levels of economic development. Institutional forms are crucial for maintaining steady development within a structured framework. Increasing an economy's productivity is crucial for advancing it to the next phase and approaching the technological frontier. The different growth models that each country employs are the primary factor that determines the distinctions between the countries that are capable of delivering faster economic development than the rest of the world. Productivity level significantly influences growth performance. Enhancing a nation's export productivity is essential for improving its quality of life, creating employment opportunities, and establishing a strong presence in the global economy. Countries with high productivity growth are more likely to increase efficiency and output over time compared to those with weak productivity growth. There are mainly two methods to enhance productivity. The first factor is market demand, and the second factor is innovative production. For developing countries, foreign demand may lead to the production of high-tech goods and generate income via exports. This suggests that the country might enhance efficiency in using labor, capital, and resources to create production. Institutional forms have an essential function in promoting competitiveness, efficiency, and exports. A country should refrain from imposing barriers to hinder its involvement in global trade. Nations that prioritize exporting often have much greater economic growth compared to those that prioritize protectionism. Schumpeter asserted that elevated productivity and innovation are the primary drivers of economic progress. However, this increase in productivity may be noticeable due to a revolution in the economic growth paradigm. Technological improvements occur when traditional production processes or organizational structures become obsolete or fail. This is known as creative destruction. Advanced technologies and industrial practices are slowly supplanting outdated ones. The working class can encounter challenges due to the closure of established firms, but certain segments of society might potentially gain advantages from this situation (Ricci, 2020). Creative destruction leads to the emergence of a new institutional form, which reflects prevailing economic conditions. Politicians should engage in self-reflection and make changes in preparation of this process. Insufficient institutional change might impede the reform process. Countries influenced by backward populism tend to have slow and unsatisfactory economic growth compared to those that focus on enhancing productivity and technological advancement.

The emergence of a new accumulation regime for gathering resources and the creation of new models for economic growth in reaction to changes in the global environment might pave the way for new institutional reforms. Modifying the growth model throughout this stage may be challenging if there is a lack of institutional complementarity, hindering the model's intended operation. Focusing on preserving the institutional structure of a closed economy while other nations are pursuing export growth strategies would impede the nation's wealth and economic performance. Institutional complementarity involves collaborative functions across different forms and if they are aligned with a growth strategy. Enhanced productivity only would not be sufficient without appropriate institutional forms and macroeconomic factors. Manufacturing advanced products in an inappropriate institutional framework, leading to higher cost of production, cannot succeed in global trade if other countries can create similar items. Regardless of the approach, significant economic progress can be achieved via creative destruction. Simultaneously, it might endanger people associated with obsolete organizations, practices, and enterprises. The working class may experience substantial difficulties due to creative destruction and the need to adapt to the new economic landscape. This might result in growing resentments and the promotion of populist measures that undermine progressive institutional improvements. Sacrifices are necessary for economic advancement. It is unrealistic to expect a competitive growth strategy to be pleasant and kind. Countries in East Asia, whose economy heavily relied on exports, had to make sacrifices in their lifestyle and time to shift to a new method of manufacturing. The Chinese people exerted significant effort and decreased their consumption. Reducing their expenses was necessary since their earnings remained modest. The country often experienced low wages and unfavorable living conditions, indicating that it was not an exceptional incidence. Japan and South Korea had similar historical trajectories. Resistance to transformation is evident in economies that are founded on populism. A change in the fundamental way economies operate might lead to people feeling unsatisfied. The growth model should be employed as a guiding concept for the working class. Any further change can lead to more self-degeneration. Nations that managed to negotiate and complete this path experienced an increase in GDP per capita and improved living conditions. Hence, performing an investigation on various growth models is quite necessary. It is the productivity approach that serves as the foundation for the wage theory and growth models (Hicks, 1963). This methodology allows for comprehending the mode of production, the level of sacrifice a nation is ready to make, and the living standards of the people. A country has several alternatives to pursue for economic progress. Economies of scales can choose a development pattern that most effectively serves their requirements.

A model that focuses on the growth of domestic consumption predicts that the growth rate in productivity of nontradable goods ($\hat{q}_n^A$) is expected to be greater than the growth rate in productivity of goods destined for export ($\hat{q}_e^A$). Subscripts *n* and *e* represent nontradable goods and export goods, respectively. The symbol ($\hat{\ }$) shows the growth rate.

The following is an example of an economic model that can be used to represent a closed economy:

$$\hat{w}^A > \hat{q}_n^A > \hat{q}_e^A \qquad \text{and} \qquad \hat{q}_e^B = \hat{q}_n^B = \hat{w}^B \tag{1}$$

Because large-scale social welfare systems in nation *A* serve to defend trade unions and boost domestic consumption, the proportionate wage rate growth ($\hat{w}^A$) is larger than the productivity growth of nontradable commodities in the model (1). Furthermore, the growth in productivity of nontradable goods is larger than the growth in productivity of export goods. This is due to the fact that international trade is a secondary issue, and it is not promoted. Hence, the productivity of the export goods sector is low, which in turn causes lagging advancement. In nation *A*, inflation is high, and the country's economy is less competitive than the economy of country *B* due to the use of a fixed exchange rate. The economy of country *B* is completely stable, with all of its macroeconomic elements in a state of equilibrium.

In the 1980s, when many nations abandoned closed economic policies and instead concentrated on export growth to strengthen their competitiveness in international trade, growth in export became the major priority. To eliminate inflation and lower unit labor cost (ULC), nations eliminated social programs and diminished the strength of trade unions.[2] Compared with the 1960s and 1970s, wage growth had a decreasing tendency in the 1980s.

$$\hat{q}_e^{\,A} > \hat{q}_n^{\,A} = \hat{w}^A \qquad \text{and} \qquad \hat{q}_e^{\,B} = \hat{q}_n^{\,B} = \hat{w}^B \tag{2}$$

A low-cost production model is shown in the model (2). This model fixes the rise in wage rates to the growth in productivity of nontradable goods. This results in low ULC growth in the export goods sector, which leads to a gain in international competitiveness. If the exchange rate is allowed to float, then the purchasing power parity (PPP) of country A will continue to rise. This will result in an appreciation of country A's national currency since the change in PPP will move in tandem with the change in exchange rate.

$$\hat{w}^A = \hat{q}_e^{\,A} > \hat{q}_n^{\,A} \qquad \text{and} \qquad \hat{q}_e^{\,B} = \hat{q}_n^{\,B} = \hat{w}^B \tag{3}$$

The Balassa-Samuelson growth model is represented by the model (3). This model makes the assumption that wage growth continues to be proportionate, but productivity growth would remain to be disproportional. In this model, the increase in wage rate is tied to the growth in the productivity of export goods, which is greater than the growth in productivity of nontradable goods under a system with a fixed exchange rate. In this scenario, excessive inflation is the outcome of disproportional productivity growth between two sectors (Balassa, 1964; Samuelson, 1964; Uni, 2007, 2012: Ünal, 2016a, 2016b).

$$\hat{q}_e^{\,A} > \hat{q}_n^{\,A} = \hat{w}^A \qquad \text{and} \qquad \hat{q}_e^{\,B} = \hat{q}_n^{\,B} = \hat{w}^B \tag{4}$$

The export-led growth demonstrated by the model (4) generates an advantageous scenario for the expansion of competitive power in a nation with a fixed exchange rate. In such a scenario, wage growth is restrained and connected to the increase in productivity of nontradable goods under plans for export-led development. If the trade partner country B has $\hat{q}_e^{\,B} = \hat{q}_n^{\,B} = \hat{w}^B$ and if the exchange rate is fixed, then country A with this model has the potential to create an increasing PPP and a trade surplus. This is possible because the country with this model can have a decreasing export goods price, which makes it more competitive in international trade. When describing models in economics, it is a common practice to take into consideration certain simple instances. Nation B is an example of a nation that has a well-functioning economy. In other words, the elements that affect the macroeconomy are completely equivalent to one another. The rise in productivity of goods exported, the rise in wages, and the rise in productivity of goods consumed domestically are all equivalent to one another. On the other side, there is another nation that is in direct competition with the perfect economy. A country adopts an export-led growth strategy. When wage growth in country A is maintained at a level that is lower than the increase in productivity in exported goods, the price of exported items will be comparatively lower in comparison to nation B. While this circumstance results in a surplus of foreign trade for country A, it results in a deficit of foreign trade for country B. This country may have a disadvantage in international competitiveness compared to a nation with a fixed exchange rate due to the association between wages and higher prices. Since the other nation is keeping the wage rise low, the prices of its goods go down, and there will be a greater demand for its products. Therefore, there is a positive effect that occurs as an outcome of wage increases on price levels. A wage rise can also result in an increase in the price of goods that are purchased and consumed inside the country. In particular, the most significant component that will be contributing to inflation is a wage rise that is greater than the growth in the productivity of domestically produced goods. There will be a price-lowering impact brought about by increased productivity. This may result from either advancement in technology or an increase in demand. In summary, a rise in productivity tends to have a deflationary impact.

Türkiye and other populist economies, which were unable to implement the necessary institutional changes, tipped into the 'over-valued currency model' when the other countries in international trade moved to the low-cost production model and the Balassa-Samuelson model, in the 1980s. Due to relatively open economic policies, this results in high productivity growth of export goods in comparison to that of nontradable goods. If a country is unable to implement necessary institutional changes because of high production costs and an overvalued currency, the country will experience high inflation, a loss of its competitiveness, a high trade deficit, and the formation of an economy that is vulnerable to economic turmoil and large devaluations in its exchange rate. The following is a definition of the overvalued currency model:

$$\hat{w}^A > \hat{q}_e^{\,A} > \hat{q}_n^{\,A} \qquad \text{and} \qquad \hat{q}_e^{\,B} = \hat{q}_n^{\,B} = \hat{w}^B \tag{5}$$

In this concept, the system of exchange rates may either be determined or allowed to fluctuate, but either way, central banks actively work to keep the system overvalued. This model largely reflects the populist economies that emerged after the 1980s. Wage growth remains higher than productivity growth of both export goods and nontradable goods. An economy following this growth model has high inflation, significant currency devaluations, low competitiveness, and a large trade deficit when contrasted with country B. In this scenario, a nation's currency is deemed overvalued when its appreciation rate exceeds the rate of PPP. Wage rate growth must decrease to match the level of productivity growth of exported goods to establish institutional complementarity between macroeconomic and institutional factors that enhance export development.

The perspectives of Hicks provide credibility to the idea of a competitive economy. Hicks noted that a country chooses a principal currency for commerce, like the pound sterling historically or the dollar currently. Increased exports lead to a larger accumulation of foreign currency reserves in the nation. A trade deficit of a country suggests that other nations in the trading bloc have experienced an increase in the productivity of their export goods. The competing nation's undervalued exchange rate might lead to a rise in its trade surplus as a result of heightened demand from another country (Hicks, 1989). Thus, it is a method employed to intentionally reduce the value of the national currency to a certain level in a country facing trade imbalances.

The rise in wages may put pressure on the exchange rate, causing it to decrease in value. Maintaining a high value for the nation's nominal exchange rate would, on the other hand, prohibit the country from becoming more competitive. It can also diminish the country's purchasing power since it will restrict the country from earning more foreign currency via exports. Because of this, any rise in wages that does not correlate with a gain in production creates the illusion of an increase in consumers' overall purchasing power. Because it gives the impression that people's purchasing power is growing, it really puts downward pressure on the value of the exchange rate. Even in the event that the exchange rate is maintained at its current level, this will result in a decline in the value of the currency. When the nominally valued exchange rate is no longer able to resist this pressure and continues to lose value, it will eventually reach the point of equilibrium, which is where the real exchange rate is situated. This is the primary driver behind the periodic currency devaluations as well as the extreme depreciations that take place in populist economies. In spite of significant wage gains that is unrelated to advances in productivity, the exchange rate is maintained at its previous level or valued higher. The pressure on the nominal exchange rate intensifies in tandem with the widening gap in the nation's trade deficit. In response, the weak exchange rate suddenly surges toward its true value. When the rate of wage growth is restrained in comparison to the rate of growth in the productivity of the export goods, this will result in the exported goods being comparatively affordable, which allows the nation to accumulate foreign currency. If wages are kept at a level that is lower than the productivity that is reached, then the cost of the workforce will be kept to a minimum. In other words, the workforce will create less money for themselves than they make through their labor. Therefore, in global commerce, the price of exported products remains inexpensive. Raising salaries will lead to price increase, while boosting productivity would lower prices. Increased purchasing power is another advantage of this. When a country is growing because of exports and keeps its exchange rate stable, it will prevent its national currency from appreciating and lead to an undervalued exchange rate system. The objective of the nominal exchange rate is to keep the currency's value lower than its existing market value. This circumstance may create the perception that goods in the nation are very affordable and that labor costs are lower. However, it will lead to the country being more affluent in reality, resulting in an increase in its purchasing power. Over time, it will become clear that the per capita income of this nation is increasing. Once the nation focused on export-led growth adjusts its exchange rate, its currency will quickly increase in value. These countries choose for a gradual adjustment of the currency rate instead of a sudden and immediate transformation, which is the alternative approach. As a result, they will be able to maintain the exchange rate at a competitive level. Ultimately, a country will experience an increase in its ability to purchase products and a surplus in its international trade if it sustains wage growth that is lower than the rise in productivity of export goods. Foreign trade imbalance will occur, leading to a fall in purchasing power due to costly goods produced in countries that consistently and excessively increase salaries in ways that strays from rational policy. A country should carefully observe the economic situations of other countries before deciding on its macroeconomic strategy and base its plan on specific compatibility. This relies on possessing the required knowledge, expertise, motivation, and willpower.

In the history of modern global economics, growth models evolved into various forms. Before 1929, a more conventional kind of competition was present. After the Great Depression, a monopolistic form of competition emerged alongside the Fordism accumulation regime. By 1970, an evolution toward a neoliberal competitive approach occurred. Due to heightened competition, it is crucial to achieve a more optimal equilibrium among several macroeconomic indicators while considering international commerce. When growth models are considered, a certain economic populist trend may become more noticeable. Populist economic policies aim to redistribute income by generating significant budget deficits, mostly reflected in wage increase. Substantial increase in wages does not align with improvements in the economy's overall productivity. The discrepancy between wage increase and productivity growth influences a country's economic policies toward populism.

Comparison of growth models

Comparing growth models in industrialized nations can provide insight into their strategy and allow for comparison with populist economies. The growth models include the elements outlined in the theoretical framework. Table 6.1 provides an overview of the growth patterns of the nations that were chosen. Table 6.2 indicates the real exchange rate based on PPP and the nominal exchange rate in each country. The growth in productivity of nontradable goods in Canada between 1971 and 1976 was 1.2% greater than the growth in productivity of export goods. The rise in the wage rate was 11.0%, while inflation was 7.4%. The rapid acceleration of wage rates persisted until 1980. However, between the years 1981 and 1986, the Canadian economy had characteristics of the Balassa-Samuelson model. During this time period, the productivity growth of export goods climbed significantly, reaching 5.4%, while the productivity growth of nontradable goods was just 0.9%. Additionally, the rate of inflation was lower compared to earlier time periods, as was the pace of change in the PPP and the currency.

The rate of increase in productivity of nontradable goods in France between 1972 and 1977 was 6.0%, which was higher than the rate of growth in productivity of export goods, which was 5%. During that time period, the rise in wage rates was an unusually high 13.5%, while inflation was at 9.5%. On the other hand, there was a noticeable slowdown in the pace of wage increase over the years 1985–1990. France leaned toward the low-cost production model due to its decreasing wage rate growth in comparison to the productivity growth of nontradable goods, and its currency adjusted in line with its purchasing power parity. France, albeit not a perfect example, tended to proceed in this direction. During the 1980s, France focused on boosting its exports through curbing domestic consumption and limiting wage growth.

Even though Japan's productivity growth in export goods was greater than the productivity growth of nontradable goods, its wage rate increase was

Table 6.1 Domestic consumption growth and export growth by country (annual rate, unit: %)

Country	*Period*	*Growth of mark-up rate* $(1+\hat{m}n)^a$	*Productivity growth of nontradable goods*	*Productivity growth of export goods*	*Wage rate growth*	*Inflation*
Canada	1971–1976	−0.6	1.2	−0.4	11.0	7.4
	1976–1981	0.8	0.8	−0.9	8.6	9.4
	1981–1986	0.4	0.9	5.4	5.3	6.9
	1986–1990	−0.7	0.8	3.5	5.5	4.5
France	1972–1977	2.8	6.0	4.5	13.5	9.5
	1977–1980	0.0	2.6	3.0	12.8	10.7
	1980–1985	0.7	1.7	2.1	9.8	10.3
	1985–1990	1.0	2.2	5.6	4.2	3.5
Japan	1970–1980	−1.6	3.8	6.6	13.3	8.9
	1980–1990	3.0	6.2	9.2	4.5	2.5
Netherlands	1972–1977	1.5	3.5	3.4	10.7	8.4
	1977–1981	2.5	2.1	1.4	4.4	5.5
	1981–1986	4.2	4.5	7.0	2.3	3.5
Türkiye	1973–1985	3.8	3.8	2.0	34.2	38.5
	1985–2003	0.4	3.0	5.3	66.2	63.5
United Kingdom	1968–1979	−2.6	2.9	2.1	13.4	11.4
	1979–1984	0.5	1.0	4.8	9.8	10.2
	1984–1990	0.3	1.8	2.3	7.2	4.9
United States	1972–1977	0.9	1.1	−1.5	7.3	7.0
	1977–1982	0.1	0.4	0.7	8.1	9.2
	1982–1985	−0.1	1.5	5.9	5.1	4.3
	1985–1990	3.3	4.7	11.1	4.5	3.8

[a]Because mark-up rates are not constant in the countries, approximate inflation or nontradable price increase comes as follows: $\hat{p}_n = (1+\hat{m}_n) + \hat{w} - \hat{q}_n$.
Note: Author's calculations based on Ünal (2018).

Table 6.2 Change rate in the currency and PPP against the United States (annual rate, unit: %)

Country	*Periods*	*Change rate in the currency against the US dollar*	*Change rate in PPP against the United States*
Canada	1971–1981	−1.8	−3.4
	1981–1990	0.2	−0.7
France	1972–1980	1.8	−1.1
	1980–1990	−3.8	−4.4
Japan	1970–1980	4.4	3.4
	1980–1990	3.6	2.2
Netherlands	1972–1981	2.2	0.6
	1981–1986	2.5	0.3
Türkiye	1973–1985	−49.5	−30.9
	1985–2003	−59.3	−64.3
United Kingdom	1979–1984	−7.5	−4.5
	1984–1990	5.2	−2.3

Note: Author's calculations based on Ünal (2018). Nominal exchange rates were collected from the Federal Reserve Bank of St. Louis (exchange rate to US dollar). If the hypothetical real exchange rate, as represented by PPP, exhibits a greater level of appreciation compared to the nominal exchange rate, it signifies that the country's exchange rate is undervalued.

disproportionately high: Around 13.3% between 1970 and 1980. As a consequence, inflation was rather high, hovering about 8.9%. However, in the years that followed, the increase of wage rates slowed down dramatically, and between 1980 and 1990, a model of production with low costs became prevalent. The nation's currency continued to be overvalued, but it moved in tandem with its PPP.

The Netherlands followed the growth of domestic consumption until 1981, but between 1981 and 1986, wage growth dropped dramatically to 2.3%, and most crucially, the productivity growth of export goods, which was 7.0%, was greater than that of nontradable goods. Because of this, the economic system in the Netherlands was based on the low cost production model.

The United Kingdom had increasing levels of domestic consumption between 1968 and 1979. Between 1979 and 1984, this country had a significant wage gain of 9.8%, surpassing the productivity growth rates of nontradable goods at 1% and export goods at 4.8% over the same period. Furthermore, the inflation rate was at 10.2%. By 1990, the inflation rate in the United Kingdom decreased to 4.9%, while the wage rate growth dropped to 7.2% between 1984 and 1990.

The United States experienced poor productivity growth and high wage rate growth during the period of 1972–1977, both of which contributed to an increase in the country's overall inflation rate. Between the years 1977 and 1982, there was a little rise in wage rate growth, which brought it to 8.1%, and inflation, which pushed it to 9.2%. These were unfavorable circumstances for an economy like the United States, which was suffering poor productivity growth of nontradable goods and export goods. After 1977, the United States transformed itself into an export growth nation, meaning that the rate of increase in the productivity of its export goods surpassed that of its nontradable goods. The United States adjusted its wage rate growth from 1982 to 1985 to align with the increased productivity of exported goods, according to the Balassa-Samuelson model. From 1985 to 1990, the United States transformed to a low-cost production model by connecting wage growth to the productivity growth of nontradable goods.

Türkiye experienced the highest ULC rise in both nontradable and export goods compared to industrialized economies. It had been using a similar approach to other countries in its efforts to boost domestic consumption due to its protectionist economic policies. Between 1973 and 1985, the wage rate increased by 34.2%. Additionally, the productivity growth of nontradable goods exceeded that of export goods by 3.8% and 2.0%, respectively. In addition, the inflation rate in Türkiye exceeded that of other countries. Türkiye had a significant increase in wage growth, reaching 66.2%, surpassing the inflation rate of 63.5% between 1985 and 2003.

In the 1970s and 1980s, the institutional forms of industrialized countries exhibited a similar trend. During the 1970s, the industrial sectors of these countries maintained a significant workforce, and trade unions were more robust and influential compared to the 1980s. Following the collapse of the Bretton Woods System in the 1970s, the fixed exchange rate system experienced a substantial institutional transformation. The manufacturing sector was the important source of economic activity in industrialized countries. Domestic consumption fueled economic expansion, except for Japan, which focused more on export policies. In the 1950s, the Netherlands focused on enhancing its manufacturing sector by using cost-effective production techniques. During the 1970s, a decline in the percentage of workers in the manufacturing industry was associated to a reduction in union density. The phenomenon was characterized as the Dutch Disease and was connected to the process of deindustrialization (Thelen, 2014).

During the 1970s, there was substantial government intervention across multiple economic areas. The government aimed to create price stability but failed to achieve this objective. The government needed to promote and support domestic industry since agricultural output had diminished in importance in most industrialized countries. In the 1970s, developed countries were ready to implement deregulatory policies influenced by neoliberalism. These initiatives facilitated economic growth throughout the 1980s. Neoliberalism became the prevailing approach for creating adaptable labor forces and open, highly liberal economies in many countries, leading to a substantial weakening of trade unions. The 1980s witnessed the emergence of an era characterized by deregulation and globalization, which led nations to adopt the idea of free market. Deregulation measures employed in industrialized nations to manage inflation contributed to significant changes in the institutional forms of those countries. In the end, the expansion of exports became the cornerstone of the development policies that were implemented by authorities. The weakening of trade unions resulted in a deceleration in wage growth. Furthermore, trade unions lost power, as the fraction of the workforce that was employed in the industrial sector dropped, which resulted in a decrease in the density of unions. The significance of establishing strategies to control inflation has increased throughout time. The deceleration in the growth of labor costs significantly contributed to the reduction in inflation. The exchange rate system became more flexible. The countries primarily focused their production on the export goods sector. Public services were ultimately deregulated as part of government strategy. A significant factor that contributed to the decline of labor unions was the rise in privatization (Nakakubo, 2015). Industrialized countries have adopted an economic structure that is characterized by an excessive degree of openness and a concentration on competitiveness on a global scale. When compared to the preceding period, the role of the government in providing assistance to the export goods industry became much more important. On the other hand, the engagement of the government in the economy had a less overall impact. Industrialized countries experienced a significant technological transformation in the 1970s, as workers transitioned to the service sector. The nations effectively moved to export-oriented growth strategies in the 1980s.

Economic transformation

The evolution of economic systems can be analyzed through the perspective of institutional economics using growth models and institutional forms. One of the primary goals of this strategy is to conduct an investigation into the circumstances under when or as a consequence of which capitalism transitioned to a new accumulation regime. Hence, this methodology facilitates comprehension of crises. It offers insight on the internal dynamics of the crisis as well as other dynamics that are evolving it, under what circumstances and in what cause-effect connection, why the transition to another accumulation regime or which regulatory style is fit for the new conditions occurred. Analysis depends on having access to specific information. In addition to delineating the distinctive framework of idealism, Aglietta posits that the advancement of this theoretical perspective can be facilitated by an examination of the regulatory theory of capitalism within the purview of dialectical materialism, drawing upon the methodologies espoused by Marx (Aglietta, 1979). This theory effectively establishes a systematic framework for analyzing the origins and consequences of crises by critically assessing capitalism from a Marxist standpoint. Aglietta, Lipietz, and Robert Boyer are regarded as the pioneers who initiated the development of this methodological approach and contributed significantly to the theory of regulation. Jessop (1990) commonly incorporated the regulatory method into his scholarly works by critically analyzing the role of the state. Harvey (1991) employs the theory of regulation as a conceptual framework for shedding light on the historical transformations that have taken place not only within the realm of the economy but also in the domains of art and architecture. These scholars have conducted several research using the assumptions that are the foundation of the regulation theory. They have endeavored to elucidate and examine the notion that capitalism undergoes transformations throughout different time periods and perpetuates itself in accordance with prevailing circumstances. Regulation theory encompasses two key components: The accumulation regime and the institutional structures. This theory does not prioritize the impact of technological advancements on regulating the economic system nor does it recognize that certain institutional forms are solely accountable for this task. The examination of crises in capitalism, within the framework of regulation theory, involves the utilization of various concepts. These concepts are not unfamiliar to the principles of Marxism. Through the application of these concepts, this theory aims to analyze the different historical periods that the capitalist mode of production has undergone, the emergence of specific accumulation regimes during these periods, the corresponding modes of regulation that have facilitated the resolution of crises, the mechanisms through which capitalism sustains its reproduction, and the analytical structure of diverse crises. This approach classifies capitalism as a system characterized by periodicity and historical evolution.

During the 1970s, wealthy nations witnessed a notable structural transformation. Because production had reached its maximum inside the boundaries of the nations, and because there was a pressing need to expand into international markets, the government was compelled to leave control of the economy to the free market. Consequently, the element that previously contributed to a rise in effective demand became a production cost inside the domestic market. The primary factor contributing to the continued decrease in revenues was the organization's failure to implement workforce reductions. The domestic market was unable to generate sufficient effective demand. The transportation industry experienced significant advancements as a result of technological developments. It became relatively possible to offer the products on the global market. Hence, the workforce inside the domestic market has lost the advantageous position it formerly had in terms of generating effective demand. As a consequence, labor, which had a diminishing impact on the rate of revenue started to become marginalized. Because of the increase in employment cost, the expense of maintaining the social welfare state has increased. Due to the rise in government spending, the comprehension of well-being inside economies started to diminish. For capitalist economies to mitigate costs, the need was to implement requisite modifications or reforms in institutional forms that align with the flexible accumulation regime, as guided by neoliberal policies. The global dissemination of the flexible market model was regarded as a direct consequence of the successful execution of these reforms. The Bretton Woods agreement was no longer in effect. A transition took place in the exchange rate system, which went from maintaining a fixed exchange rate to one with a floating exchange rate. The labor rights that were acquired by unions in the aftermath of the Great Depression subsequently emerged as a detrimental factor for economies. It became imperative to eliminate the rigidity of labor and establish a labor market characterized by flexibility. The industrial methods were going through a period of significant transformation. After a period of time, conventional commodities that were not offered started to be supplanted by technology that could create according to the preferences and desires of individual consumers. The majority of the organizations that held old means of production and public industries were losing more functionality as a result of the quantity of obsolete means of production and public industries, and they were allocating excessive funds out of their budget to update them. The assumption of production by the private sector was contingent upon the gradual erosion of workers' power. The ideas put out by Keynes were no longer effective in maintaining a functioning economy. There arose a need for growth-oriented changes that would facilitate the popularity of flexible production methods. The nations that were unable to successfully accomplish this transformation continued to struggle with persistent macroeconomic issues. During this time period, inflation continued to climb higher. On the other side, as businesses attempted to boost their revenue by raising the pricing of their goods, trade unions were advocating for an increase in the minimum wage and other employee benefits. Wage rises on one side and price increases on the other were contributing to a major rise in inflation. The system was starting to get congested. There was no way to bring down the wages. A lesson might be drawn from 1929. Again, this might lead to a decrease in effective demand. It would not be possible to increase the expenses. This time around, earnings would decline, but inflation rates would rise. Because of the inflexibility of the system and the complexity of the bureaucratic structure, it was impossible to reduce the size of workers despite the fall in revenues. In addition, there were significant increases in expenditures for public services. The formation of inflationary pressure would result in cost increases.

The intensification of the oil shock in 1973 resulted in a subsequent escalation of inflation. The pricing of items had an upward trend as a result of fluctuations in oil prices. The sharp rise of oil prices by the Organisation for Economic Co-operation and Development (OPEC), in light of the Arab-Israeli conflict, prompted industrialized nations to adopt energy conservation measures. The aforementioned circumstances resulted in significant alterations to the economy. The reduction of wages and the imposition of credit restrictions were mostly attributed to the purported impact of oil prices, particularly by both governmental entities and corporate organizations. Consequently, it was assumed that there would be a decline in purchasing power. Despite a significant number of individuals experiencing unemployment, there was a little reduction witnessed in the overall demand for consumption. Since the social welfare program was not suddenly abandoned, a potential economic downturn was avoided. Nevertheless, the attempt to mitigate the impact of the oil shock and eradicate stagflation led to the demise of outdated institutional structures. In response to the potential impact of an external shock, regulatory mechanisms in the form of institutional intervention were implemented with the aim of lessening the ensuing crisis via measures such as cost-cutting or workforce reduction. The transition of the external crisis to an internal one has impeded the economic growth performance of economies. According to Krugman (2009), after the end of the Second World War, there was a fall in the prevalent sense of economic vision, which ultimately led to the revelation of the inadequacies of the full employment policy during the 1970s. It was mentioned that the reason why there is an increase in inflation is because the central bank puts an excessive amount of money into circulation in an effort to generate employment. In the same manner, he stated that there must be a significant increase in unemployment to eliminate inflation from the economy. The introduction of exogenous shocks, such as abrupt increases in oil prices, has the potential to precipitate economic downturns but not necessarily on the scale of a depression. In essence, the simultaneous management of internal challenges and the emergence of external crises may lead to significant structural implications for economies. Each of these challenges represented the difficulties encountered throughout the transformation to the new era. Institutional reforms were implemented using a practical approach to mitigate inflationary consequences, without taking into account any political risks.

The establishment of trade unions was formulated in response to the evolving flexible circumstances, diverging from a rigorous disciplinary approach. Various consumer groups emerged depending on the output. The initiation of production was based on the perspectives and ideas of individuals. Consequently, the inflexible framework of societal organization was eliminated. The proliferation of many social groups has facilitated the transformation from a modern society to a postmodern society. The phenomenon of individualization has witnessed a notable rise. Individuals started to distinguish themselves from society by adopting modes of production that allowed them to manifest their unique identities in response to evolving production circumstances. By adopting such a flexible structure, the economies were able to sustain continuous production processes. The labor demand of enterprises has begun to take shape in response to changing economic circumstances. Because of this, the businesses would be able to dismiss workers whenever they needed at times when there was a low demand for the products that they produced. There was a more concentrated effort to exert control over the employees. Therefore, the workforce was available for employment in whatever capacity was required. The absence of labor rights in some regions resulted in the weakening of workers' organizations, as a consequence of the intensified flexible accumulation regime. The efficacy of government involvement in the economy was diminished, resulting in a decline in the working class's influence and authority. The working class lost its ability to have a substantial impact on power distribution.

In contrast to the industrialized economies, which adopted deregulatory policies, the emerging nations, such as Argentina and Türkiye, were delayed or unwilling to adopt institutional reforms. The processes of economic transition in Argentina and Türkiye are quite comparable to one another. The economies of both nations began as agricultural growth that lacked an accompanying industrialization. Nevertheless, the agricultural sector had a significant impact on the development and growth of manufacturing industries. Subsequently, the pursuit of import substitution industrialization was initiated. During this historical era, there was a notable emergence and growth of labor movements. A robust correlation between the government and the working class was discovered. The time was a critical juncture that established a profound degree of path dependency. Starting with the 1980s, both nations witnessed a transition in their developmental trajectories toward policies that prioritized export-oriented strategies. During each era of transition, the implementation of required institutional reforms was characterized by a restricted and gradual pace. Subsequently, the nations once again found themselves confronted with recurring macroeconomic difficulties. Following the end of the Second World War, Argentina and Türkiye implemented protectionist policies aimed at fostering industrialization by promoting the production of essential components and intermediate products inside their respective domestic markets (Waisman, 1989; Beccaria and Carciofi, 1982). However, the outcome did not align with the anticipated expectations. The projected improvement in productivity did not materialize. Furthermore, the implementation of import tariffs and the regulation of capital emerged as prevalent characteristics in both nations. The period under consideration had a notable increase in wage growth, while concurrently noticing a deliberate suppression of the exchange rate. This phenomenon resulted in an increase in the cost of domestically produced goods in the context of international trade. Basically, newborn sectors had disadvantages as compared to those in developed economies. Following the 1980s, both nations continued to exhibit a path dependency toward the import substitution industrialization era. The import taxes maintained a significantly elevated level, resulting in a restricted level of openness. The accession of Türkiye to the EU resulted in its participation in the Customs Union, leading to an expansion of trade operations with European nations and the establishment of facilities by multinational corporations inside Türkiye to access European markets. The identical situation was witnessed in Argentina as well. The implementation of a comprehensive reform process could only occur after undergoing a severe episode of hyperinflation. After implementing trade and financial reforms in the 1970s, Argentina started the process of integrating into the global economy. This process was further intensified in the 1990s when the Peronist administration transferred ownership of state-owned firms to private entities and reduced import tariffs and export taxes (Galiani and Somaini, 2018). Nevertheless, the extent of this transformation remained modest in comparison to that of other regions of the world.

Neither Argentina nor Türkiye was able to create a strategy for economic development comparable to that which is practiced in industrialized nations. Because of this, the two countries' ability to compete in international trade lagged behind that of many other nations. Therefore, the development of their export competitiveness did not go according to plan. Two nations that have previously experienced exceptional economic growth have started sliding more and further behind many other developed and emerging economies. During the 1970s, in particular, the Turkish economy did all it could to discourage exports. The high cost of production became more obvious. The exchange rate was pegged and consistently devalued, both of which contributed to the breakdown of the institutional forms near the end of the 1970s. The economy of Latin American countries was not an exception to this rule. It quickly escalated into a state of hyperinflation. The exchange rate systems did not have a favorable adjustment. Both nations' constitutional systems were developed to protect and promote the interests of the working class. It is quite interesting to note that there is not a single period of time during which one currency might appreciate in relation to the other. For many decades, there has been a consistent depreciation in value. After the 1970s, industrialized nations underwent a transition to becoming economies focused on export growth. They significantly reduced the amount of duties and limitations. In addition, the nations of Europe began coming together to form a customs union to boost the mobility of both labor and capital. The top economies of the world have begun making preparations for globalization and easier mobility across nations. It is generally accepted that more openness may lead to higher levels of economic output. Moreover, it may assist nations in the process of transferring technologies and enterprises to their domestic economy. The decade of the 1980s was a time when nations began to emphasize openness and less restriction in trade across borders. This shift has the potential to promote both development and competitiveness. The significance of the connection that exists between openness and macroeconomic stability gained prominence. It is often assumed that economies in more open nations have the potential to make greater progress than those in more closed economies. For instance, when compared to North Korea, which pursued isolationist economic policies while operating under a harsh communist dictatorship, South Korea's openness, liberalism, and democracy resulted in far more progress being made than in North Korea. Additionally, China, which had previously been a closed economy, achieved significant advances in economic performance with the implementation of deregulation strategies and the establishment of free zones for trade and investments. A nation that was producing goods with low and medium levels of technological sophistication could dramatically expand its production facilities to generate higher-quality goods with medium and high levels of technological proficiency. Hence, the increasing amount of its exports boosted the production of industrial goods within the economy. The people experienced a dramatic improvement in their standard of living. In 20 years, the country's GDP per capita caught up to that of Argentina and Türkiye. The economic performance of China demonstrates that protectionist measures may hold a nation back economically and keep it in a position that it does not deserve to be in.

In Argentina and Türkiye, the implementation of institutional changes with the goal of enhancing openness resulted in an increase in exports, indicating a positive outlook. Nevertheless, both of these countries made grave mistakes by permitting their currencies to maintain an overvalued price for a prolonged duration. If a country intends to implement more liberal and export-focused development strategies, it should also undertake institutional reforms that align with this new strategy and the evolving economic model. To facilitate openness and trade, it is necessary to have a competitive exchange rate that is flexible enough to adjust based on the performance of the economy. Another major mistake would be made by these countries was their effort to eliminate import restrictions and tariffs while also dealing with an overvaluation of their currencies. The situation became far direr as a result of this. Regarding international trade and economic performance, the two countries have entirely forfeited their capacity to compete with other nations. The nature of the problem was internal. Both the working class and populist regimes attributed their failures on globalization and neoliberal economic policy. When a nation's currency is overvalued, it hampers the competitiveness of its economy against other economies. This statement represents a basic truth and a core concept in the field of economics. Moreover, eliminating import duties and quotas would inevitably pose an economic risk, manifesting as an expanding trade imbalance and a decline in productivity. Both of these countries, however, are misled by populist policies that they are unable to grasp this economic reality. Their exchange rate was either maintained at a constant level or controlled. As a result, there is no space for fluctuation in exchange rates. Keeping a fixed exchange rate for an extended period of time had negative consequences for the domestic economy and impeded the progress of productivity. The two countries possess immense potential, but their strengths have been eroded due to inadequate institutional reforms. The countries were required to address the escalating inflation to offset their current account deficits. In Türkiye, the media often characterized inflation as an evil and formidable monster. It failed to highlight the erroneous institutional issues that are brought about by populist administrations. These countries committed another error by mistakenly believing that variations in the exchange rate were the primary source of inflation. Consequently, they implemented efforts to avert the depreciation of the exchange rate, resulting in an even greater overvaluation than before. By maintaining a fixed exchange rate, it was believed that this measure would effectively curb the rise of domestic prices and costs. Specifically, the countries were unable to develop their domestic industries to a level where they could effectively compete in the global market during the era of import substitution industrialization. The industrial sectors failed to achieve its maximum capacity for expansion. The problem of heavy dependency on imports persisted under approaches that were more liberal. The last significant mistake was a lack of acknowledgment that inflation was being influenced by efforts aimed at appealing to the general public rather than being caused by policies related to exchange rates. The rising wage growth is surpassing the rise in productivity, resulting in increased expenses. Despite the increase in the price of exported commodities caused by the rising wages in the country, the currencies remained overvalued.

The fluctuations in currency exchange rates that have occurred in these nations cannot be attributed to the neoliberal economic doctrine. The obligation rests with populist regimes since they are incapable of establishing institutional complementarity while considering macroeconomic factors. Nevertheless, the proposals put out by neoliberal researchers are inadequate in addressing the problem. Their actions might exacerbate the situation in the countries, leading to significant consequences in politics. It is possible for there to be large macroeconomic imbalances brought on by openness that are not accompanied by genuine institutional transformation. Joining a customs union, establishing a free trade agreement, or joining an economic and monetary union when macroeconomic conditions are unfavorable may lead to catastrophic events. It is not sufficient to just adhere to open economic principles. There are a number of other factors besides openness that contribute to advances in economic output and employment. It would be in the best interest of the nation to undertake institutional changes to bring down its labor costs and minimize currency overvaluation. A trade imbalance may be exacerbated, and overall economic output would suffer if open economic policies are allowed to continue. Even the United States is helpless in the face of China's economic policies, which promote low production costs and an undervalued currency. This explains why Argentina and Türkiye are unable to implement a fixed exchange rate while China is able to. China was able to successfully conduct institutional change in the field of wage–labor relation before it opened its economy and established free zones. Because of this, the nation was able to witness an enormous decline in inflation. After that, the simultaneous implementation of the fixed exchange rate occurred. When the rise of wages is limited, a country might potentially establish the circumstances required for a currency to be undervalued. This was an economic strategy employed in global trade, resulting in uncertainty among developed countries, particularly the United States. Subsequently, China undertook a proactive step to reorganize its institutional framework and introduced a managed exchange rate system. Hence, it is an illusion to assume that emerging countries can resolve their issues by embracing liberal economic policies. This is an exceedingly naïve anticipation. There is no way that it could be easy and fast. If the necessary improvements are not implemented, the country might face failure.

Notes

1 Source: In the case of Türkiye, statistical indicators from TurkStat could be checked.
2 The method of ULC growth rates of export goods and nontradable goods: $\widehat{ULC}_e = \hat{w}_e - \hat{q}_e$ and $\widehat{ULC}_n = \hat{w}_n - \hat{q}_n$.

7 The nexus between economic populism and political aspects

The demand for institutional reforms was not an issue that was confined just to the administration of Alfonsin in Argentina. Numerous political parties often provide statements on the imperative need for institutional change, although their progress is hindered by the inherent political risks involved. The situation in Türkiye had similar characteristics. The people had a negative response toward suggestions for deregulation in the context of institutional transformation. The use of political campaigns to oppose institutional reforms was a favorite activity of left-wing parties. Both extreme left-wing and extreme right-wing regimes have been very critical of any potential institutional reforms that may lead to a more stable economic environment. Persuading the working class and trade unions has proven to be a formidable challenge. In the Argentinian context, subsequent to 1987, there was a notable emergence of discourse around the implementation of institutional reform. However, the tangible impediment of social costs posed a significant challenge to the advancement of progressive ideologies. The inquiry was designed based on the ongoing discourse around the feasibility of implementing institutional transformation while also emphasizing the need of assessing the societal and financial implications associated with such reforms. The working class had a mostly negative stance toward the implementation of liberal policies in Türkiye. The trade unions expressed divergent perspectives, although their stance on changes fell short of providing the necessary impetus for political parties to enact policy measures. There was a prevailing notion that markets would be liberalized to accommodate global investments. This notion stood in direct opposition to the nationalist stance of right-wing political parties and the antiimperialist position held by left-wing political parties. Implementing institutional transformation in the absence of support from the working class and its affiliated political parties posed a significant challenge. Large demonstrations might be planned by trade unions in both nations. During the era of any reform legislation, political parties in Türkiye were confronted with significant demonstrations and strikes. The political leaders of the major parties strategically used antiinstitutional reform rhetoric as a means to appeal to the working-class electorate with the objective of securing victory in the elections. Despite the aspirations of politicians such as Eduardo Angeloz and Carlos Menem to reinterpret economic changes, their efforts did not yield sufficient influence to effectively contribute to the implementation of these reforms throughout society. These were regarded as the only viable alternatives

DOI: 10.4324/9781003438090-7

for the economy in the areas where they were employed for political campaigns. Nevertheless, there was an increase in speculations, which further exacerbated the macroeconomic imbalances and ultimately led to the economic downturn. A wave of societal discontent had arisen in response to political decisions, leading to a substantial increase in inflation. During the first years of the 1990s, the peso was pegged to the US dollar. The central bank's ability to engage in money supply for the purpose of covering budget shortfalls was limited. In the event of need, it was essential to ensure that the newly generated money supply was adequately backed by gold or foreign reserves. Furthermore, the currency achieved full convertibility with the US dollar (Barros, 2005).

During the 1970s, a regulation was introduced in Türkiye with the aim of maintaining the stability of the lira by prohibiting the possession of foreign currency. However, the aforementioned restriction was abandoned in the 1980s. Both individuals and corporations had the liberty to own foreign currency. The provision of freedom for convertibility was granted. Candidates for public office were helped in their quest for popularity by rhetoric that emphasized liberty and transformation. The implementation of reform initiatives in Argentina had favorable outcomes for the economy. The rate of inflation had a dramatic fall. This was not the situation with regard to the Turkish economy. The inflation rate has emerged as a significant factor with profound implications for the economy. Nevertheless, the impact of economic populism on electoral results is evident. In both Argentina and Türkiye, wage dynamics have been used for this purpose, resulting in a substantial boost in wage growth either before or after elections. This particular approach, used as a means to garner electoral support, has subsequently resulted in eras characterized by an inevitable upsurge in inflation and volatility in currency rates.

Political structure

Both countries have democratic institutions that are distinguished by a wide range of political parties across the ideological spectrum from left wing to right wing. Each political party develops its economic policies according to its ideological viewpoints. However, the concept of economic populism remains relatively consistent. The political alignment of the ruling party in any country is insignificant since no party can avoid being influenced by economic populism. Therefore, the issue at hand is not just attributable to political parties but rather stems from institutional forms. The profound interrelation between the government and the working class compels all ruling political parties to engage in the manipulation of wages, currency rates, interest rates, and price levels within the economy. The impetus to enact institutional reforms aimed at diminishing the interdependence between the government and the working class can only materialize when governments adhere to liberal economic principles, such as the privatization of institutions to subject them to market forces, or when novel regulations are devised to stabilize the economy.

Without a doubt, Juan Domingo Perón in Argentina emerged as a prominent figure within the realm of populism, making a lasting impact on the country's historical trajectory. Perón is widely recognized as the progenitor of the Peronist movement and the subsequent establishment of the Partido Justicialista (PJ), both of which had a profound effect on the political landscape of Argentina over an extended period of time (Muno, 2019). In the field of populist study, his ideas were referred to as Peronism. Peronism had a phase of rapid industrialization, marked by significant social and economic changes. The nation shifted its economic focus from agricultural output to industrial production. This led to the establishment of a large-scale organization whereby members of the working class congregate and collaborate. The modernizing of the nation contributed to the rise in popularity of the Perón movement. Perón was born in 1895 and passed away in 1974. He adjusted his lifestyle to accommodate his involvement in politics. His journey started as a member of the Argentinian armed forces. He spent time in Italy and had been influenced by the ideological principles espoused by Benito Mussolini and the political movement known as fascism. Furthermore, he became involved in a military coup in 1943 orchestrated by a collective of officials. He assumed the position of Minister of Labor inside the coup administration. This event marked a significant juncture in the nation's history, during which he was presented with a favorable opportunity to exert influence on governmental policy, particularly in the realm of labor organization, and garner support from the working class. Finally, he obtained the position of the president of Argentina in 1946. This action had a profound impact on the equilibrium of power inside the economy. However, his initiatives rooted on populism proved to be unsuccessful. Following a military takeover in 1955, he was compelled to live in exile until 1972. Following his return, he was victorious in the elections in 1973, and he passed away the following year in 1974 (Anselmi, 2018). The followers of his populist ideology were unable to achieve the desired level of macroeconomic stability. The occurrence of confrontations among political factions, including Marxist movements and left-wing and right-wing societies, culminated in a repressive military takeover in 1976. Following a protracted period of military governance, Raul Alfonsin became the president of Argentina via a democratic electoral process in 1983. This year also occurred to align with the circumstances in Türkiye. In 1980, a combination of conditions, including a severe economic crisis and increasing tensions between right-wing and left-wing organizations, led to the emergence of militarist elements that sought to seize power in the country. In 1983, a political party that aligned with democratic principles took control of the nation's government responsibilities. Nevertheless, Türkiye's experience was of a brief duration. Alfonsin's primary goal was to restore the democratic system after a seven-year era marked by military control in Argentina. The government's power was weakened due to hyperinflation and societal turmoil, leading to its resignation and eventual substitution by a populist party. The protracted political conflict between militarists and unions in Argentina led to a substantial loss of life, resulting in the deaths of thousands of individuals. The political polarization between left- and right-wing factions in Türkiye caused a situation of instability and peril inside the country. Nonetheless, in the 1980s, there was an important evolution in economic priorities, as countries sought to reduce conflicts and give greater attention to economic transformation. The Peronist political party suffered a decline in power after the military takeover. Peronist movements had shown their effectiveness throughout time, ultimately culminating in the ascension of a populist leader to a position of power.

The election held in 1989 resulted in the victory of Carlos Menem, a candidate affiliated with the Peronist party. The event was widely regarded as a pivotal moment that marked a significant turning point for the democratic system in Argentina. The nation had seen an extended period of unbroken democratic governance since achieving independence. It was asserted that this leader had backing from preceding authorities. Typically, he engaged in communication with those living in local communities and smaller urban areas. The promises made by him exhibited no noticeable variation. He asserted that he would increase wages and productivity to create employment (Barros, 2005). However, he was regarded as a politician adhering to neoliberal principles. The economic policies implemented by Menem and Özal exhibit notable similarities. Following the military coups, both politicians observed an increase in their political influence. They persisted in adhering to the outdated economic policies of preceding populist administrations. Despite their hopeful rhetoric of economic reform and opposition to established norms, they persistently implemented irrational policies. Two presidents, despite the limits of their policies, made steps to reduce the influence of public enterprises, promoted policies that were more democratic and liberal in character, and attempted to reduce the role of the government in the economy. In both nations, the concept of liberalism was not a novel phenomenon. During the 1950s in Türkiye, there was a notable increase in the visibility of liberal ideas as a result of political reforms that fostered a more democratic system and allowed for the participation of parties in elections. During the period of the Menderes administration, the nation endeavored to enact liberal economic policies. Nevertheless, the level of industrial growth remained insufficient to effectively compete in the global market. The competitiveness of agricultural goods experienced a decline subsequent to the conclusion of the Korean War. There had been a substantial reduction in the demand for certain items. During the early 1960s, a military coup occurred with the objective of halting the democratic movement. Rather than enhancing democratic principles and fostering economic equilibrium, the nation experienced a transformation toward a more closed economy and a gradual erosion of its foundations due to the implementation of protectionist policies. The doctrine of liberalism originated inside the country throughout the 1950s. The threat of military action decisively halted this perspective. There was an increase in populism in the country, which led to a lack of success in achieving a fair allocation of power between the working class and industrial sectors.

The political system has a significant role in determining the economic policies that are implemented in both Argentina and Türkiye. The role of leadership and its associated charisma has significant relevance for both of these countries. Their defiance toward the global society has the capacity to cultivate a feeling of oneness among people, motivating them to unite toward a shared objective. Peronism places a significant emphasis on the centrality and widespread nature of the charm possessed by the leader. In the Turkish context, the leader is viewed as a guardian of the interests of the general population, protecting them from the perceived control of the elite groups as well as from foreign opponents. The qualities related to leadership are based on previous cultural norms and traditions. The leader should openly denounce the current culture of elites, regarding it as tainted and devoid of ethical principles. The emergence of this movement may be attributed to the ideological resistance of Kemalism against the institutions of the empire. Over the course of several decades, this specific political system had a substantial impact on the Turkish economy. The economic crisis that transpired in 2000–2001 provided a favorable circumstance for conservative political organizations to acquire dominance. The new governing party demonstrated his capacity for leadership and used his political sway to back those who were against old institutions and secularism. Conservatism became the dominant force in the political system during this time. All political bodies inside the country have pledged to develop a welfare state and promote a prosperous society. Peronism included two separate political strategies and ideologies, namely the mobilization of the working class and the integration of Catholic doctrines. His goal was to strengthen the Catholic faith's dedication to education. The Turkish government under the conservative party has developed its political strategies by taking into account the interests of the working class and the principles of Islamism. The ideology of Chavismo in Venezuela has comparable traits to those commonly associated with populism. Thus, in the realm of populist rhetoric, these two prominent attributes of the countries were employed to attract the support of the people. Populist governments must proactively challenge the privileged class who exploit the working class and promote nonreligious values, which are regarded as disloyal. Within the framework of two political systems, governments may efficiently use social and technical tools to actively interact with the middle and lower socioeconomic strata. The aforementioned factors resulted in the formation of a consensus throughout society and the handling of large groups of constituents by both the Peronists and the conservative party in Türkiye, even if both political entities may have functioned during distinct historical periods. During the 2000s, after a severe economic crisis in Argentina, Néstor Kirchner and his spouse Cristina Fernández de Kirchner had a significant influence on the political landscape. They were populist politicians who claimed to be on the left and whose political techniques were influenced by Peronism. During the term of President Menem, the Peronist strategy underwent a transformation, shifting toward a more liberal approach with the implementation of deregulation policies. During the 2000s, the Kirchner government made efforts to appeal to those who were unemployed as well as neopopulist factions. For a long period of time, the administration made efforts to attract the working class by implementing left-wing policies. The Peronist party was unable to break free from its reliance on established patterns and habits. The nation's efforts to enhance its global economic standing proved to be futile. In the 2010s, with the death of Néstor Kirchner, who became a revered figure in Argentina, his spouse took on a more prominent role in running the country and leading initiatives. Nevertheless, significant modifications were not witnessed. The productivity level had a consistent decrease while inflation showed a significant rise. During this period, the currency rate displayed considerable volatility, and the fiscal measures that were implemented experienced continued difficulties.

While not all populist parties in Argentina adhere to Peronism, it is noteworthy that the policies rooted in Peronism exhibit populist characteristics inside the country. A conflict exists between the Peronist factions and others who oppose the Peronist ideology. The movement was associated with the working class. The significance of the working class was heightened with the establishment of the Worker's Party by Perón in 1946. Subsequently, the political organization underwent a transition, adopting the appellation of the Peronist party, which subsequently evolved into the denomination of the Justice Party. The political landscape in Argentina has been significantly influenced by the legacy of Peronism, which has been characterized by the leadership of prominent figures such as Juan Domingo Perón, Carlos Menem, and Néstor Kirchner–Cristina Fernández de Kirchner (Muno, 2019). Recent political parties in Argentina have persisted in pursuing expansionary fiscal policies. The Peronist political faction continues to have significance in the context of the Argentinian economy. Representative democracy was the prevailing political framework in both nations. Numerous ideologies and political organizations might potentially find a suitable platform for their own political activities. The underpinnings of populism in Türkiye can be traced back to the principles of Kemalism and conservatism, whereas in Argentina, it has its roots in Peronism. Both political spheres became as influential forces in the economics of the respective nations. During the 1980s, the Özal administration emerged as a prominent proponent of neoliberal populism. However, based on macroeconomic indicators, his adherence to liberal economic policies proved to be short-lived. During the 2000s, the administration led by the government endeavored to build upon this established practice. Nevertheless, the duration of the performance was relatively short, leading to the adoption of heterodox policies in the nation throughout the 2010s. Populist leaders has the ability to establish a feeling of connection between themselves and the people. They adopted a specific role in shaping the ideologies of their successors. When their tactics prove ineffective, they adeptly position themselves as victims of political institutions or unidentified foreign adversaries. Therefore, they are highly regarded and recognized as the savior of their 'we.' The people hold the belief that the leaders, via the act of sacrificing their lives, played a crucial role in the survival of the nation. Populist political movements strategically use the passionate connection with the people for their own political agendas. This assertion has validity just within the realm of populism's political dimensions. Economic populism has a much greater capacity to appeal to individuals, particularly those living in less prosperous and developing nations, as well as developed countries experiencing economic recessions. The populist movements in both nations are primarily oriented toward peripheral regions, smaller urban centers, rural areas, and the working class residing in major metropolitan areas. This political maneuver is employed with the aim of persuading individuals that they have not been neglected. The silent majority is a collective that remains unnoticeable until election season. Populist leaders serve as a vital channel for people to voice their desires, highlighting their importance. Populist governments have garnered support from the Central Anatolia

Region and remote urban areas of Türkiye. Urban and isolated cities often generate significant numbers of votes in favor of conservative, nationalist, and protectionist populist governments. Left-wing organizations and secular individuals have the capacity to garner support from residents in highly populated and economically developed metropolitan regions.

The political institutions in both nations were shaped by democratic principles. Populism has emerged as a persistent concern since the advent of import substitution industrialization, which facilitated the mobilization of the working class and subsequently led to the formulation and implementation of policies aligned with this evolving socioeconomic landscape. However, the primacy of institutional change in the wage–labor relation persists in modern times. While the political landscape in both nations may be influenced by left-wing or right-wing forces, the persistent challenge of populism and its entrenched historical legacy remain resistant to transformation. The society has a propensity to support hyperpresidential and charismatic leaders who enact protectionist and expansionist policies to demonstrate that they are serving the interests of ordinary people rather than those of the powerful industrial elites. This notion is also a fundamental topic within the field of institutional economics. It can require a significant amount of time to change the legislation, regulations, norms, and traditions into a framework that is more progressive. The political structure of both nations was further impacted by extreme militarist forces before 2000. The escalation of political unrest and conflict among various political factions, along with the increasing polarization of political parties, provided a rationale for militarists to orchestrate a coup d'état and dismantle the democratic framework inside the nation. Subsequently, with the implementation of significant institutional reforms, the newly established administrations endeavored to sustain governance under the framework of representative democracy. Although populism rejected democratic institutions, it did not ultimately support severe authoritarian governments in these countries. Although aggressiveness has sometimes increased, the commitment to democracy has consistently been a core value in countries, where people have voiced their resistance to the possible advent of authoritarianism promoted by populist leaders. There are many political factions inside economies. Nevertheless, it is important to note that the political system remains protected by the implementation of limited democracy and pluralism. Irrespective of the circumstances, populist governments maintain the conviction that decision-making should not be entrusted to the people. This implies that there remains potential for these countries to transition into more democratic states and adopt more pragmatic institutional frameworks to pursue advantageous economic strategies. It is essential to recognize within the realm of economic knowledge that the adoption of economic populism as a driving force in shaping the political structure does not possess the capacity to provide prosperity for individuals unless accompanied by the implementation of institutional reforms that align with the underlying economic dynamics.

The institutional revision in Argentina throughout the 1940s intensified the polarization between Peronists and anti-Peronists. The influence of Peronism on politics and society generates an impression of significant polarization, which is shaped by the previous authority's policies that encouraged a coalition of individuals unified by an identical idea (Manzetti, 1999; Little, 1973). This historical transformation was also a process to build a direct connection between the government and the people. Türkiye underwent a constitutional change that included transitioning from a parliamentary democratic system to a presidential democratic one, enabling a solitary leader to wield more authority and swiftly adopt and modify laws, surpassing prior limitations. The effectiveness of a parliamentary body, which aimed to enhance the connection between public opinion and political parties, was diminished. Consequently, a direct connection between the government and the people was developed. This implies that a government has the authority to enact changes or modify institutions as deemed necessary. Nevertheless, a state of division became evident among those who expressed support for the governing party and others who had opposing views. In both nations, democratic elections may be facilitated by the use of institutions on behalf of the populist administration that has governing authority. There are often two options that are provided to the people. There is a potential for individuals to experience a duality between prioritizing the maintenance and liberation of their country or giving in to a condition of disorder and the eventual erosion of their collective identity. The Manichaean approach is characterized by a fundamental dichotomy between forces representing good and evil, as well as conflicts between the people and the ruling elites, or between the working class and industrial establishments.

Polarization has the potential to turn competitors in other political arenas into adversaries. Therefore, the government has to act against these adversaries to maintain the nation free and secure. The impact of polarization instigated by populist administrations serves to foster political engagement among the people. They may exhibit tendencies toward authoritarianism. The power of individuals may be enhanced via the cultivation and development of their inherent characteristics. Leadership ought to align with the collective desires and preferences of the people. Democracy should be employed for referenda and polls. The triumph of adversaries in electoral contests may be regarded as a precarious circumstance with potential implications for the future trajectory of the nation. Furthermore, populists put onto the people the need to organize and protect the nation from adversaries. Therefore, polarization is successful to generate a decision-making in channeling the energy of political will. However, this scenario might escalate disputes and limit opportunities to implement fresh institutional reforms aimed at achieving an equilibrium of authority and division of power in the field of economics. With the use of referendums, representative democracies should legitimize their authority and position, which are assumed to be provided by the people, rather than focusing on implementing favorable institutional reforms. Charismatic leaders are regarded as the genuine representatives of nations. Their remarks should not be debated, and their authority should be respected. The ideals of the populist party are crucial to organize the society and may interfere into decision-making process. The disregard of democratic institutions might occur. In this context, populists have a tendency to oppose established institutions. However, they may employ institutional reforms to expand their power. Therefore, populism may be regarded as a phenomenon that operates within institutional frameworks, particularly in the economic domain. The manipulation of institutions for political purposes and the expectation that the justice system should prioritize the interests of its followers are prevalent concerns. The principle of separation of powers is not upheld. It can be witnessed that Perón made attempts to exert influence over the Supreme Court due to its composition of conservative adversaries, who posed a potential threat to his policy agenda (Muno, 2019).

The concept of the rule of law pertains to the degree of institutional excellence that determines the amount to which individuals have trust and feel secure in abiding by the laws and regulations of a given society. Based on the World Bank statistics related to the percentile rank of the rule of law, it is evident that both Argentina and Türkiye had relatively low rankings. The ranking scores show a higher degree of proximity to one another. Two nations are far worse than the rest of the industrialized world and the growing Asian nations. The rule of law encompasses crucial elements such as contract enforcement, property rights, policy, the courts, crime, and violence. Both nations witnessed an increase in their scores when they deviated from populist initiatives and instead prioritized the implementation of more pragmatic programs. Following a decline in their growth performance, there was a further decrease in their ratings. The rule of law in Türkiye had a notable upsurge throughout the 2000s, coinciding with a period characterized by suppressed wage growth and the implementation of a more stable exchange rate policy. In the years after 2010, there was a notable decline in the score regarding the rule of law, resulting in a relative lag behind several other nations. Moreover, it is worth noting that Argentina had much higher scores prior to the 2000s. Following the occurrence of an economic crisis, there was a notable decline in its score. In the early 2020s, their rule of law remained lower than that in China, which has been regarded as an undemocratic nation in which the rule of law cannot operate effectively. In 2021, the percentile figures for China, South Korea, Argentina, and Türkiye were around 53.8, 86.4, 35.1, and 36.5, respectively. The percentile was much lower in other emerging economies with populist tendencies, such as Venezuela. In these countries, governments have a significant propensity to intervene in economic matters. Nevertheless, it is commonly recognized that such interventions in the market have an adverse effect on democratic principles. Furthermore, these efforts exacerbate division since they only endorse certain factions.

The mobilization of society

There are multiple ways that power is exerted in different countries, and it is crucial to pay attention to these distinct methods. In a great number of countries, the power of the government is quite widespread, and it exercises control over every area of the institutions. From this point of view, China is a particular notable case. It is not possible for a government to be driven to embrace populist policies as a consequence of political competition when there is no democratic system in place. Consequently, this makes it possible for a governing body to exert influence over the economy with the purpose of accomplishing certain objectives. The Soviet

Union provides an additional example of this particular political framework. East Asian countries possess diverse political frameworks, although they exhibit a common trait in their endeavor to achieve economic development driven by exports. The political system has the ability to assume several forms. However, this limitation does not pose a significant obstacle to macroeconomic systems. Effective institutional changes that develop a growth-oriented framework in a country result in heightened prosperity. The process of achieving the technological frontier comprises several discrete stages. The first phase of a nation's industrialization is characterized by a primitive level of development, mostly reliant on the agricultural sector. Subsequently, the manufacturing sector starts its development. This phenomenon stimulates both employment rates and production levels. The proportion of GDP contributed by the manufacturing sector rises while the proportion contributed by the agricultural sector falls. Following this, growth models become more significant, eventually becoming an integral component of both productivity and efficiency. As the service sector experiences growth, there is an increased emphasis on innovation, capital investment, and operational efficiency. This level of development may be attained by an export-led growth strategy. East Asian nations that have implemented export-led growth strategies have shown notable improvements in efficiency and innovation. Following this stage, countries move away from export-led growth and have a moderate improvement in productivity along their natural trajectory. Consequently, the sustenance of development increasingly relies on the significance of education, innovation, efficiency, human capital, and skill. Nevertheless, in political systems characterized by democracy and the presence of multiple competing parties, the implementation of potentially unpopular policies may provide significant challenges for governing bodies. Political parties in developing countries lack significant institutionalization and face intense competition. Governments often exhibit a strong inclination to regulate institutional forms to maintain their temporary tenure in power, with the chosen mode of production functioning as a critical institutional determinant. Hence, governmental policies exhibit diversity based on whether a nation operates under a free market economy or a closed economy. By structuring the mode of production according to Communist ideals, a government is protected from the effects of competition. Typically, such nations are governed in a permanent manner by a single political party since the absence of an electoral mechanism prevents the participation of ordinary residents in the political decision-making process. It can be stated that populist ideas have gained traction in democratic nations as a consequence of increased competition.

Argentina and Türkiye both have democratic elections, but the democratic institutions in both nations are very nascent. Multiparty systems may sometimes result in fierce rivalry between political parties with contrasting values and philosophies. These countries' political environment is mostly defined by the existence of three prominent ideological factions: Liberals, nationalists, and social democrats. Hence, institutional elements are employed as economic tools to enact populist policies with the objective of obtaining popular endorsement. Populism is characterized by a number of variants and may be classified into two separate forms: 'backward' populism and 'forward' populism. The phenomenon of backward populism entails the reemergence of traditional values inside the economic framework, hence impeding the progress of a nation. Forward populism refers to a scenario when the people are actively engaged in promoting development and economic progress. Under such circumstances, institutional modifications can have a substantial influence on the economy. Following the end of the First World War, Türkiye implemented a series of progressive populist reforms. The people exhibited a significant level of mobilization in favor of the government's objectives. During this period, there was no multiparty system, which prevented political parties from engaging in any kind of rivalry. Therefore, the government found it feasible to enact substantial institutional modifications to facilitate economic expansion. Both countries have substantial and sizable corporations that were established during the era of protectionism. However, the amount of production is far lower when compared to East Asian countries such as China. Moreover, the process of setting up a business is hindered by significant challenges such as exorbitant costs, restricted availability of financial capital, bureaucratic red tape, and a shortage of skilled workers. Small- and medium-sized firms face operational inefficiencies as a result of difficulties related to entering the market. The political framework of a nation plays a crucial role in shaping the condition of that country. Political stability, security, and a free market are essential elements that contribute to both economic growth and overall stability in the economy. Investors can be worried about the economic situation due to heated rivalry between political parties and important political problems. Anticipating future results and implementing strategies in alignment with the current political environment presents considerable difficulties. Countries that have more political stability tend to demonstrate superior performance in economic endeavors. It is difficult to conceive of a scenario in which investors are inclined to direct their capital toward a nation whose economic policies are driven by populist tendencies. In a democratic society, there is a greater likelihood that investors will have opportunities to engage in innovation and make contributions to economic development. Economic agents need to engage in long-term economic forecasting with the expectation of overall stability within the economy. In a hypothetical scenario, in a nation where either a left-wing or right-wing political party has governance, there may be a potential adverse impact on overseas investors, as it might convey the message that their assets are susceptible to nationalization or restrictions on economic operations. Hence, it is essential that the political framework be founded upon the principles of power equilibrium, protection of property rights, a democratically controlled economy, and robust government incentives and protections.

In both Argentina and Türkiye, the need to mobilize society before elections has often resulted in the adoption of economically populist campaigns by all political parties. The influence of election periods on macroeconomic indicators and news is evident. News reports have shown a significant correlation between salaries and election campaigns as well as the consequent escalation of inflation. Furthermore, several governmental bodies have had difficulties in successfully executing austerity measures. Prime Minister Çiller resigned in the 1990s when a party left her coalition government in protest over austerity measures that led to the largest labor strikes in Türkiye's history. The adoption of liberal economic measures, such as the privatization of state enterprises, with the implementation of austerity policies aimed at managing inflation, resulted in an escalation of labor disputes. The administration sought to enact a policy aimed at reducing economic instability via wage reductions, but it encountered an unprecedented surge in strike activities and faced immense political pressure. Ultimately, the party was unsuccessful. Due to the fact that she was unable to settle the present strike by public sector workers about their salaries, the news reports suggested that Çiller was encountering difficulties in her efforts to build a new minority administration. The prime minister found herself constricted in terms of political possibilities on 20th September, a week after the breakdown of Çiller's coalition government that had been in power for four years. At the same time, the country was faced with the possibility of shortages in a variety of essential items. Following the event, the prime minister said that her political party had been subjected to repercussions as a result of their failure to succumb to the demands of striking workers for a significant increase in their salaries. Furthermore, she highlighted that their activities were driven by the principle of placing the welfare of the country ahead of their personal self-interests. In addition, she remained adamant in her unwillingness to feel regret, claiming with self-assurance that our sense of self-worth continues to be enhanced, reaching heights that are comparable to the heaven above. The concept of path dependency was demonstrated by this specific historical event, which was provided as evidence. It was primarily owing to the existence of high inflation and major depreciations in the currency rate that the administration was unable to adequately implement its economic goals, which eventually culminated in the subsequent election loss.[1] In 2015, heightened rivalry among political parties pushed the government to implement a policy focused on promoting robust wage growth, which consequently resulted in an upsurge in inflation. The news states that the ruling party obtained enough members in the Turkish parliament during the 1st November election to form a government without needing to have a coalition with other parties. As part of their campaign platform, the party pledged to raise the minimum wage by a 30% increase. However, it is not rational to expect a 30% economic growth rate since it has been and is very improbable. Countries classified as developing countries, such as Argentina and Türkiye, often encounter potential growth rates of about 3%–5%.

The government and the people have developed a tremendous bond. The populist administration employs the plebiscitarian linkage as a means to validate its governance and policy choices. This grants authority to the government, enabling it to organize the labor force and enact policies that appeal to the general population. During the 1940s and 1950s, there was a notable surge in the democratic movement in both Argentina and Türkiye. The presence of political conflict has had a transformative impact on the public's view of politics. More democratic rhetoric has been at the core of every political conflict that has taken place on the globe. The working class experienced a higher degree of economic democracy as a direct consequence of the transformation implemented. On the other hand, in contrast to the privileged elite, the working class is defined as having little financial means, despite the fact that it is the most prevalent group inside the country. An important empowerment of the working class was achieved as a consequence of the adoption of institutional reform, which made it possible for them to establish a social framework that was more collaborative. The execution of the economic democracy regulations has resulted in the growth of populism as a form of economic representation. Not only does this imply that the working class is attempting to claim their entitlement to higher wages and improved purchasing power, but it also indicates that they are expressing a desire for the government to levy additional taxes on industries and elites while simultaneously redistributing income and transfers. This move is in direct opposition to the ideals that underpin a free market economy.

Note

1 For additional source: 'Turkish prime minister loses vote in parliament' (CNN World News).

8 Crises and policies

Numerous elements contribute to the interpretation of economic crises. The aspects under consideration include the inherent characteristics of labor and its correlation with output, the amount of wages, the means by which production is acquired, as well as the connection between banking and credit relations, among other factors. Each of these characteristics exhibits interconnectivity and may mutually influence one another. While it is important to note that economic populism cannot be attributed as the main cause, it is worth considering that the presence of certain institutional factors might contribute to the stimulation of economic crises. In economies characterized by populism, the occurrence of crises may be attributed to the significant interdependence between the labor sector and the government. Industries are disregarded in this particular kind of interaction. The absence of a balanced distribution of power within the markets contributes to the occurrence of crises. These crises may be clarified using economic concepts, such as the substantial devaluation of the currency rate, imbalances in the current account, or persistent inflation. A government that tries to impose austerity measures may encounter a negative public response and face the potential consequence of losing political power. Consequently, governmental entities may exhibit hesitancy in implementing actions. A dilemma of cohabitation arises between established institutions and developing ones.

Nations exhibit diverse economic frameworks and possess unique inherent challenges. Crises may manifest as an outcome of financial difficulties or economic circumstances. The Great Depression of 1929 has remained a significant subject of discourse in the field of economics within the context of economic history. Deflation emerged as a primary factor contributing to the occurrence of this catastrophe. Furthermore, the energy crises that occurred in the 1970s and the mortgage crisis of 2008 had a direct effect on industrialized nations while also exerting an indirect influence on emerging nations. Furthermore, it is noteworthy to mention that Argentina and Türkiye have encountered several economic crises, mostly instigated by persistent inflationary pressures and volatility in currency rates. Every crisis was characterized by significant devaluations and challenges in maintaining a favorable balance of payments. A notable crisis emerged in both nations throughout the early 2000s. This factor significantly contributed to the implementation of reforms intended for mitigating macroeconomic instability. Türkiye had a significant economic crisis during the year 2000–2001, which resulted in a transformative

DOI: 10.4324/9781003438090-8

impact on the government and initiated a series of reform measures. The economic crisis and recession experienced in Argentina between 2001 and 2002 resulted in widespread protests that led to the overthrow of the government. Following the crisis, Kirchner effectively implemented measures that led to economic recovery. The prospective Peronist-style administration had the potential to revitalize the economy via the implementation of measures such as debt reduction for creditors, mitigation of social unrest, and the establishment of a reasonably stable pricing mechanism. The occurrence of severe crises in two nations necessitated the formulation of new policies by their respective governments. The government had a significant role in facilitating the transformation to the new growth model. The matter about the government's use of the authority it will acquire may only arise in the aftermath of a significant crisis that has had serious consequences. The currency crises, then, contributed to the emergence of this opportunity. Therefore, the government would possess the capacity to address the shortcomings of past political leaders by implementing the needed changes throughout the whole economic landscape, therefore facilitating the emergence of novel institutional structures inside the economy.

Economic crises have significant importance due to their propensity to engender a sense of mistrust among the people toward the governing authorities. Therefore, during periods of crises, it becomes convenient to attract support from the general public by making unrealistic pledges of prosperity, increased wealth, and a stable economy. Nonetheless, the absence of institutional adjustments may provide a conducive environment for the emergence of a future populist administration. Both Argentina and Türkiye are susceptible to experiencing high levels of democratic discontent while witnessing economic crises. The phenomenon of societal unrest leads to the resignation of administrations that have been unable to formulate effective policies. In December 2001, Fernando de la Rua tendered his resignation from his job. Argentina witnessed a distressing devaluation of its currency, leading to a complete default on its financial obligations. The aforementioned observation holds true for Türkiye as well. Following the economic crisis of 2000–2001, the political party voluntarily abandoned its governmental role, prompting the legislative body to make the decision to hold an early election. Both nations established a fixed exchange rate regime, pegging their respective currencies to the US dollar. However, the nations were compelled to face currency crises as a consequence of significant depreciation. Neither country was able to identify effective leadership capable of resolving the issue. Both nations experienced an increase in poverty, inequality, reduced demand, and less purchasing power among the middle class as a consequence of the crises. Left-wing organizations were drawn to this issue, contending that the adoption of capitalism economic policies was responsible for significant economic issues. Nevertheless, they were unable to acknowledge macroeconomic instability and the recurrence of catastrophic crises as elements of economic populism. Left-wing political parties implicated globalization, privatization, and deregulation policies as the root causes of economic issues rather than exclusively concentrating on mitigating economic uncertainty and acknowledging the issue as an internal problem.

During times of economic crises, it becomes imperative to use institutional frameworks to identify and analyze the inherent inconsistencies within the growth model. The government has the capacity to deal with the shortcomings inherent in the components of the growth model, thus enabling its optimal functioning. For a model of growth to operate effectively inside institutional forms, it requires the presence of diverse economic and social structures. This discourse encompasses various aspects pertaining to the regulation of production and labor as well as the wage relationship. It also explores the correlation between the evolution of labor organization and the means of production. Additionally, it delves into the determination of capital prices, which serves as the foundation for the development of management principles. It examines the distribution of value, which ensures the reproduction of diverse social classes and groups. Moreover, it considers the formation of social demand in alignment with the advancement of production capacity, emphasizing the necessity of maintaining a balance between production and consumption. Finally, it addresses the context in which relationships are established with capitalist and noncapitalist economies as well as different national and regional economies. These forms perform a crucial role in outlining a growth model. However, it is important to recognize that the configuration of the growth model is subject to variation based on specific temporal and spatial factors (Boyer, 1990; Jessop and Sum, 2006). The structure of these components undergoes modifications and exhibits distinct features while transitioning from one growth model to another. To provide perspective on the periods, it is essential to take into account these criteria. Nevertheless, it is necessary to establish structural or institutional mechanisms to maintain economic stability. Hence, it is essential that the growth models be managed primarily via the institutional forms of the nation. To fully comprehend this phenomenon, it is important to consider the historical transformations in institutional forms, as they play a crucial role in determining the existence of path dependencies and complementarities.

Following the Great Depression, the concept of Keynesian economics gained prominence among industrialized nations. The promotion of mass consumption was advocated as a means to achieve economic stability. Therefore, the implementation of policies aimed at enhancing consumption had emerged as a prominent aspect inside society. This particular viewpoint is referred to as demand-side policy. According to the Keynesian perspective, an economy is inherently incapable of achieving stability on its own and is susceptible to becoming entangled in crises. Consequently, the influence of supply-side economics diminished. Keynesian demand-side economics emerged as a replacement for it. Economic policies were formulated in accordance with this prevailing notion. Following a notable advancement in technology and production, there arose a need to overcome the issue of insufficient effective demand in the context of mass production. Thus, there was a rise in salaries and a strengthening of employment policies. Workers gained power as an outcome of their attempts to achieve social and union rights. The notion that the economy would naturally generate full employment and operate independently started to diminish over time, leading to the contention that stability in the economy could only be attained by government involvement. Government programs were adopted to enhance employment rates. This initiative represents a significant milestone in addressing mass consumerism. The policies in question were abandoned by developed nations throughout the 1980s. The resurgence of liberalism has become significant once again. The combination of high inflation and decreased productivity prompted governments to adopt a more open policy toward foreign trade. Developing nations have made challenging efforts to align themselves with emerging trends in development and economic policies. They were not successful in catching up to developed economies. Argentina and Türkiye are classified as developing nations. It is challenging to conceive that two nations would serve as hubs of prosperity, stability, and economic advancement. Neoliberalism was attributed as the scapegoat due to its perceived shortcomings. The assertion was of such significant magnitude and had a radical nature that the people refrained from acknowledging the fact that the issue at hand did not just stem from neoliberalism and institutional flaws. The International Monetary Fund (IMF) has consistently been regarded as the entity responsible for the failures. The presence of populist regimes and the prevailing political system posed significant challenges in the implementation of essential reforms. Consequently, the impact of crises was further intensified. Despite the assertions made by the indicated nations about their freedom from economic crises, it is evident that such claims are unfounded due to the absence of any significant institutional reforms aimed at mitigating systemic failures. The solution was not complex, but the realm of politics continued to provide a significant challenge. For many decades, Latin American nations and Türkiye had pursued a policy of pegging their currencies to the US dollar. The subsequent populist administrations did not give up on imposing a fixed exchange rate, despite the fact that their attempts to fix their currency rate throughout the course of the periods were unsuccessful. The severe economic crisis that occurred in the early 2000s had a transformative impact on government policies. The implementation of a fixed exchange rate, rigid labor policy, and expansionary monetary policy were not consistent with the principles of neoliberalism. These measures were intentionally enacted by administrations with populist tendencies. The implementation of these unfavorable policies had been associated with several economic disasters. Indeed, it is common for nations to encounter economic crises. The paradox is that these nations, which are retrograde examples of the global economy, are having the same kind of economic crises over and over again.

The economic crisis that occurred during 2001–2002 can be attributed to a series of unsuccessful institutional reforms. The nation observed a significant depreciation of its currency, leading to a recurrence of debt defaults. These failures were prevalent in both nations over a prolonged period of time. Countries have often entered into agreements with the IMF to deal with issues such as debt default, inflation reduction, and economic stabilization. Initiation of all program agreements had begun with the goal of enacting more market-oriented policies. Despite initial attempts, all plans for agreements were unsuccessful subsequent to the attainment of financial assistance from the IMF. The orthodox policies of stabilization were disdained. Instead, populist economies have embraced heterodox stabilization measures, even though they have never been implemented in any nation and have never been examined by any study. These policies are regarded as fresh alternatives. The assertion was made that neoliberalism did not provide the anticipated outcomes. The measures in question were deemed inappropriate due to the perception that they reflected an attempt by Western powers to exert control over the nation. Nevertheless, policies that are often referred to be heterodox have also shown to be ineffective. The lack of alignment between heterodox ideas and economic reality contributed to this outcome. Despite the efforts made by governments to regulate macroeconomic factors, their attempts to adopt policies and exercise control over expansionary measures were ultimately unsuccessful. Therefore, the issue of what the answer is to the problem of populist regimes continues to be an open one.

Argentina and Türkiye have been adversely affected by persistent macroeconomic instability. Inflation has been a longstanding concern for both countries, but starting in the period of import substitution industrialization, it became a chronic problem for both nations. An unusual plunge into an inflationary spiral was observed by Argentina throughout the decade of the 1980s. Advanced economies worldwide have embraced liberalization over protectionism and implemented progressive economic reforms. There was a broadening of the extent of global trade across diverse economies. The following years witnessed a significant decline in the inflation rate. Governments in developed countries had a crucial need to expedite wage rise due to the necessary nature of demand-side measures. The outcome was stagflation, which occurred when this problem intersected with rising energy prices. Argentina and Türkiye, unlike more developed nations, have not implemented substantial institutional changes to stabilize variables and mitigate inflation. In the late 1980s, Argentina had a hyperinflationary episode that reached a staggering 3000% level. Because of the high level of inflation, regular and consistent devaluations of the currency have become the norm. In the 1960s, the annual rate of inflation was lower than 10% in Türkiye. In spite of this, inflation skyrocketed during the 1970s and developed into a significant issue. For decades, nations had to cope with inflation rates in the double digits. The issue of inflation was not resolved throughout the 1980s. During the 1970s, when industrialized nations were experiencing oil crises, they faced severe inflation, which forced them to implement policies of deregulation. The outcomes were remarkable. The majority of developed nations in Europe and the United States could implement a sustainable fiscal strategy. Through the elimination of import duties, openness evolved into a powerful tactic. These nations were able to bring their inflation rates down significantly while also achieving improved economic results. As a consequence of the free trade agreements that were made available to them by the World Trade Organization (WTO) and the EU, exporting their products became their primary focus. Both Argentina and Türkiye continued to struggle with high levels of inflation. The persistent rise in prices has several unfavorable repercussions. It leads to an increase in price levels, which discourages industries from adapting to the changing dynamics of the market. Under the circumstances of a free market, it is difficult for both consumers and producers to arrive at an accurate price determination. Investments become less appealing as uncertainty rises. When people's purchasing power and savings rapidly decrease, political risks increase due to dissatisfaction.

The occurrence of inflation might be traced back to the rudimentary implementation of fiscal measures. As a result, it became unavoidable that the purchasing power of the working class experienced a substantial erosion, while the pressure on the exchange rate intensified, leading to depreciation. This dynamic had led to a distinct and volatile economic situation. Furthermore, the socioeconomic impact of hyperinflation contributed to a significant reduction in earnings, thus exerting a profound influence on those belonging to the lower- and middle-class strata of society. During the 1990s, Argentina used a currency board system. The implementation of a fixed exchange rate regime had a favorable impact on the economy. Nevertheless, the economy exhibited vulnerability to external shocks. Rather than implementing a fixed exchange rate system, it is advisable for the nation to address fiscal imbalances via the adoption of austerity measures, enhance labor market flexibility to mitigate rigidity, and align policies with the principles of globalization. Reduced budget deficits would facilitate the implementation of appropriate programs without imposing excessive pressure on the government. Furthermore, this measure serves to mitigate the political risks associated with the implementation of increased taxation, which has the potential to generate discontent within society. The creation of a flexible labor market would facilitate the process of recruitment and termination of employees for enterprises. This will foster a competitive and equitable working environment in accordance with macroeconomic circumstances. This will provide enterprises an opportunity to make adaptations in response to evolving market conditions. Implementing economic policies in alignment with global strategy has the potential to provide significant advantages. Understanding the growth model of a trading partner has significant importance. Otherwise, it would pose significant challenges for the economy to effectively engage in global trade and maintain competitiveness. Under a fixed exchange rate regime, the economy is constrained in its capacity to use political tools. Therefore, the enforcement of expansionary fiscal policies may exert further pressure on the exchange rate system.

Argentina's reform efforts have not yielded satisfactory outcomes. Despite the initiation of discussions for new electoral changes in the late 1990s, the significance of this objective gradually diminished. Exporters always had a disadvantageous position in international trade, which aspired to become a competitive power. The currency rate sustained an overvaluation for a period of ten years. Occasionally, when the currency experienced a collapse and then returned to its equilibrium state, this transient condition proved to be short-lived. Furthermore, throughout the 1990s, there was a notable rise in the competitiveness of developing countries in global trade, which might be attributed to the effective implementation of their exchange rate systems, exemplified by the case of the yuan. Consequently, the peso exhibited an overvaluation not just in relation to the US dollar but also when compared to other currencies. Macroeconomic imbalances, such as elevated levels of unemployment, remained prevalent. The persistence of a high interest rate continues to contribute to the overall level of risk associated with the nation.

The circumstances were similar for the Turkish economy. The nation had a substantial economic crisis as a result of the depreciation of its currency. The Çiller administration, which assumed power by electoral means by adopting populist strategies, had significant challenges in effectively implementing deregulation programs aimed at mitigating the economic turbulence. The export showed a lack of competitiveness in the realm of international trade. The nation experienced instability in its current account balance. The economy suffered due to the overvaluation of the currency rate. The decision to maintain a high interest rate was made to encourage the inflow of speculative capital with the aim of mitigating the potential depreciation of the exchange rate. In 1994, the economy experienced a dramatic economic crisis. Expansionary policies have been attributed to the emergence of a substantial budget imbalance, necessitating its financing via the intervention of the central bank. The level of inflation experienced was considerably severe. During that time, however, there was a record-breaking surge in wage growth.

To establish stability, the 5th April austerity plan was implemented. The objective of the strategy was to stimulate economic recovery via financial support from the IMF. Türkiye was compelled to adopt deregulation measures, reduce inflation, provide stability in the currency rate, and undertake a comprehensive austerity program. Despite the country's concerted efforts to mitigate the impact of the crisis, it was unable to effectively undertake the necessary institutional reforms. The working class exerted substantial pressure on the government. The presence of political risk had hindered the implementation of comprehensive market reforms. The measures exhibited similarities to the neoliberal policies that have been applied in countries throughout Latin America. In the mid-1994, there was a significant increase in strikes and the number of workdays lost due to strikes reached an unprecedented level (Ünal, 2018). The populist administrations proved incapable of withstanding the internal pressure exerted by the working class. There was no other option available to maintain agreements of the terms offered by the IMF in exchange for loans, and it was also necessary to keep populist policies in place for the next years. The lack of comprehensive reforms resulted in a significant economic crisis throughout the early 2000s. The outcome remained the same as Türkiye found it necessary to enter into a fresh agreement with the IMF to implement neoliberal policies including privatization and deregulation across all sectors of the economy. The initiative is referred to as the Transition to the Strong Economy Program. During the first years of the newly formed administration, there was a notable inclination toward rejecting populist measures and instead adopting a more pragmatic approach that aligned with the economic requirements. The potential for a substantial decrease in inflation, together with the relative stability achieved in the exchange rate system, had contributed to reduce the fiscal deficit reaching the limit set by the Maastricht Criterion of the EU. A decrease in wage growth was observed. There was a significant reduction in the rate of growth in the labor costs. The nation demonstrated enhanced competitiveness in contrast to previous periods. The economy witnessed an unprecedented surge in both economic growth and export expansion. However, the nation has been unable to achieve a reduction in inflation to the target rate of 2%. According to the World Bank, the economy could only reach a 6.25%

inflation rate in 2009, which was much lower in comparison to past time periods. Despite the relatively low level of volatility, the currency rate exhibited a progressive depreciation. The trade imbalance had substantial growth. Following the global crisis of 2008, the nation had a significant decline in its growth performance. The economic policies of populism have reemerged. The reason for this is that the rise in wages was not sufficiently adaptable to the conditions of the market. The slowdown in economic growth should have exerted downward pressure on wage increase. Nevertheless, this desired result was never attained. Inflation had a notable surge throughout the 2010s. The volatility in the currency rate had once again emerged as a significant concern. In conclusion, the anticipated effectiveness of institutional transformation was not accomplished.

It is essential for these nations to implement measures aimed at curbing expansionary fiscal policies since such policies might pose significant risks under a fixed and overvalued exchange rate framework. Despite the recurring economic issues, no political party has ever improved its policies to avoid the repetition of the same errors. Populist regimes have shown a lack of resolve in addressing the factors contributing to fiscal imbalance. Any measure taken regarding this issue is likely to result in a decline in the government's popularity among the working class. The governments showed a lack of capacity to implement fiscal adjustment measures that would evoke a significant response inside the nation. The debt was created to consciously drive the economy into instability as an alternative for effectively tackling the deficit via the implementation of sound economic policies. In other words, a financial burden was postponed until the next administration took office.

Despite the implementation of import substitution industrialization, there was a large increase in the trade imbalance. An overvalued exchange rate policy led to severe pressure on prices as an outcome of the excessive generation of liquidity. The amount of debt that the government owed also increased. On the other hand, there was no rise in tax revenue, which might have helped lower the national debt. When it comes to populist governments, wage-setting policy may be a deciding factor in whether or not expansionary policy is pursued. The government modified wages in response to rising expenses of rent, the cost of living, energy, and materials to lessen the possibility of political unrest. This suggests that international trade could suffer because of the system of fixed exchange rates. Countries eventually ran out of international reserves. As a severe alternative, this results in a significant decrease in the value of the exchange rate. Due to the escalating financial instability, currency crises resulted in numerous bankruptcies. In addition, the IMF often provided these two nations with financial assistance to meet the demands of their respective governments. The government can have a greater degree to intervene in the currency market as foreign reserves decline. In the past, this was done by making it more difficult for businesses and individuals to obtain foreign cash. The introduction of capital restrictions was necessary because there were insufficient amounts of foreign currency available to meet the requirements of businesses and people. To achieve this goal in modern times, governments and financial institutions increase transaction fees and spreads when purchasing and selling foreign currency. However, neither strategy would be sufficient to eliminate the risk posed by draining reserves since populist regimes tend to use unfavorable institutional forms that are the root cause of the issue. Hence, populist economies continue to experience this dilemma or déjà vu for decades. In spite of the fact that both nations' economies grew throughout the decade of the 1990s, this trend did not last for very long. The underlying cause of the path dependency could not be removed. The nations continued to use exchange rate regimes that were either controlled or fixed. The competitiveness of exports was harmed as a consequence. Currency crises affected both Argentina and Türkiye in the early part of the new millennium.

The rapid progress of technology, the swift flow of money, and the lack of capacity to handle loans give rise to financial concerns that result in instability in the economy. In the past, there was no need for establishing institutional arrangements about the linkages between money and credit. Over time, the importance of institutional structures began to grow significantly. The pivotal role in this can be attributed to the exponential progress of technology. The rapid advancements in technological innovation and the diverse range of manufacturing methods have led to the development of instruments that may be employed to impact the financial markets. In the modern world, financial markets have become more open, and money has reached a point where it can move more quickly from one location to another. The significance of the free market has expanded, which has led to an increase in the number of people investing their money in the financial markets. New financial instruments started to be employed. There has been a noticeable acceleration in the rate at which complicated financial products are transferred from one nation to another. Because of this factor, the connectivity of nations has risen even more as a consequence of the growth of financial markets. Furthermore, advancements in technology have taken this link to a new level. Cryptocurrencies and the digital economy have greatly simplified the transmission of capital compared to the past. Therefore, it is difficult to manage exchange rates and price levels in an economy by capital limitation. For these nations to be able to eliminate their macroeconomic volatility, therefore, institutional complementarity is a must. The idea that these two nations need to liberalize their economic systems to establish unrestricted movement of capital has been discussed for decades. Attempting to construct a free financial system, on the other hand, while the macroeconomy is in a state of instability, might lead to greater problems. This is the reason why politicians in these two nations have been critical of the IMF. The recommendations made by the IMF were relatively favorable. Nevertheless, to be effective, they need to be put into place using the appropriate institutional forms that are consistent with the growth model. Increasing financial integration can render these countries more susceptible to shocks from the outside as well as a high degree of speculation, both of which have been experienced by these nations on several occasions in their currency rates and during severe economic downturns. The assumption that in order for a nation to develop, there must be free market reforms is disproved by the case of China, which implemented a system of a fixed exchange rate and regulated the movement of capital. During the 1990s and 2000s, this nation avoided being directly impacted by the currency crises and economic recessions that occurred in other nations. However, the loosening of restrictions on the movement of capital without the simultaneous implementation of constructive institutional reforms gave rise to severe financial crises in a number of emerging nations, including Argentina in 2002 and Türkiye in 2000–2001. These countries faced continuous macroeconomic instability as a consequence of their failure to establish institutional complementarity.

In economic populist countries, a recurring pattern of economic crises is the depreciation of currency rates at different stages of the crises. Because economic populism was the organizing principle behind each era, it does not matter which historical period is examined. Populist countries employ either interest rate policies or exchange rate regimes to curb the depreciation of their currency. This is a historical pattern that is being followed even in contemporary times. A constantly appreciating exchange rate is indicative of a trade imbalance in a nation. Nevertheless, attempting to prevent changes in the currency exchange rate may have negative consequences for an economy, ultimately necessitating a devaluation or substantial depreciation. The currency is very volatile, which makes it prone to speculation. These countries must develop a currency strategy that is viable to reduce their trade deficit and mitigate the inflationary effects caused by the exchange rate on their economy. The import substitution industrialization had a lasting impact in the form of an overvalued exchange rate regime. When governments choose for a fixed exchange rate system to mitigate the inflationary effects of imports, the export industries would suffer not just due to excessive protectionism and restricted trade openness but also because of an exchange rate that is considerably overvalued. Due to the high costs associated with manufacturing, it is unfeasible for a country to maintain a policy that ensures a consistent exchange rate. Over time, if the currency appreciates, it would make imports cheaper, hence incentivizing import industries to make investments. This would eventually lead to a deterioration of the trade imbalance. When the currency's value is artificially appreciated, exporters can only get a restricted quantity of the foreign income they may potentially earn via free market and trade activities.

Transformation and institutional reforms

The implementation of the institutional approach facilitates the examination of how capitalism managed to endure the many crises it encountered in the complex relationship between its growth model and regulatory mechanisms. The modifications in the techniques adopted for economic advancement have a significant effect on both the interactions among individuals involved and the resources utilized for production. Institutional forms need modification after a certain duration or during a transitional phase. The capitalist mode of production effectively evades the crisis and perpetuates its own existence in this manner. The underlying cause for the transformation in regulatory mode throughout time is the relatively slower pace at which economic systems adapt compared to the rapid evolution of new economic production contexts. However, in the event that nations come to recognize the essential institutional forms that are required and adopt them in an extensive way, the process of transformation can be characterized by greater ease and a higher likelihood of achieving success. In accordance with the growth model and appropriate economic policies of nations, institutional reforms need to arise. To successfully implement changes, it is crucial to develop a well-organized distribution of authority and implement favorable regulations. To counteract political and populist pressures, it is essential to restrict the government to a subordinate position and reduce its intervention in the economy. Therefore, under this system, pricing is no longer influenced by the government but instead determined by market forces. To accomplish price determination that is influenced by market forces, it is necessary to execute privatization steps and remove regulatory restraints. Monetary and fiscal policies have to be used in an approach that ensures minimal government interference in the economy and mitigates the potential risks associated with inflation. It is necessary to liberalize international trade. This can assist businesses compete better in the global market. This can promote the renewal of resources, foster technological advancements, and enhance production efficiency. It is furthermore advised that nations consider depreciating their exchange rates. To encourage the influx of capital investments into the country, it is necessary to take a more liberal approach toward the balance of payments, focusing specifically on the capital account. The elimination of inflexibility in the labor market, the decrease in the power of the working class, and the evasion of protective laws would weaken the basis of economic populism in these countries. The lack of scrutiny of these modifications or the inability to enforce limited adjustments has led to the ineffectiveness of measures designed to promote neoliberalization or attain economic stability. Argentina and Türkiye attempted to implement institutional reforms with the objective of promoting a transition toward a more liberal economic policy. The countries have chosen to discard fixed exchange rates and opt for floating exchange rate systems as an approach to address the problem of currency overvaluations. Additionally, both countries have adopted inflation-targeting policies, which might be regarded as a recent institutional reform. An absence of substantive institutional adjustment to address path dependency persisted despite the successful development of more stable economies in both countries. Furthermore, there was a deficiency in the institutional complementarity between monetary policy and fiscal policy. Hence, the institutional reforms were limited in their scope and did not succeed in establishing enduring stability in either economy. The efforts made by the IMF and the World Bank to mitigate the onset and proliferation of the crisis in developing nations proved to be ineffective. It is evident, in particular, that these institutions are unable to fulfill the necessary function of international regulation. The IMF and other relevant organizations continue to actively pursue a resolution to crises, with the primary objective of establishing stability within the international markets. Nevertheless, it is worth noting that the actions implemented have been inadequate in achieving the desired level of market stabilization in these populist countries. These international entities pay little attention to the diverse patterns of growth and institutional forms that are employed by nations. Consequently, whenever a political party achieves power, it tends to undermine any previous reforms via the implementation of economic populism.

To combat the continued trend of dollarization, populist regimes and their economic ministers are pursuing alternative tactics to encourage liraization and pesofication. In countries with these characteristics, when the local currencies experience a loss of trust in the market, economic actors begin using a different currency that is more widely accepted and stable (Craig and Waller, 2004). The US dollar has consistently been the primary currency of choice in both nations. In the context of persistent inflation, a nation may have significant challenges in maintaining the stability of macroeconomic indicators due to the declining availability of reserves over time. Furthermore, the potential occurrence of significant depreciations in the nominal exchange rate might lead to an increase in external debt repayments. This phenomenon might potentially pose substantial political concerns for administrations with populist tendencies. Moreover, these nations may lose their appeal to potential investors. Despite the relatively low levels of minimum wage and GDP per capita in both nations, they have challenges in attracting substantial investments to their respective domestic economies. There is a misconception that low pay, when denominated in US dollars, may be appealing to overseas investors. The first consideration is to establish a robust growth model that has the potential to attract multinational corporations focused on export growth to establish their operations. For decades, the reports propagated the notion that China had a labor force with lower costs, which has led firms to establish their operations in this nation. While there is a certain merit to the statement, it is important to note that the explanation provided is somewhat limited in its scope. If the reason for lower labor costs is really the case, it would be expected that many enterprises would be present in economically disadvantaged regions such as Africa, Latin America, or Southeast Asia. China's capacity to maintain a steady currency rate for a prolonged duration might effectively showcase its economic stability and robustness to the international community. This phenomenon may be explained by China's implementation of an export-oriented development plan. This allows global firms to participate in future predictions and carry out cost studies. Nevertheless, implementing this work presents difficulties in both Argentina and Türkiye. A government with populist inclinations may, at any time, raise wages, which would then need current corporate plans to be modified due to the resulting increase in production costs and inflationary pressures in the market. The levels of limited productivity may continue to exist, along with low savings rates, stagnant GDP per capita, and the ongoing issue of poverty. Both Türkiye and Argentina experienced substantial economic stagnation throughout the 1980s and 1990s (Nataraj and Sahoo, 2003). During these particular time periods, two countries experienced repeated instances of similar economic turmoil.

In Argentina, hyperinflation was brought under control by the implementation of significant institutional reforms between 1991 and 2002. This principle is referred to as the Convertibility Law. Based on the provided institutional form, the exchange rate was determined based on a fixed value relative to the US dollar. The modification received commendation inside the nation. The fixed exchange rate system provides only a temporary improvement in nations characterized by high manufacturing costs. The significant reliance on imported commodities and the socioeconomic pressures faced by the working class force authorities to adopt measures may be regarded impractical. The legislation was widely acknowledged for its potential to mitigate the inflationary impact of the exchange rate and stimulate short-term economic growth. The design of institutional forms should be aligned with the growth model of the economy. Otherwise, the manifestation of failure will gradually become evident over an extended period of time. This particular institutional form paved the stage for the onset of the economic crisis in the early 2000s. The successful implementation of a fixed exchange rate regime is dependent on the systematic undervaluation of a currency via artificial methods. The exchange rate, when overvalued, will strive to converge toward its equilibrium or natural rate throughout various political, social, or economic circumstances. The peso suffered from a lack of credibility and confidence. Carlos Menem implemented legislation aimed at fixing the exchange rate. It was believed that the implementation of this legislation had the potential to alter the public's impression of the domestic currency since it would convey a sense of stability in the economy. The exchange rate was determined to be one peso equivalent to one US dollar. The enactment of this legislation put considerable strain on the central bank since it was tasked with maintaining the exchange rate system in the absence of a robust economy capable of attracting substantial foreign reserves to the nation. The Chinese growth model facilitated the development of such capability. The implementation of appropriate economic policies and regulations, aligned with the strategic objectives, has the potential to provide internal resources for the accumulation of reserves. Argentina and Türkiye, two countries characterized by limited resources and lacking a sustainable growth model, demonstrated a high degree of confidence in their decision to adopt a fixed exchange rate regime throughout their economic trajectory. To maintain the value of the national currency at an appropriate level, there must be a restricted money supply and a low overall inflation rate. It was hypothesized that this legislation would also impose restrictions on any loans provided by the central bank to the budget. In essence, the pegging system can be regarded as a kind of export growth strategy that forced domestic economic entities to engage in production for the purpose of accumulating foreign reserves, thereby serving as the only means of expanding liquidity. This institutional form might be considered a radical measure aimed at restricting the influence of both the central bank and the government on the national currency. In particular, the presence of a tight fiscal policy would result in the establishment of an institutional complementarity for the given institutional form. Argentina and Türkiye might maintain their economic progress via the implementation of export-led growth policies. To effectively implement this strategy, it is essential for a central bank to attain independence and possess sufficient authority over the money supply, enabling it to resist governmental pressures for political objectives. This is an important way for Argentina and Türkiye to avoid the kind of economic crises and instabilities they have had in the past. Otherwise, populist governments would exploit economic instruments, and the central bank would be unable to serve as a balancing force. In reality, nations where populist policies may dominate the head and political instruments for their own gain are the only ones that need a central bank with a high degree of independence. A nation that is capable of implementing stringent restrictions to enhance institutional complementarity between monetary and fiscal policy may not necessarily need central bank independence. When a bank effectively aligns its operations with fiscal policies to mitigate economic volatility and maintains robust regulatory measures, the market may not necessarily need complete independence. The institutional framework of the bank might provide a justification for the position that it has taken. In this scenario, democracy may be regarded as a valuable attribute, yet not an essential need. China does not possess a political system that adheres to the principles of democracy. There is a lack of autonomy at the central bank. However, the exchange rate strategy of this country remained comparatively more effective than that of the countries often referred to be democratic states.

The system of economic populism was devised with the intention of minimizing dissatisfaction among the people. Furthermore, as stated by Barros (2005), the implementation of the legislation contributed to economic strain due to the heightened opposition from certain interest groups and trade unions, which expressed greater opposition toward the reduction of salaries. The attempts to implement expected institutional reforms encountered resistance from unions and workers who tried to protect their employment in the context of deregulation initiatives. They were accused of being agitators who wanted to undermine the law. The story suggests that the strategies used in both nations are flawed. Following their success, they endeavored to make further institutional reforms aimed at promoting deregulation policies and liberalism. Nevertheless, their tactics were overwhelmed by large demonstrations, making it impracticable for them to implement the subsequent phase. Consequently, they were compelled to adopt populist economic policies due to the lack of other options. However, it is recommended that the first approach focuses on diminishing the influence of the working class, followed by the implementation of a fixed exchange rate system. These two institutional modifications should ideally be executed concurrently and in alignment with one another. During the term of the Menem administration, Argentina endeavored to implement policies aligned with the principles of neoliberalism. This political strategy proposes that nations in Latin America should adopt extensive privatization and deregulation measures to enhance labor flexibility. Nevertheless, the Convertibility plan was fundamentally incongruous with these principles. The US dollar has been widely favored by officials in Argentina. It was extensively used, its value inspired confidence, and it served as a reserve currency for developing nations, including Türkiye. As a consequence, the decision was taken to utilize the US dollar as the currency to which the peso would be tied. The execution of this institutional reform was hypothesized to result in economic progress, the reduction of inflationary pressures, the maintenance of a stable currency rate, and the attraction of investments. On account of the existence of macroeconomic imbalances, the national currency may be subject to shocks from other countries as well as activities that include speculation. It was in the year 2001 that there was a discernible increase in the amount of pressure that was being applied to the currency. It was common practice to denominate debts in terms of the US dollar. In 2002, the Convertibility Law was terminated from all of its provisions. Every single account that was held in

US dollars was converted into the appropriate local currency. One term that has been used to describe this phenomenon is pesofication. This institutional reform did not prevent further erosion of the currency's value against other currencies. The designer of the Convertibility Law was a highly educated economist based in the United States. Nevertheless, the concept of institutional complementarity between monetary policy and fiscal policy was not taken into consideration. The problem in Argentina and Türkiye cannot be solely attributed to currency rate fluctuations. The fundamental reason may be ascribed to the control of fiscal policies by politicians in pursuit of their political objectives. It is not practical to consider adopting a foreign stable currency or tying the national currency to a financial instrument. A practical solution to reduce institutional flaws is to create a policy framework that promotes balance and cooperation between fiscal and monetary processes.

For a developing country to successfully participate in international trade, it may improve its competitiveness by focusing on two important factors: Maintaining lower export prices and holding unique production capabilities or resources, such as oil. Türkiye and Argentina have little impact on worldwide energy production. Hence, it is essential to conduct a modernization process to develop skills and bolster competitiveness in the field of international trade. Nevertheless, the endeavor to bring about institutional reform encountered resistance from political factions on both the left and right sides of the spectrum. These organizations aimed to capitalize on this situation by using populist strategies to attract support. The trade union has always resisted proposals for privatization and initiatives aimed at enhancing productivity. In the framework of a more interconnected global society, the endeavor of participating in competitive activities has grown significantly more challenging. The complexity of production has expanded, resulting in the establishment of multinational businesses that wield power on a global scale. Therefore, the process of competition presents substantial obstacles for a developing country in the domain of international trade. Technological progress is reducing employment opportunities that were historically carried out by human workers. The 1990s were characterized by favorable circumstances that facilitated the use of cost-effective manufacturing methods. Nevertheless, in the contemporary world, there is a heightened need for capital to expedite the production process. Hence, it is crucial for developing countries to promptly implement institutional reforms. Otherwise, underdeveloped nations would continue in lagging behind industrialized countries that possess the capacity to employ advanced and modern technology in their industrial operations. In an era that is highly advanced in terms of technology, the use of export-led economic policies may no longer provide favorable outcomes as it did in the past. In the context of globalization, it is critical for countries to have a labor market that exhibits a high degree of expertise, adaptability, and versatility. In light of this, it is of the ultimate need to formulate new regulations that are in accordance with the industrial adaptability that is necessary in the modern competitive environment. It is essential for the system to function in synchronization with the demands of the industrial sector. Establishing a suitable harmony between the working class and industry is of utmost importance since the latter has to adjust to the changing environment. The workforce should demonstrate adaptability in response to improvements in productivity in line with a growth-focused strategy. Nevertheless, it is imperative to acknowledge that the working class must not be overlooked, and their rights should not be eliminated. It is suggested that a close connection between the government and the working class should be avoided since this leads to less economic activity and therefore increased expenses for society. A global context must be taken into consideration when designing institutional reforms in the wage–labor relationship.

European nations have implemented essential legislation to establish a more scientifically informed wage negotiating process. Furthermore, the acceptance of the Euro as the only currency fosters the generation of economic activities. Despite the presence of overvaluation in some nations, the adoption of a more realistic approach to wage–labor relations did not inflict as much harm on their economies compared to Argentina and Türkiye, which opted for fixed or controlled exchange rate regimes (Ünal, 2017). The working class displayed a significant level of inflexibility and was included into the economic populism but in a unique way compared to European nations. The phenomenon of wage growth surpassing productivity growth might be regarded as a similar means of explaining inflexibility. In both Argentina and Türkiye, the process of laying off workers can prove challenging due to the absence of wage flexibility in accordance with productivity growth rates. Hence, the task of locating or resigning from employment poses significant challenges. Due to substantial wage growth, it is quite likely that two nations possess a significant proportion of their workforce engaged in informal employment, lacking established job arrangements. It was estimated that approximately 50% of the workers worked informally (Beccaria and Groisman, 2015). Moreover, it might be inferred that these corporations are exempt from the need to fulfill tax and social security contributions on behalf of their employees. The high cost of manufacturing necessitates that employers adhere to these guidelines and adopt a freer market economic structure. The poor use of labor stands as a significant issue within the context of Türkiye. This nation characterized by its youthful demographic had the potential to develop a model for growth that aligns with its unique dynamics. However, it lags behind many other nations in terms of worker productivity. Based on statistics from the OECD, Türkiye exhibits the highest working hours among its member countries in relation to working time. It is significant that Türkiye's productivity level ranks at the lowest position when compared to other member nations. The analysis suggests that the implementation of institutional reforms in the wage–labor relationship fails to provide optimal productivity outcomes and lacks the ability to effectively incentivize workers to actively participate in production activities. The expenditure associated with hiring a worker is elevated. Nevertheless, it is crucial to note that the rate of labor cost increase surpasses that of nations. Therefore, companies have difficulties in formulating their strategy due to the challenges posed by increasing prices, inflation, and volatile currency rates. The lack of flexibility and productivity in the labor market poses constraints on further investments from multinational corporations and international entities. Populist policies fail to instill a sense of trust and assurance. The Foreign Direct Investment (FDI) tends to prioritize nations that exhibit higher levels of democracy and a more conducive free market environment for companies to establish and operate.

Every country is vulnerable to facing economic difficulties. Occasionally, developed economies have episodes of economic instability. The problem lies in the fact that despite the widespread awareness that these countries would inevitably face currency crises either today or tomorrow, no measures were implemented to bring about institutional reform, and there was a lack of political determination to inform society and economic participants to the imminent risk. These crises have more similarities to classical rather than modern situations. They exemplify many economic issues that are covered in academic courses. Nevertheless, the countries persisted in their demand to adopt an identical institutional framework. The economies failed to effectively achieve their process of economic transformation. Although it started early, the process of reformation showed a consistent lack of speed. Moreover, the populist governments impeded the execution of institutional reforms. Some changes were limited because of retrograde populism since the government pledged to increase its economic intervention in society. Consequently, the crises had a detrimental effect on the economy. The competitiveness strategy was founded on a mistaken concept during the period of globalization. In the past, it was possible to adopt closed economic policies, especially when developed countries followed similar approaches and communist governments placed strict restrictions on their trade with other countries. In contemporary times, the manufacturing process has become more intricate and diverse. It is difficult to consider a situation in which every part of a product is made solely inside one country. Hence, implementing higher import tariffs in the context of a maintained currency and significant wage hikes would not be a suitable strategy. The intensification of speculations arises from the belief that the government's ability to maintain exchange rate stability has diminished. In response to the loss of confidence in the economy, the general population chooses to withdraw their savings from financial institutions. A decrease in savings results in reduced investment levels, which in turn leads to diminished economic growth and increased unemployment rates. This event occurred in Argentina during the period when the Convertibility Law was dismantled, and in Türkiye, when the nation faced significant devaluations that resulted in an escalation of debt for domestic enterprises. In 2000, the de la Rua administration, faced with a decline in its credibility, requested assistance from international organizations such as the IMF in an attempt to receive support. The Ecevit administration in Türkiye had a similar outcome. The administration requested assistance from the IMF to pursue neoliberal economic policies. The IMF made the assumption that both countries had the potential to implement reforms aimed at bolstering confidence and enhancing their credibility.

9 Economic populism from the 2000s

The formation of economic populism took place in two countries as an outcome of an incorrect institutional shift that occurred during the period of industrialization that was characterized by import substitution. The reality remained unaltered despite the efforts to implement institutional reforms in the 1980s. In the 1990s and 2000s, there were significant economic crises that impeded the execution of important institutional changes aimed at ensuring macroeconomic stability and shifting society away from economic populism. Conversely, the IMF and the officials it appointed were deemed responsible for the circumstances in both nations. The adverse consequences of international institutions and neoliberal policies include elevated levels of unemployment, which are far higher than those observed in developed countries, a decline in purchasing power parity, persistent inflationary pressures, an unstable currency rate, as well as heightened levels of inequality and poverty. Populist administrations have the capacity to effectively instill this perception throughout the working class. Therefore, the legitimacy of government involvement is established to implement policies that counteract globalization and the principles of a free market economy. If this scenario continues, people would get trapped in circumstances of poverty and social injustice. Customs duties would be levied on global trade, the inflation rate would be represented as much reduced, and the process of transferring ownership from public to private hands would be suspended. Moreover, there would be a notable growth in the interconnection between government policies and corporate entities. Despite the portrayal of a free market economy, the prevailing reality reveals a market that is effectively controlled by firms that maintain strong ties with government programs. Public institutions continue to impose a strain on the budget. The use of employment as a populist strategy serves as an indication that the administration is committed to providing secure and suitable work opportunities. Consequently, the implementation of these policies has the effect of diminishing productivity within the society, thus necessitating the coexistence of higher rates of inflation, substantial trade deficits, widespread poverty, and diminished purchasing power.

During the 2000s, the Turkish government implemented institutional reforms in response to the demands brought forward by left-wing parties. Previous administrations showed hesitancy in adopting initiatives that correspond with the ideological tenets of left-wing political parties. The government has implemented a policy of providing free education, including the provision of textbooks. The tuition fees

DOI: 10.4324/9781003438090-9

charged by universities have been abolished. The health service has emerged as a prominent institution within the government. Affordable healthcare services are offered. Furthermore, 1st May, a day historically associated with communist, revolutionary, and extreme left-wing movements, was officially designated as a public holiday in 2009. This particular day was marked by several clashes and conflicts that have significant historical importance for the nation. The implementation of government involvement in the economy garnered the support and empathy of the working class. The policies promoting freedom and worker welfare had a surge in influence throughout the 2000s. Furthermore, the implementation of transfers for those belonging to the lowest socioeconomic class emerged as a notable catalyst for expansionary policies. The prevalence of economic populism was relatively constrained throughout the early 2000s. Following the occurrence of the economic crisis, both nations adopted a pragmatic approach in their policymaking endeavors. This phenomenon resulted in a state of relative stability in both economies. Nevertheless, throughout the 2010s, there was a noticeable shift away from these pragmatic approaches toward a resurgence of economic populism. This phenomenon might be connected to severe competition among political parties since economic policies confronted political polarization and considerable ideological differences. Consequently, economic populism emerged as a prominent strategy for attaining political power. Both nations began to experience persistent depreciations in their currency rates throughout the 2020s. The economies once again witnessed the emergence of severe chronic inflation issues.

In 2023, Argentina was decisively working to establish a renewed deal with the IMF. The unresolved issues may be attributed to the influence of government interference and the desire of the working class for their own interests. To mitigate Argentina's economic instability, it was expected that the country would make an effort to persuade the IMF to grant it a loan package.[1] The country's competitiveness in international trade had been substantially reduced as a result of extreme macroeconomic uncertainty, which also posed the risk of causing the economy to enter a recession. Furthermore, the fluctuation in climatic circumstances had led to drought conditions, which had a negative influence on the principal export commodities, including soybeans and maize, which in turn made the economic downturn even worse. According to estimates, the agriculture business is projected to experience a decrease in exports compared to the previous year. Moreover, the meteorological conditions led to a significant decline in the output of key agricultural commodities. The nation witnessed a significant increase in inflation, surpassing the 100% threshold. To lessen this impact, the IMF emerged as a viable option for finding resolution. Protests were observed across the nation, as people voiced their dissatisfaction with the policies that were adopted by the IMF. The decrease in purchasing power was the basis for their grievances. The working class was demanding a larger salary hike in response to the rising inflation since they believed that their existing earnings were not increasing and were negatively affecting their lives. Disagreements emerged among the coalition governments on the negotiation and execution of agreements with the IMF. Essential elements of the agreement were the central bank's accumulation of reserves and efforts to decrease the budget deficit as a percentage of the GDP. The administration explicitly appealed to the IMF, underscoring that this drought is unprecedented in recorded history. The politicians declared that they drained reserves due to a desperate need for imported goods and a decline in exports.

The populist rhetoric in Türkiye has been focused on the IMF, the EU, and several other foreign organizations. Political parties often use slogans assuring that they will not be subject to arrest by foreign organizations, which are viewed as potentially exploitative entities that exert control over the governance of a nation. The tensions that arose between coalition administrations and their divergent views on reform have bolstered the position of the government, enabling to pursue a program aimed at implementing a presidential system inside the nation. The administration stated that the counterproductive practices of coalition governments, together with their tendency to engage in misguided policy pursuits, had exacerbated the economic challenges. Therefore, the persuasive language used by the presidential administration in its efforts to resolve the political party disagreements inside the coalition instilled in the people a sense of hope that the destiny of the nation and its economy would undergo transformation subsequent to a vote. The US system was indicated as an illustrative example. Nevertheless, it was essential to ensure that the presidential system was tailored to reflect the distinctiveness of Turkish culture and traditions. The presence of representative democracy and coalition administrations posed challenges in the implementation of new reform measures. The assertion posited that the existing parliamentary system had challenges in reaching decisive outcomes. A significant proportion of the population chose to be governed under a presidential government. A majority of 51.41% of the population cast their votes in favor of the constitutional amendment. The government did not function in accordance with the traditional framework of a political party. The entity made a deliberate effort to establish direct contact with individuals to obtain their support. Consequently, the legitimacy of constitutional amendment might be established. The prime ministerial system was discontinued. There was a significant delegatin of power to president, who was given the exclusive responsibility of managing the government. In a parliamentary system, it is possible for a political party that has a majority of votes to form the government. In a presidential system, it has become crucial to secure a majority of votes above 50%. Alternatively, the party can lose its influence in regulating both economic and political affairs. Consequently, the level of competitiveness did not diminish. The people reached a consensus to institute a presidential government and confer more powers onto the governing party. Hence, during a crisis, adherence to agreements with the IMF would result in the failure of all these rhetorical statements. Despite the many economic challenges faced by the country, entering into an agreement with the IMF continues to be regarded as a last recourse. This institution has long been a subject of criticism by populist administrations over the course of several decades. This occurs because when a political party suffers a defeat, its opponent will get a higher degree of authoritative influence compared to their former position. Thus, it is crucial for the current government to maintain its position and not relinquish it to the incoming party, regardless of the situation.

Prior to the upcoming elections scheduled for 14 May 2023, a very intense rivalry emerged between the present administration and the opposing political parties. Within the hundredth year of the existence of the republic, the political factions wanted to win the election and govern the nation. Consequently, they adhere to various economic policies to attract the attention of the working class. The present administration has introduced a multitude of economic policies aimed at benefiting the general populace. The provision of early retirement privileges was extended to those who were eligible to receive pensions. The older demographic was experiencing a decrease in their earnings in comparison to prior time periods. The process of the population becoming older is a well-recognized occurrence. The birth rate is slowing down. Nevertheless, they did not have to wait until they were 65 to start enjoying the advantages of retirement. This strategy is implemented with the aim of garnering the electoral support and endorsement of those within the middle-age demographic. Türkiye is host to two significant religious festivals. A decision was made to provide retired individuals with incentives to enhance their enjoyment of national fests. The aggregate payment sum represents a significant monetary supply disruption resulting from fiscal policy measures. Additionally, there was a notable rise in earnings for those receiving pensions. Minimum wage workers noticed a two-fold rise inside a single year. Prior to the election, the administration made a commitment to implement a rise in the minimum wage by the month of July. Furthermore, it was reported that there would be an increase in the salaries of public employees. The government has initiated a recruitment process to fill posts inside public institutions, offering employment opportunities to a significant number of individuals. This approach may be characterized as an economic populism aimed at formulating an employment strategy that lacks a thorough assessment of the existing employment structure inside institutions, as well as the impact of technology advancements that have diminished the need for public sector employment. A significant portion of job opportunities were directed toward teachers and healthcare professionals across sectors. An assertion was made about the discovery of a new natural gas resource region. Thus, the government made a commitment to provide complimentary access to natural gas for residential use. Türkiye experiences a notable impact as a result of elevated taxation rates imposed on electronic devices and motor vehicles. The government has made a commitment to provide tax exemptions on electronic devices, including smartphones and computers, to young people on a one-time basis. The opposition party has no significant distinction from the existing administration. The proposed policy pledges to augment retirement pensions by over 100% and raise the minimum wage at a pace above the present rate of growth. The statement included a commitment to increase the number of teachers and public workers by two-fold. Furthermore, it made a commitment to decrease the special consumption taxes imposed on motor vehicles specifically for younger people. A commitment was made to ensure that the salaries of public employees would be 2.5 times greater than those of the minimum wage. All of these measures serve as a conspicuous manifestation of a populist paradigm inside the nation. The two distinct political parties use comparable strategies in their pursuit of electoral support. The measures in question exhibit a lack of realism and bear resemblance to a metaphorical act of undermining the economy of the nation. Two political factions exhibited a notable emphasis on economic populism. In the first stage of the presidential election, neither the ruling party nor the opposition party managed to get a majority of votes, as both candidates obtained less than 50% of the total votes cast. The ruling party obtained a voting share of 49.52%, while the opposition party received 44.88% of the votes. The remaining fraction of votes was divided among other political candidates. The subsequent round of the election, scheduled for 28 May 2023, included just two political parties, with the objective of deciding the definitive winner. The ruling party was triumphant in the election, gaining a vote of 52.18%. The continued existence of economic populism persisted throughout the subsequent period. This phenomenon of populism extends beyond the typical characteristics associated with economic populism. The rapid development of technology and the prevalence of digital lifestyles, along with significant salary growth and escalating inflation rates, have prompted individuals to increasingly rely on credit cards and accumulate debt for future financial needs. The opposing political party has pledged to eliminate the debt resulting from interest rates and provide individuals with a significant chance for installment payments. Several organizations had made the assumption that the currency rate would experience depreciation subsequent to the conclusion of the elections. Consequently, individuals engaged in the acquisition of foreign currency or gold via the use of credit cards or the conversion of credit into cash from financial institutions. As a result, the central bank had a restricted allocation of credits available for the purpose of cashing or acquiring further assets. Nevertheless, this development may have negative implications in terms of vote acquisition. Specifically, the central bank reversed its decision overnight, which might potentially impact the party's ability to attract support. National banks persisted in implementing comparable practices. The discernible consequence of implementing populist measures is a decrease in the level of support for the governing party. The presence of economic populism and macroeconomic imbalances can have a substantial impact on the government's electoral support.

The implementation of institutional changes is challenging even in the current period of the 2020s. For many decades, the working class has derived advantages from periods characterized by protectionist policies. The policies of globalization and deregulation continue to pose significant dangers to the class. This issue persists as a significant barrier impeding innovation, competitiveness, development, and output. Therefore, every effort to enact changes has the potential to be overturned. While many nations have moved away from the period of protectionism, the trajectory of this stage persists. During the productionist time, consumers had limited opportunities to express their preferences for imported items, in contrast to the present day. The advent of globalization and technical improvements has facilitated the accessibility of global items for local clients. Hence, a significant portion of wages allocated toward imported goods presents a persistent concern that has the potential to exacerbate trade imbalances inside countries. It is essential for nations to adopt realistic strategies to develop their international economic frameworks. The absence of appropriate institutional structure and macroeconomic considerations might give rise to challenges in the context of free trade agreements and participation in a customs union, leading to the stimulation of trade imbalances. However, to reduce government participation in the economy, it is possible to conduct a process of deregulation and allow public institutions to operate as private enterprises, even if they are not fully privatized. The central bank needs to engage in institutional complementarity, aligning its efforts with a stabilization program aimed at eliminating inflation. Nevertheless, it would not be appropriate to devalue currencies without the implementation of a suitable institutional framework and structure for a growth model. While there is a claim that currency controls have been relaxed, it seems that statistical institutes and central banks actively strive to maintain an overvalued exchange rate. The current policy deserves reconsideration since it is suggested that the use of the currency rate should be directed toward export policies rather than imports. The rigid correlation among the peso, the lira, and the US dollar needs to be abandoned.

Türkiye was able to halt the rise of its wage growth between 2003 and 2011, bringing it down to 11.2%; this rate is still much higher than the increase in productivity of both nontradable and export goods, which were 2.7% and 3.7%, respectively, as indicated in Table 9.1. However, the productivity of exported goods had a considerable decline of 1% throughout the 2010s, while wage growth surged to an average of 16.6%. Inflation rose slightly from 10.6% to 11.1% on average, indicating a modest rise. With each passing year, Türkiye's inflation rate began to exhibit signs of becoming a more persistent issue. It is possible to detect a circumstance that is comparable in Argentina. The rate of wage growth was around 21.1% between 2004 and 2011, but the pace of productivity growth was much lower. Specifically, they were 3.3% in nontradable goods and 5.3% in goods that were exported. Wage growth reached 34.7% during the 2010s, while productivity growth rates went into the negative throughout the same decade. The result was an increase in inflation from 17.1% to 36.4%. The policies of both nations were designed with export growth objectives. Consequently, compared to nontradable goods, the productivity increase of exported goods was much greater. On the other hand, the economy was founded on the high cost of production that resulted from the significant wage rise. The nations were severely affected throughout the COVID-19 period, including

Table 9.1 The structure of growth models in the 2000s

Countries	*Period*	*Growth of mark-up rate* $(1+\hat{m}_{\pi})$	*Productivity growth of non-tradable goods*	*Productivity growth of export goods*	*Wage growth*	*Inflation*
Argentina	2004–2011	–0.2	3.3	5.3	21.1	17.1
	2011–2021	1.6	–1.1	–1.1	34.7	36.4
Türkiye	2003–2011	0.7	2.7	3.7	11.2	10.6
	2011–2021	–1.5	2.5	–1.0	16.6	11.1
United States	2003–2011	2.0	0.5	1.4	2.3	2.5
	2011–2021	–2.8	1.2	–0.3	3.2	2.0

Note: Authors calculation. EORA database is used for deriving data for 2011–2021. The detail of other information is given in Table 6.1.

the United States, which experienced a negative increase in the productivity of exported goods during the 2010s. In Argentina and Türkiye, the disparity between the rates of productivity growth and wage growth remained much larger than in other countries. Furthermore, according to the data shown in Table 9.2, it is evident that although the real exchange rate experienced significant depreciation, the nominal exchange rate was effectively suppressed from losing value.

The social contract has significant importance in establishing a harmonious equilibrium of power and delineation of authority inside the market. In other terms, it may function as an optimal rate that facilitates economic democracy. Instead of favoring one faction, it might be used to mitigate the influence of political interests on economic players. Furthermore, it is essential that fiscal and monetary policies provide support for this institutional shape. This measure will aid in maintaining control over inflation. Numerous economists have emphasized the need of monitoring the currency as the foremost determinant in Latin American nations. Nevertheless, the most important objective is in the establishment of an institutional framework that fosters a harmonious distribution of control and effectively eradicates the prevalence of economic populism inside a nation. This entails addressing the tendency of politicians to use economic instruments, such as wage and exchange rate adjustments, for their own personal gain. If this issue is resolved and nations begin formulating policies based on actual economic results, it is likely that the problems of inflation and unstable exchange rates will improve significantly. In the absence of appropriate institutional reforms, subsequent governments possess the ability to use economic instruments to further their own ideological agenda, political affiliations, personal commercial interests, and social networks. Populist narratives prevalent in Latin American countries and Türkiye revolve around the implementation of an unstable fiscal policy, exerting control over the central bank and monetary policy, establishing targets against other countries and industries, and government intervention in the economy. These measures aim to attract public support by redistributing national wealth, not necessarily as a means of incentivizing productivity, but rather to serve political interests. The classical outcomes for all nations exhibit similarities. In light of the prevailing default and high debt levels within the economy, efforts are being made to identify an entity that can provide financial support to stimulate economic growth and mitigate the risk of recession in the nation.

Table 9.2 The real exchange rate and nominal exchange rate

Country	*Periods*	*Change rate in the currency against the US dollar*	*Change rate in PPP against the United States*
Argentina	2004–2011	−5.2	−10.2
	2011–2021	−35.7	−39.8
Türkiye	2003–2011	−1.8	−9.1
	2011–2021	−14.7	−16.0

Note: Authors calculation. EORA database is used for deriving data for 2011–2021. The detail of other information is given in Table 6.1.

Wage populism and minimum wage policy

Wages have consistently been used as a strategic instrument by governments in each political campaign to attract the support of the working class. In 2015, there was a significant increase of 20.3% in Türkiye's minimum wage for the elections. Following the scheduling of the 2023 Turkish election, there was a significant rise of 54.7% in wages.[2] This resulted in a widespread increase in national wages across all sectors of the economy. As a consequence, the inflation rate experienced a significant surge of 72.3% throughout the course of 2022.[3] A situation quite similar to this one exists in Argentina. Economic populism is a chronic affliction that is widespread in many countries. As one of the contributing reasons, the lack of comprehensive institutional reforms that attempt to eradicate entrenched institutions and customary practices is one of the causes that contributes to the problem. Intense competition between political parties leads to changes in market circumstances due to the campaigns they conduct. This characteristic is absent in developed countries. In contrast to countries with a populist economic system, industrialized nations seldom experience inflationary pressures as an outcome of the adoption of wage growth actions. The prevalence of protests is a result of a decrease in purchasing power. Particularly, people such as medical officials, teachers, minimum wage workers, and farmers living in rural regions demand for an increase in wage growth to enhance their income levels. There is a notable presence of labor lobbying. Therefore, it is not always necessary to participate in trade unions. The notion of wage institution embraces all sectors of society within a certain country.

When compared with industrialized nations, which have labor markets that are more flexible, it is more difficult to recruit workers in countries due to the involvement of the government and the large public sectors that exist there. These sectors contribute to a higher level of safety as well as longer-term job prospects that pay higher earnings. In the context of the Turkish economy, it is important that the predominant aspiration among the people is to get employment inside state institutions. Making adjustments in these institutions, particularly during times of economic crisis, poses significant challenges. Public institutions provide stable job opportunities, extended periods of vacation, and a more comfortable working atmosphere. Nevertheless, commencing employment might be a multifaceted process, whereby references assume significant importance. This implies that the presence of employment possibilities inside public institutions does not guarantee equitable access to them. The people are required to successfully complete a series of tests administered by central institutions. It often takes many months to get a post. In addition, populist administrations often use employment institutions as a means of attracting electoral support. The labor market does not exert control over employment dynamics. The emergence of a substantial lobbying class can be attributed to government interference, wherein the class operates without generating any tangible value or production. Therefore, the implementation of institutional change aimed at reducing overemployment and fostering a more balanced labor relationship poses significant challenges. Despite individuals being engaged in various occupations, a significant portion of the population may nonetheless experience unemployment. The industries exhibit a reluctance to generate more employment due to the absence of market dynamics in the economy and the presence of elevated production costs. Argentina and Türkiye have much higher levels of unemployment in comparison to other industrialized and emerging nations. Based on the statistics provided by the World Bank, Argentina exhibited an unemployment rate of 8.7% in 2021, while Türkiye recorded a rate of 12%. However, the rate in China was far lower, roughly 4.6%, while in South Korea, it was even lower at 3.6%. The high unemployment rate provides an opportunity for populist governments to deliberately embrace this situation to gain support from large segments of the populace. There is a prevailing belief among the people that those in positions of privilege exploit the work capabilities of the general population only for the purpose of amassing personal fortune. A government characterized by populist inclinations has the capacity to modify this preestablished result. Nevertheless, governments exhibit little endeavor to alter this sequence of occurrences and instead persist in depending on outdated institutions for their operations.

Individuals from these nations migrate to developed economies with the aim of securing employment opportunities. Germany is now home to a significant population of the Turkish people. A considerable number of individuals hailing from Argentina and other Latin American nations characterized by populist governance have a propensity for exploring employment opportunities inside the United States or Canada. The issue is to the insufficiency of means of production and resources inside these nations. The lack of adequate institutional structures in these nations is the reason for this phenomenon. There seems to be a lack of political will to undertake the necessary risks involved in implementing institutional changes. The tax rates in Argentina and Türkiye are significantly high. Certain items that fall under the middle-class category have higher price in these countries compared to their counterparts in industrialized nations. According to the OECD report, Argentina had a tax rate of around 29% on other goods and services, which was much higher than the OECD average of 12%. Furthermore, the value-added taxes were set at a rate of 24%, although the OECD had a lower rate of 20%. This is a result of legislation pertaining to taxes. Upon closer examination of the special consumption tax, it becomes clear that the rates inside the Turkish economy, are at an unprecedented level (Ünal, 2021b).

In their study, Ünal and Köse (2019) conducted an analysis on the influence exerted by the working class on wage increase in both Türkiye and the United Kingdom, spanning the time period from 1963 to 2015. It was in 1963 when the wage–labor connection was institutionalized, and this year serves as the foundation year. The research revealed that wage levels were influenced only by short-term fluctuations in real GDP growth. Nevertheless, the levels of wages were subject to the impact of inflation, both in the short term and the long term. In addition, it was discovered that the number of workdays that were missed due to strikes had a favorable effect on wage levels over the long term. This suggests that the influence exerted by the working class could play a significant role in driving substantial increases in wages. During the era characterized by prevalent government interventions up to the 1980s, increases in wages were determined by considering the impact of inflation. Over the course of time, the aforementioned policy was abandoned due to its observed correlation with the occurrence of stagflation. Consequently, there has been a shift toward implementing a wage strategy that incorporates the consideration of actual economic expansion. Consequently, a strategy of export-led development was implemented with the aim of mitigating inflation and enhancing global competitiveness. When determining wage increases in developing nations, it is conventional to consider the inflation rate. This approach became obsolete throughout the 1980s due to its propensity to disrupt the economy by inducing inflation and devaluing the currency rate in times of sluggish real economic expansion. The primary objective of trade unions in Argentina and Türkiye is to have a wage growth rate that surpasses the rate of inflation. Nevertheless, this strategy has the potential to adversely impact the economy via inflation, a trade imbalance, diminished competitiveness, and exacerbation of income inequality. Furthermore, it is worth noting that employers' organizations actively strive to minimize the pace of wage increases. The implementation of this specific strategy may result in unfavorable outcomes, such as preventing those living inside the borders of the country from receiving the benefits of economic growth and causing a drop in social welfare. It is not uncommon for political parties to use populist strategies when it comes to determining the pace at which wages should be increased. Additionally, these parties may face external pressures that discourage them from adopting politically risky actions. In the context of political competition, people without enough economic understanding can elect an alternative political party that employs a populist campaign, thereby opposing a government's efforts to maintain an optimal annual wage growth rate. The outcome presents a potential political risk for the governing body. As a consequence, political parties often aim to reduce their exposure to political risks and embrace populist politics to maintain their status quo regardless of the outcome of an election.

The primary purpose of minimum wage levels is to ensure the living standards of the working class, and they are under the direct jurisdiction of governments, regardless of prevailing market circumstances. The determination of wages often occurs via a process of negotiation between trade unions and employers' organizations. However, the balance of power that is believed to be ideal may be disrupted under circumstances in which one of the parties has a greater degree of influence or authority. Economic populist administrations often exhibit a reluctance to adopt free market policies, which leaves wage determination to market forces. The potential occurrence of this event results in a diminished government impact on wage–labor relations, which gives rise to political risks in the context of electoral processes. Therefore, the implementation of a minimum wage policy in Argentina and Türkiye is regarded as a compelling populist measure by the respective governments. Minimum wages have the potential to increase above the inflation rate either before or subsequent to elections. Regrettably, to safeguard the purchasing power of labor, it is essential to acknowledge that, due to the prevailing market dynamics, any increase in purchasing power is inherently temporary. In contrast, in situations when there is a decrease in economic growth, it is possible for inflation to be stimulated. This implies that in succeeding time periods, if governments raise salaries above the rate of inflation in the medium term or toward the end of the year to appease the working class, the outcome is a spiral of wage-induced inflation. Typically, this phenomenon is observed in Argentina and Türkiye. Köse and Ünal (2021) pointed out that the cost of labor has been one of the most significant factors contributing to inflation in Türkiye. In spite of the fact that its influence was relatively minor in the first months, it eventually became one of the most significant factors in determining the significance of high inflation. In addition, it was also stated that the cost of labor becomes a significant variable in inflation and that this influence continued to emerge over the course of months. The impact of labor costs on inflation is more long-lasting. For the purpose of providing an explanation for this conclusion, the impact of wages is highlighted as being important and positive. This is due to the fact that large wage increases promote high labor costs. A significant increase in wages might cause inflation to rise. It is possible for wages to have a more significant and long-lasting impact since they are not flexible.

From an institutional standpoint, the international organization failed to effectively convince these governments to implement sufficient institutional reforms. Moreover, these countries did not successfully execute a detailed plan designed to reduce the likelihood of such problems happening again. However, the IMF has the capacity to help alleviate immediate economic difficulties. It is justifiable for countries to temporarily mitigate the current economic crisis. Over time, the reappearance of identical problems might become evident once again. The loans provided by the IMF have the potential to alleviate the budgetary burden experienced by governments. The constraints imposed by the IMF have the potential to contribute to a modest level of economic success for the affected countries. The primary responsibility for the current situation lies with the policies implemented by the government. The effective implementation of the conditions set out by the IMF is based on the willingness of governments to reach a consensus and adhere to prescribed economic reform measures. The IMF was subject to criticism. The policies show a lack of efficacy in promoting economic development via the implementation of disciplined budgetary measures, labor market reforms, and trade competitiveness strategies. Both Argentina and Türkiye have engaged in a discourse of attributing their economic issues on the IMF. Populist rhetoric has been an often-adopted approach by politicians. Peronist administrations, as well as the Turkish governments, directed their attention toward the IMF due to their concerns over the constraints associated with IMF agreements. In the context of these administrations, the IMF does not possess the authority to determine economic policies since it does not have governing power over the countries. The establishment of an institution that facilitates the financial support of nations' policies via loan agreements is vital. The attempts that this international organization made to assist nations in overcoming their economic issues and integrating into the global economy were ineffective.

The heterodox policies of these nations have a resemblance to social experiments. There is currently a lack of research or theoretical frameworks that provide justification for economic strategies that deviate from the established principles of economics. The end of heterodox initiatives resulted in disappointment and heightened resentment. The actions enacted in these countries have formed an essential component of their historical account, marked by the existence of detrimental political trials. Unfortunately, the heterodox measures were often regarded as conventional policies or neoliberalism. Nevertheless, the implementation of monetary policies, such as the fixed exchange rate regime, did not correspond with the objectives of neoliberalism. The use of fiscal and monetary policies for the purpose of strengthening the exchange rate system is not apparent when the latter is implemented in the form of a fixed rate, ultimately leading to its failure. Maintaining an overvalued exchange rate is not driven by economic necessities. One characteristic of economic populism is the mitigation of political risks and the creation of a perception that the imported goods contribute to an enhancement of the purchasing power of the working class. These nations lack advanced industrial sectors. A significant proportion of high-tech items is sourced from industrialized countries. The domestic economy has adverse effects due to an overvalued currency since it faces challenges in effectively penetrating the home market, which is mostly filled by imported goods. Populist administrations make commitments to achieve exchange rate stability, although they often fail to consider the necessary institutional reforms. Therefore, it is essential for individuals to choose a specific target on which to assign blame. Possible examples of such entities include past administrations with populist tendencies, democratic political parties, or international organizations.

After the economic crisis, Nestor Kirchner became the president of Argentina in 2003. The policies implemented had characteristics reminiscent of the Peronist ideology. His populist rhetorics were centered on globalization, international organizations, and the previous administrations who were accountable for macroeconomic imbalances. Erdoğan's conservative party in Türkiye was victorious in the election by securing a significant proportion of the votes in 2002. The emerging administration demonstrated a strong inclination toward embracing globalization, fostering a positive relationship with the EU, and demonstrating a commitment to implementing liberal economic policies. Therefore, the newly formed administration garnered support from a majority of nations and investors. Furthermore, the global economy has operated in a manner that has yielded advantages for both of these nations. The emergence of this state might be attributed to the growing influence of the Chinese economy via its export-oriented development strategy as well as the detrimental economic crises experienced worldwide that led to a slowdown in economic activities. Due to its relatively undervalued currency, China has become a major exporting force across the world. The recent series of economic crises in the United States, Russia, and East Asian countries, subsequently affecting emerging nations like Argentina and Türkiye, had prompted these governments to implement interest rate reductions as a means to stimulate economic growth. Because of this, Argentina and Türkiye were able to benefit from a worldwide trend that led to a decline in the value of the US dollar. Furthermore, the introduction of debt restructuring procedures had a substantial influence on the economy. The countries being examined exhibited positive economic growth and implemented policies aimed at promoting expansion, which had a role in their overall performance in terms of GDP and GDP per capita.

Any significant movement in the exchange rates in these nations had the potential to cause widespread panic in the market. The economies rely heavily on consumption, and overdependence on imported items may pose significant challenges for both businesses and individuals. This nightmare began when Argentina's Convertibility Law was overturned, and Türkiye's attempt to impose a fixed currency rate in the early 2000s ended in failure. The unsuccessful measures paved the path for the new governments in Argentina and Türkiye. In both nations, the administrations used populist rhetoric and implemented programs aimed at increasing income in the following periods. The injection of the US dollar into the global market might be attributed to the prevailing low interest rate inside the United States before the onset of the 2008 economic crisis. This approach mitigated the exchange rate volatility experienced by the economies. The implementation of institutional reforms, along with a rise in purchasing power and the maintenance of reasonably stable currencies, which are bolstered by US policy, could give rise to an appreciation in the exchange rate. This, in turn, might enhance support for economic measures. However, this condition was of short duration. The United States had a significant impact on interest rates as a result of the preceding crisis. Following the stock market bubble in 2001, Alan Greenspan, who was widely regarded as the primary figure accountable for the crisis and faced persistent criticism, implemented a reduction in interest rates as a preventive measure against an economic downturn (Greenspan, 2004). This fall served as the foundation for subsequent price increases and the stimulation of the housing market. Particularly after the collapse of the housing market bubble, there was a deliberate focus on fostering development within the industry. The process of facilitating loans was undertaken. Consequently, there was a notable rise in the demand for homeownership, mostly attributable to the reduction in borrowing costs. The working class, who aspired to homeownership, was able to achieve this goal via the use of borrowing mechanisms. This presented a significant opportunity, particularly for those belonging to the middle socioeconomic level. Due to their inability to amass sufficient economic resources over an extended period, they were unable to acquire a residential property. This scenario exemplifies the absence of a wage–labor relationship within the context of economic populist countries. The onset of inflation coincided with a relaxation in loan demand. A gradual increase in interest rates was inevitable due to the difficulties in maintaining stability caused by the rise in uncertainty. Nevertheless, as a result of the substantial borrowing and concerns of a potential economic downturn, the decision to refrain from increasing interest rates was deemed appropriate (Bernanke, 2012). This event inside the United States served as a pivotal moment for populist nations attempting to maintain stability in their currency rates vis-à-vis the US dollar. Following the outbreak of the 2008 financial crisis, the previously established stability within the exchange rate witnessed a significant decline. The economies once again found themselves struggling due to the depreciations.

The governments of the two countries have faced challenges in conveying favorable impressions to the international community due to their excessive expenditures. This has resulted in an imbalanced relationship between the working class and industries, instability in exchange rates, interference in judicial decisions, and a reduction of business sector interests. As a consequence, industries have struggled to operate with optimal efficiency and attract substantial investments. Two countries have had difficulties in luring international firms and harnessing technological progress, in contrast to China, which is often regarded as an undemocratic and communist society. Both Argentina and Türkiye have notable shortcomings in cultivating a favorable business climate. This is a matter that pertains to institutional forms. The industrial sector in these countries suffers from a deficiency in robustness. The working class demonstrates resilience and retains a substantial degree of reliance on government programs. Based on the institutional analysis of politics provided, it is concluded that the institutions in both nations are inadequate in generating opportunities for entrepreneurs. Furthermore, they exhibit quite a diminished degree of competitiveness in comparison to other countries involved in highly competitive activities in the domain of global trade. This problem leads to poor economic performance and reduced competitiveness. Both countries must prioritize strengthening the rule of law, safeguarding property rights, creating favorable conditions for entrepreneurial activities, and improving the efficiency of bankruptcy resolution procedures. Promoting a democratic reputation and nurturing a congenial business environment might potentially enhance the economic performance and prosperity of the two countries. When sectors are devoid of support, entrepreneurs have difficulties in launching new enterprises. According to data from the World Bank, the density of new enterprises was found to be very low in both countries. Türkiye had a density of 1.8 in 2020, while Argentina had a density of 0.2 in 2018. The reported rate in the United Kingdom was 18.1, in China, it was 8.6, and in South Korea, it was 2.6. A limited availability of manufacturing opportunities hinders industries from participating in the market. Argentina's ease of doing business was rated 126th, whereas Türkiye's was placed 34th. In 2019, the United Kingdom had the 8th position, South Korea held the 5th rank, and China held the 32nd rank. Based on the most recent statistics, Argentina was ranked 140th, and Türkiye was ranked 77th in terms of the ease of starting a business. The United Kingdom, China, and South Korea were placed 18th, 27th, and 33rd, respectively. The time and costs associated with constructing a warehouse, often referred to as the process of obtaining building licenses, are of paramount importance for a nation's entrepreneurial endeavors. Within this particular category, the rank attained in Argentina was 104, whereas in Türkiye, it was 53. The respective figures for the United Kingdom, China, and South Korea were 23, 33, and 12. In addition, it took 2.4 years in Argentina and 5 years in Türkiye to resolve insolvency. Time spent in the United Kingdom was 1, South Korea was 1.5, and China was 1.7. The postponement of resolving corporate bankruptcy hinders entrepreneurs from reallocating their resources toward more effective investments or economic activity. Consequently, entrepreneurs encounter more challenges in the two populist nations when compared to the United Kingdom, acknowledged for its considerably more liberal economy, as well as in China, which remains a communist country, and South Korea, an industrialized economy.

The countries struggled to attract substantial FDI that may possibly improve efficiency, productivity, and the production of high-tech products. This issue remains a substantial obstacle for both economies. These countries are categorized as developing economies and need significant financial resources to efficiently govern their respective economy. The existence of protections, elevated tax rates, rigid labor markets, macroeconomic imbalances, and political rivalry provide substantial obstacles for multinational firms intending to invest and engage in production in these countries. Both of these countries provide significant growth potential for multinational firms at the global level. However, the difficulty of precisely forecasting the future path of these economies reduces the attractiveness of their markets. Türkiye functions as a physical and cultural bridge between the continents of Europe and Asia. It is located in close proximity to Russia, Middle East, and North Africa from a geographical standpoint. The nation has a mostly young population and demonstrates a more sophisticated economic framework when compared to its surrounding countries. Nevertheless, the entity's ability to produce and compete remains significantly restricted.

Argentina, a country that faced challenges in advancing its industrial sector and reducing its reliance on agricultural exports, encountered the implementation of export levies on its agricultural goods during the Kirchner administration. The generated income resulting from elevated tax rates might be used toward compensating public employees, facilitating transfer payments, and promoting the implementation of expansionary measures aimed at benefiting the working class. Peronist leaders did not refrain from implementing taxation measures on industrial activities. The Turkish economy has a comparable situation but with distinct characteristics. The substantial increase in the special consumption tax imposed on essential commodities and primary items inside the economy has resulted in domestic enterprises refraining from engaging in production activities for the domestic market (Ünal, 2017). The people attempted to get a significant portion of their commodities via imports from neighboring nations. For instance, the tax rates associated with the purchase of a new car are considerably increased. Therefore, global corporations that have established their facilities in Türkiye prioritize the exports of goods to nearby regions and European nations. Imports are used to satisfy the demand of the population. There is the potential for a significant widening of the trade deficit in the country. Alternatively, it is appropriate for the government to decrease taxes on commodities and promote domestic firms to emphasize the well-being of the people. Consequently, individuals would satisfy their needs via domestic production rather than relying on imports from other nations. Globalization is a phenomenon that operates in conjunction with policies aimed at promoting the expansion of exports. Hence, diminishing the significance of exports and introducing substantial tariffs would result in inefficiencies and reduced productivity inside industries. The implementation of essential institutional reform would provide advantages for individuals and industries that could exhibit high productivity and contribute to economic success.

Exchange rate populism

When implementing expansionary economic policies, it is unavoidable that the exchange rate would depreciate, leading to a rise in the general cost of living (Köse and Ünal, 2021). This phenomenon may lead governments to implement high interest rate policies to offset currency depreciation and preserve the value of the currency or to consider other measures for attracting foreign capital. In Türkiye, in the early 2020s, the development of a new investment instrument was motivated by major depreciations in the currency rate. This instrument was offered as an alternative to controlling the exchange rate. This entailed the pegging of the Turkish lira to the US dollar, whereby individuals who converted their foreign currencies and deposited them in a bank would be eligible for government reimbursements to protect the real value of their bank deposits in case of a depreciation in the exchange rate. It is essential that when the value of the lira decreases, the government and central bank have the duty to reduce the financial losses suffered by investors.

The issue of exchange rate instability has prompted a discourse on the potential adoption of a stable currency by these nations as a means to mitigate their financial challenges. The economy was deemed to be more stable if it abandoned its own currency in favor of the US dollar. Due to the ongoing status of these nations as emerging economies, their industrial capacities remain insufficient for the production of complex and advanced technological goods. Therefore, their economies exhibit a significant degree of dependence on imported intermediate and final commodities. Köse et al. (2024) stated that the exchange rate is a significant determinant that can benefit imports in Türkiye. The devaluation of the currency may potentially boost imports, especially if the economy heavily relies on intermediate and final products, particularly if the imported items are resistant to fluctuations in prices. The assumption was made that the adoption of a new currency might mitigate the inflationary impact of the exchange rate on imported goods. Due to the prevalence of dollarization, the US dollar was regarded as a favorable choice. Several examples may be used to clarify the given scenario. Ecuador and El Salvador made the decision to replace their respective national currencies with the US dollar as their official currency. In their study, Köse and Ünal (2024) conducted an analysis to examine the influence of temperature, oil price, currency rate, and wages in the agricultural industry on food inflation in Latin American nations, including Argentina, Colombia, the Dominican Republic, Ecuador, Mexico, and Uruguay. The significance of the currency rate in explaining inflationary trends in Argentina was confirmed. A strong and positive correlation was observed between the two variables. The study conducted revealed that the impact of the exchange rate in Ecuador over the specified time periods was relatively limited. This demonstrates that Ecuador experienced a significant institutional reform by adopting the US dollar as its national currency. Therefore, the significance of the exchange rate on inflation was not evident. The adoption of a foreign currency necessitates significant institutional restructuring. Convincing nationalist and left-wing parties, who base their campaigns on opposition to imperialism and US policies, will provide a significant challenge. According to Edwards (2010), this pattern was identified for

Ecuador, suggesting its applicability to nations experiencing exchange rate volatility. Ecuador has effectively undertaken a comprehensive institutional reform and accepted the US dollar as its official currency. However, he expressed concerns on the potential future abandonment of the US currency by Ecuador, a development that might potentially lead to economic instability. This perspective might be characterized as simplistic and lacking sophistication. The notion that lacks a foundation in a growth-oriented framework may persist in a state of insufficient completion. The selection of a stable currency as an official medium of exchange can be effective provided that some crucial parameters are met. This strategy is postulated to be implementable in situations when inflation may be induced by significant depreciations in the currency rate. Nevertheless, the implementation of such a strategy could result in an overvalued currency, which will worsen the current account balance of Argentina and Türkiye.

In the context of institutional economics, it is essential to establish institutional complementarity between fiscal policies and monetary policies. The chronic inflation cannot be attributed to the presence of exchange rate volatility. As seen in Table 3, the underlying cause may be attributed to the significant disparity observed between the rate of wage increase and the rate of productivity growth within the export goods sector of the nations. If these nations opt for an alternative currency as their official currency, their exchange rate will be suppressed. However, in situations when high wages and poor productivity result in significant expenses, the strategy of devaluing the currency would be eliminated. This devaluation would be an efficient means of counteracting the rise in costs that are associated with international trade. In the event that this process fails to function, it is anticipated that the two nations would encounter trade imbalances. There is no exchange rate option that can devalue and solve the situation. Hence, it might be argued that these two nations, along with other economies characterized by populist tendencies, do not need the adoption of an alternative currency. To align wage growth with productivity growth, it is essential for them to implement measures aimed at suppressing wage increases. Additionally, their central banks should undertake efforts to mitigate overvaluation in their currency rates.

With the exception of Germany, the members of the EMU often encounter a similar issue. The primary objective of the euro project was to create a unified market among the member nations of the EMU. However, a single market without an adequate growth strategy may only serve to exacerbate issues. The constituents of the Eurozone were deprived of the chance to devalue their exchange rates as a means to enhance their competitiveness in the realm of global trade. Exchange rate modifications have the potential to mitigate trade imbalances. The Eurozone nations are no longer able to engage in such actions. The potential risk lies in the possibility that high wage growth or diminished productivity growth rates may lead to an escalation in trade imbalances within these nations. Germany is characterized by an economy that experiences growth mostly driven by its export activities. The country has a high level of competitiveness inside the Eurozone. The euro has persisted as a devalued currency inside this economy subsequent to the decision to abandon its national currency. Nevertheless, it may be argued that the euro is considered to be an overvalued currency in several other nations, particularly Greece, Italy, Spain, and Portugal (Ünal, 2017). The exchange rate mechanism of the EMU mandates that member nations must enforce limitations on the volatility of their exchange rates within a certain range. The effectiveness of the regulation to restrict currency rate volatility is undermined when adopted with expansionary policies. Greece has transformed into a nation lacking robust businesses capable of manufacturing sophisticated technical goods. This country regards tourism as a robust industry for economic activity due to its insufficient productivity and overvalued currency. Therefore, in the event that Argentina and Türkiye make the decision to adopt a different currency as a result of dollarization, it is anticipated that both countries would experience a worsening of the problem of their trade imbalance. Those industries that are considered to be semideveloped in the country run the danger of being eroded or relocated if they are built to compete at a level that is beyond the capabilities of the nation. Hence, the presence of economic populism poses significant challenges in attaining favorable results. Figure 9.1 demonstrates the influence of high production costs and overvalued exchange rate policies on the export price, as compared to the domestic price levels in Türkiye and Argentina.

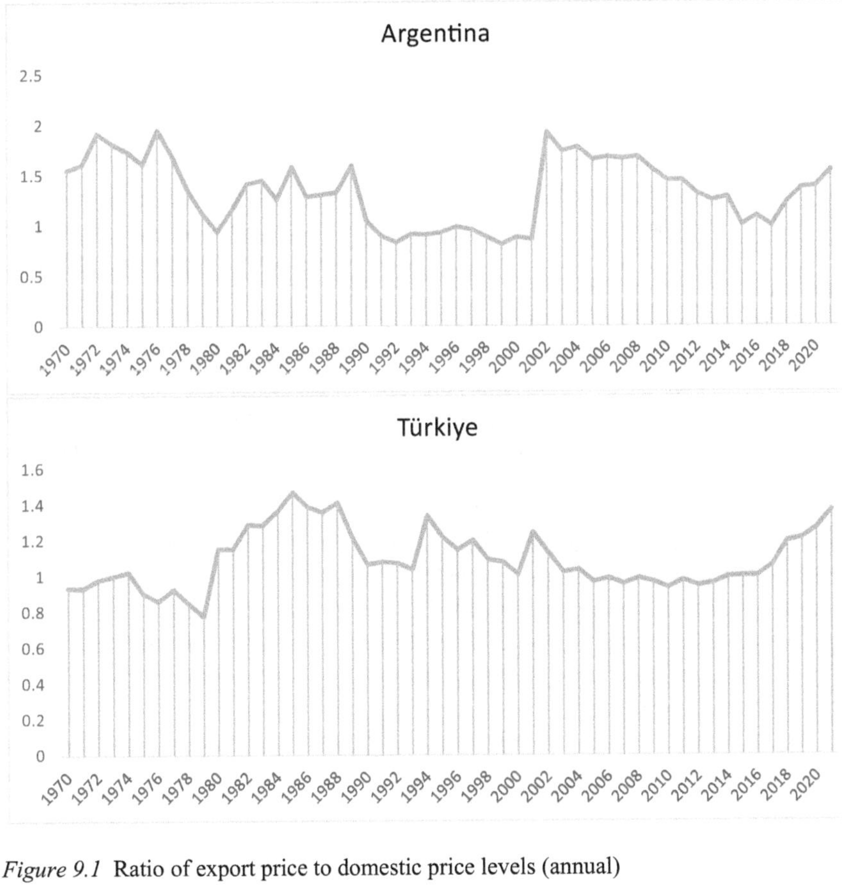

Figure 9.1 Ratio of export price to domestic price levels (annual)

The data have consistently shown the resemblance between the two nations. The primary focus should be on the fluctuation, aiming for a 1.0 ratio. The trend often stays higher than the ideal ratio. This suggests that the cost of exporting goods remains relatively high in comparison to the cost of domestic goods. During the 2000s, there was a decline in the ratio in the two nations. Starting from the mid-2010s, the ratio began to increase once again.

The exchange rate poses a significant threat to the populist governments that are in power. This dynamic has the capacity to diminish any advantages provided by a populist administration to the people. The implementation of expansionary policies, which include increasing the money supply via credits and transfers, may have a notable influence on both inflation and the currency rate. The depreciation of the lira and the peso may lead to an increase in the cost of imported final and intermediate goods. Consequently, the working class can demand high wages to maintain their purchasing power at a consistent level. The increasing pace of wage growth is expected to exert further inflationary pressures and impact the currency rate. The wage-inflation spiral presents a significant dilemma for the economy. The need to devalue currencies may arise due to the increasing wages surpassing growth in production. The fluctuation in exchange rates will lead to an increase in the pricing of imported items. Moreover, there is an additional anticipation of elevated inflation in the next period. In essence, companies aiming to secure themselves against inflation may choose to raise prices significantly by taking into account future expenses. The administration characterized by populism would find itself in a difficult position. To mitigate this issue, administrations may choose to implement a fixed exchange rate regime, pegging their currencies to the US dollar. However, it is crucial to note that this may also lead to an increase in financing costs, a worsening of debt levels, and a surge in interest rates and impose more strain on central banks (Beckerman, 1995). While the exporters get the same amount of revenue, the domestic costs continue to rise. Ultimately, this will undermine the profits of exporters, impeding their participation in the global trade arena. The current system imposes penalties on exporters, a sector that ought to get help within the context of the global economy. Consequently, the trade deficit and currency account deficits may impose a significant strain on the economy. The rise in interest rates may lead to a need for hot money flow, but this may also result in heightened economic risks. Furthermore, the issuance of new bonds that are denominated in foreign currencies to maintain an artificially overvalued exchange rate may lead to increased expenses and heightened vulnerability of the economy. Moreover, the use of swap agreements has gained prominence in both Argentina and Türkiye as a means to protect the stability of their respective currency rates. This proposed method does not provide an appropriate resolution to the prevailing economic challenges.

Countries that choose to abandon the floating exchange rate policy and instead peg their currency to another currency, such as the US dollar, should consider creating a framework that allows for labor costs to adapt in accordance with the new economic strategy. The inflexibility of wages and the labor market is likely to lead to the eventual breakdown of the fixed exchange rate system. Industries must possess the capacity to develop novel policies that enable them to adapt their costs in response to fluctuations in international prices. In both Argentina and Türkiye, sectors have challenges in effectively adapting their wage growth strategies to accommodate the changing dynamics of the economy. In both nations, it is essential for sectors to shoulder the substantial wage hikes, which subsequently contribute to a notable inflationary impact on the market. It is not unexpected to witness that both nations have implemented a significant increase in the minimum wage, resulting in a stimulation of production costs. Therefore, the industries lack control over the escalation of wages. These nations have a traditional wage structure that has persisted from the period of import substitution industrialization, with a labor market characterized by rigidity and limited adaptability. Trade union membership is quite common among public workers in public institutions, exhibit lower levels of productivity, higher rates of employment beyond what is necessary, and greater degrees of regulation. Trade unions advocate for the interests of workers within the context of populist administrations. The leader of the largest trade union in Türkiye has the authority to request support for the government via the acquisition of votes. In advance of the election on 14 May 2023, the leader of the trade union urged individuals, particularly public employees and members of the working class, to remain consistent in their commitment, especially in the face of potential declines in purchasing power and feelings of discontent. It is essential to provide support to the administration throughout the electoral process in Türkiye. This also serves as a clear indicator of the connection between the government and trade unions. Despite the attempts made by governments to implement modernization strategies and enhance labor market flexibility, the efficacy of these measures in diminishing the influence of trade unions remained constrained due to the restricted and inadequate nature of deregulation policies.

It is important to recognize that the macroeconomic conditions in populist nations are mostly influenced by internal forces. While it is indeed accurate that external shocks might have an effect on the inflation or exchange rate of nations, it can be assumed that these shocks are considered to be temporary occurrences. The absence of adequate institutional changes renders these nations more susceptible to external shocks. Prior to the occurrence of the catastrophic crises in those countries, there had been instances of economic crises that had occurred on a global scale. However, it is important to note that macroeconomic parameters cannot be arbitrarily constructed by two nations. Instead, these characteristics are determined based on the essential growth models that facilitate exports. Hence, the impact of foreign crises and shocks on these nations was mostly indirect. During the 2000s, the United States implemented a substantial reduction in interest rates, which subsequently influenced many other nations. The US dollar witnessed a decline in its value. China has taken measures to enhance the competitiveness of its currency in the realm of international trade. Other nations that wanted to stimulate economic development and enhance export performance opted to devalue their own currencies. Nevertheless, these nations persisted in enacting overvalued currency policies inside rigid exchange rate frameworks.

During the early 2000s, there was a strategic intention to alleviate the financial strain imposed by public industries on the budget, while simultaneously implementing deregulation measures aimed at mitigating debt. These measures created an opportunity for the rise of new governments that failed to sustain the implementation of reforms. Argentina was confronted with a worsening economic crisis, and funds began to leave institutions. Governments that were unable to effectively address the issue chose to step down from their positions. The credibility of the nation completely dissolved, and it was determined that the nation would be placed in the default category. Consequently, Argentina abandoned its esteemed standing on the global stage in an attempt to demonstrate the viability of its managed currency rate regime. The increased pressure around the exchange rate caused the implementation of stringent regulations governing foreign currency operations inside banking institutions. This measure did not effectively contribute to the improvement of the economy; rather, it exacerbated its decline. The value of the peso experienced a dramatic devaluation. The demonstrations resulted in the erosion of the government's reputation, ultimately leading to the resignation of de la Rua. Argentina enacted an emergency measure that allowed for the devaluation of the currency rate. The government engaged in the conversion of dollar accounts into the peso as a measure aimed at bolstering the economy. The conversion of US dollar accounts into the peso or the implementation of stringent transaction controls might provide a transient resolution that lacks long-term sustainability. The act of mitigating the effects of currency depreciation provides advantages to those who own obligations denominated in the domestic currency or who have savings in overseas accounts. Nevertheless, individuals who own foreign currency accounts may encounter financial losses as a result of the implementation of measures aimed at artificially maintaining an overvalued exchange rate. Hence, it is critical for a populist administration to mitigate any future grievances among the people. The implications of the economic crisis were attributed to international organizations. The reason for the perception that entering into agreements with international organizations suggests a country's proximity to default is the expectation that such organizations can endorse and provide support for its heterodox policies, which lack a solid theoretical foundation.

The Argentinian economy has shown to be unable to survive the consequences of populist policies implemented during the early 2000s, despite the implementation of various measures aimed at mitigating the impact of the crisis. The administration led by Alberto Fernández endeavored to mitigate the persistent devaluation of the national currency in 2023. Despite the substantial increase in inflation to 104% in March, the government continued to maintain the stability of the peso's value, a stance that contradicts fundamental economic principles. In countries characterized by populism, people have been used to experiencing economic turmoil, sudden devaluations, and the adoption of a foreign currency, such as dollarization. These events have attained the status of classics within the nations. Nevertheless, the government was criticized by past populist administrations for its alleged role in the significant increase in inflation rates and the resulting volatility in the currency rate. There were certain members of the political class who were of the opinion that an agreement ought to be reached with the IMF. It was contended that entering into any agreement with the IMF would exacerbate inflation since historical evidence suggests that the IMF's approaches have not yielded positive outcomes in similar contexts. This strategy may be considered valid in a certain context. The establishment of agreements with the IMF does not possess the capacity to engender enduring stability inside these nations. However, this is partially accurate since the populism that plagued these regimes made it impossible for them to overcome their issues. Vice President Cristina Fernández de Kirchner adhered to traditional populist rhetoric, attributing the country's high inflation on the IMF. She pointed out that the IMF cannot be regarded as a viable alternative due to its track record of ineffective ideas. Entering into any arrangement with the IMF has the potential to induce inflationary effects. She mentioned that dollarization would be an even more problematic option than convertibility.[4] A massive number of Argentinians gathered in Buenos Aires to participate in a protest against the government's reduction of funds allocated to public colleges. This demonstration marks a significant opposition to President Javier Milei's strict austerity policies.[5] The presence of high inflation has the potential to create distortions in the perception of prices within the market. Throughout time, economic agents encounter challenges in determining the appropriate price of a commodity. Consequently, the initiation of dollarization exacerbates the depreciation of national currencies. Advancements in technology, the emergence of digital currencies, and the widespread use of smartphones have significantly facilitated this procedure compared to previous methods. The local population would exhibit a prolonged reluctance to use the national currency. The domestic economy would abandon its ability to exert influence on the valuation of foreign currencies. It is evident that exchange rate markets may arise, each exhibiting distinct pricing dynamics. The real exchange rate may vary significantly from the rates published by authoritative entities such as the central bank. Under these circumstances, the most common procedure might be to convert the peso via the employment of a means that is unjustified. The significance of the agriculture sector in facilitating exports is of paramount importance for the nation. Nevertheless, it is impossible to conceive of the possibility that this sector could withstand populist initiatives. The presence of limited industrial development and the use of unstrategic growth models are significant contributors to the escalation of economic turbulence.

In modern times, technological improvements have expedited the swift execution of financial transactions, allowing individuals to quickly move funds from their bank accounts via smartphones or internet platforms. Controlling the currency rate employing political tools utilized by central banks is a difficult task. As a result, a government and its economy may gradually witness a decline in trust. In response to a significant decrease in the value of the currency during the fall of 2018, Türkiye attempted to exert significant influence over it via a measure enacted by the central bank at midnight. In the early 2020s, the lira had frequent and substantial devaluations on a daily basis. On 20 December 2021, the lira was deemed overvalued and was unable to withstand market forces that would have restored its equilibrium. The government failed to provide a thorough elucidation about the condition of the economy. There was a substantial rise in stress levels witnessed within the real economy and financial sector. The first action undertaken by the administration was the recognition that the country's economic development is contingent upon the implementation of export-led growth strategies. Consequently, the depreciation of the lira would result in a favorable exchange rate for exporters. The erosion of purchasing power posed a political risk for the administration, as citizens expressed concerns over the potential surge in inflation due to the nation's reliance on imported commodities. The government was unable to promptly identify a solution to address the issue at hand, but it maintained its stance that Türkiye would adopt a policy similar to that of China. Nevertheless, the administration continued to implement expansionary measures as part of its economic strategy. In the beginning of the new year, there was a substantial rise observed in the minimum wage as well as earnings in both the public and private sectors. Within a short period of time, the currency experienced a substantial surge, escalating from 9 lira to 18.20 lira. When the government became aware that the economy was unable to endure the impact of depreciations, it devised an alternative approach during the closure of the financial market. A novel derivative was unveiled in the evening. When investors cashed in their deposits, they would gain not only from the interest rate but also from the value of the US currency since the derivative acted as a deposit opportunity for investors. If investors exchanged US dollars for Turkish liras, they would be able to benefit from both the interest rate and the value of the US dollar. This chance presented a favorable circumstance for investors to protect their savings from the adverse effects of inflation and currency devaluations. When the investors learned about the new derivative, they intended to sell their US dollars at a higher price and buy them back at a lower price. Financial institutions refrained from offering this option due to a significant disparity between the selling and buying currency rates. The temporary measure effectively restored the currency to its original state, although creating a state of uncertainty in the market. The introduction of the new derivative denominated in foreign currencies and linked to inflation by the central bank and government led to a significant appreciation of the currency, resulting in a rapid decline of the lira to 10.20 in a single overnight period. There was a significant volatility observed in the currency rate. The discourse around export-led growth was neglected. The lira experienced a rapid appreciation, resulting in an overvaluation, within a short period of time. The people were protected from the volatility and conjecture generated by both domestic and foreign adversaries. As a consequence, the government emerged as a savior, rescuing the people from the erosion of their purchasing power and the looming economic disaster. Locating a narrative that demonstrates a sudden overnight appreciation of a currency, prompting individuals to hastily visit banks, currency exchange establishments, and use their smartphones to promptly divest themselves of the US dollar proves to be a challenging endeavor. It may be hypothesized that the lira had converged toward its equilibrium exchange rate. In essence, it could be inferred that in the near future, it is quite probable that the value of the lira would experience a decline once again due to significant costs associated with production and the implementation of expansionary measures. Over the course of a few months, the lira experienced more depreciation, reaching a level of 18.20 again and subsequently beyond this threshold.

On 19 April 2023, the central bank reported that the exchange rate between the US dollar and the lira was 19.40. In practical terms, it has become more difficult to get US dollars at a rate lower than 20 lira in the market. Banks and currency offices often maintain a significant gap between rates. It is worth noting that the exchange rate for purchasing US dollars was at 19.20 lira, while the cost for selling US dollars was around 20.66 lira at a prominent public banking institution. The substantial margin renders the conversion of US dollars without incurring any costs unfeasible. Furthermore, to impede the ease of currency exchange, the government implemented a novel institutional reform aimed at maintaining an artificially overvalued exchange rate. The exchange tax, which was discontinued in the late 2000s, was reintroduced in 2019 with a tax rate of 0.01% applied to each transaction. Within a few months, this rate increased to 0.02%. Furthermore, in 2020, there was a substantial rise in the tax rate applicable to foreign currency transactions, which rose from 0.02% to 1%. The tax application also included the transaction of gold and other commodities. This approach was a conventional method used to regulate the flow of money, representing a robust measure aimed at curbing the principles of free market and liberal economic policies. As a consequence, attempts were made to restrict foreign currency transactions, similar to the measures employed during the time of import substitution industrialization. However, the implementation of capital controls proved to be ineffective in maintaining exchange rate stability over an extended period of time. Moreover, it is evident that the lira is unlikely to maintain its current rates and would gradually depreciate over time. Due to persistent inflationary pressures, the lira experienced a substantial depreciation over many decades, culminating in an exchange rate of 1.5 million lira per US dollar in the early 2000s. To facilitate transactions within the realm of calculations and foreign currencies, the government implemented an institutional reform, wherein six decimal places were removed from the lira, resulting in the introduction of the new Turkish lira. The news was presented with the assertion that the lira had demonstrated strength in the realm of the global economy. Nevertheless, this institutional reform only resulted in a numerical alteration, failing to address the persistent devaluation of the lira and its consequential destiny.

Populism to control price levels

Price level control is a policy instrument that governments could employ to address elevated inflation rates in certain commodities or services. The existence of increasing inflation rates and a controlled exchange rate might potentially cause a decline in the competitiveness of exports, thereby leading to a sustained trade deficit. Moreover, the increase in costs generates dissatisfaction within the social structure. Contrary to the belief in liberalism that governments merely need to control trade and maintain social harmony, they have a responsibility to be proactive in defending the working class and promoting distributive justice. Hence, it could be claimed that governments play a crucial role in monitoring and upholding price levels in an economy. If this trend persists, the political risk in emerging countries, where individuals allocate a significant proportion of their money toward daily necessities, can escalate. The government's political legitimacy was closely tied to its capacity to enhance people's standard of life, making economic development a key priority. To ensure that economic development has the required attributes, the government possessed a clear and unambiguous directive, which was officially established in the regulations, to actively participate in the economy. This was evident in several ways, such as changes in wages, fiscal and monetary policies, the establishment of state companies, the implementation of price controls for commodities, and involvement in international trade, investment, and credit policies (Bazdresch and Levy, 1990). As a result, the government would take on the central position in the economic affairs of the country and would be responsible for effectively managing the competing requirements of the working class and industry, functioning as a protective entity.

It is possible to find one of the most notable cases of price controls and the potential consequences they may have prior to elections in the administration of Richard Nixon. President Nixon asserted that individuals would choose their economic preferences over the nation's foreign policy. He was presumed to be opposed to price regulations, which would contradict the principles of a free market economy. A socialist agenda might be one interpretation of his proposed institutional change. He believed that exerting control over inflation would enhance his chances of being reelected as the president of the United States. He implemented wage and price controls while simultaneously allowing for the dissolution of the fixed exchange rate system, resulting in the fluctuation of the dollar relative to other currencies. Nixon's decision to transition away from the fixed exchange rate system was a cautious alteration since it had the potential to be regarded as a failure. His initiatives effectively curbed inflation, and he emerged victorious in the 1972 election. Nevertheless, his enduring strategies to regulate inflation via price restrictions had adverse effects on the economy in subsequent years. Furthermore, inflation rose to a substantial level. Nixon harbored optimism that by mandating comparable union wages for all employees covered by federal contracts, he could disrupt the labor effect and halt the wage-price spiral. Nevertheless, it was anticipated that this would be viewed as antiunion and would not impede wage hikes. Although Nixon believed that restrictions would be effective, it seems that he was prepared to engage in a temporary measure to exert influence over the people in order to increase his chances of being reelected. A freeze or restrictions would have limited effectiveness and should thus be implemented around the 1972 election, according to Nixon (Abrams and Butkiewicz, 2017). It was reported that the restrictions had only temporary, negative impacts on inflation and that these effects were reversed by the end of 1973. Prior to the end of 1973, regulations were already having detrimental impacts on pricing, production, and interest rates. Moreover, there is evidence indicating that the enforcement of restrictions, together with the implementation of an expansive monetary policy, might result in economic circumstances that are more severe than the ones that existed before the controls were put in place (Davidson, 1983). The United States experienced a decline in its international reserves during the period when price controls were in effect. The price restrictions were denounced for their perceived effect of creating an illusion of price stability, which might potentially exacerbate inflation.

Following the 2008 global crisis, there was a substantial escalation in the level of rivalry among political parties. This problem led populist parties to return to old practices reminiscent of the import substitution industrialization period. The governments employed policies that diverged from traditional economic approaches. The rate of privatization slowed down, while the enforcement of price limitations increased. There was a significant increase in the minimum wage in both countries. These developments were regarded as improvements in social circumstances. The adoption of expansionary policies was driven by strategies related to salaries, workforce participation, and retirement benefits, in line with the demands expressed by the labor force. Nevertheless, this phenomenon led to a rise in the prices for standard consumer products. The adoption of expansive fiscal and monetary policies led to a rise in inflationary pressures in the economy. The phenomenon of inflation had a notable increase after the 2015 election in Türkiye. During this particular time frame, there was a substantial rise in the minimum wage with the intention of garnering the support of the working class. Nonetheless, statistics revealed that roughly half of the population required minimum-wage employment. In addition, a new policy was developed to provide bonuses to retired individuals in Türkiye in advance of two significant festivals. The policy represents a substantial implementation of expansionary measures. Consequently, price increases were noticeable. The persistent issue of inflation reappeared at a rate that was much higher. The people became discontented with the existing price structure in supermarkets and the total expenses associated with daily life. Populists embrace a rhetorical tactic to portray themselves as being assaulted by unknown opponents. The phenomenon of stocking and dollarization had once again shown itself as a tangible reality. Meat prices in particular became a source of considerable controversy. The governments implemented subsidies in an attempt to reduce meat prices. It was widely believed that the government had the capability to effectively mitigate the issue of escalating costs. The issue of rental housing has emerged as a significant concern in Türkiye. The influx of immigrants from the Middle East and Asia, together with gentrification initiatives aimed at demolishing older structures to mitigate potential seismic risks, as well as the occurrence of earthquakes in major urban centers, had collectively contributed to a substantial increase in housing prices due to the rise in demand for citizenship via property acquisition. The issue of living in metropolitan areas of significant size had emerged as a matter of great concern. The prices exhibited a persistent upward trend on a daily basis. However, the administration implemented a policy of price control on housing. According to an official communication from the presidential channel, it was asserted that the rate of rise in domestic prices should not exceed 25%. Despite this, inflation nearly reached above 70% in the 2020s.[6] Figure 9.2 depicts the inflationary patterns of both nations after the implementation of import substitution industrialization. While Türkiye had a longstanding issue of historical chronic inflation, Argentina plunged into a period of hyperinflation throughout the 1980s and 1990s. Both nations had the ability to

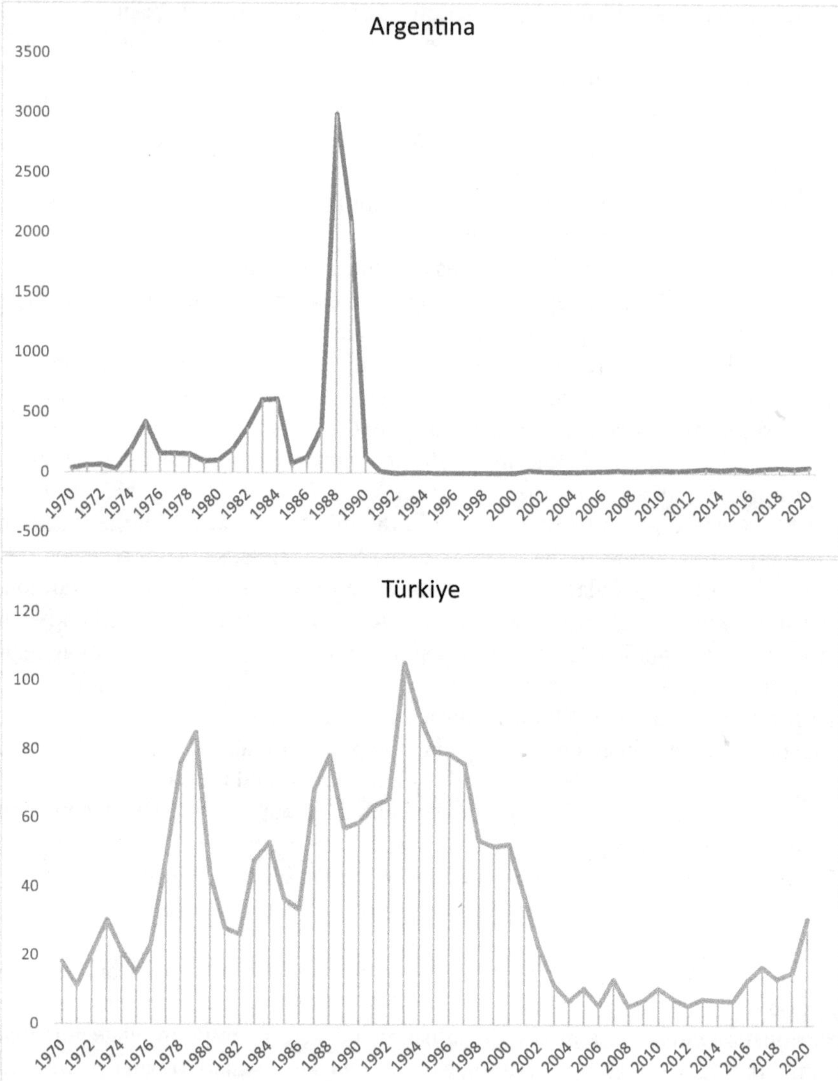

Figure 9.2 Inflation rate in the countries (annual, unit: %)

restrict the escalating costs throughout the 2000s. After a decade, both countries returned to their previous status as inflationary nations. Since the mid-2010s, inflation has turned into a persistent concern.

The neoliberal economics proposes that central banks need to be able to operate autonomously. When a central bank acts independently, it has the ability to enact policies that are in line with the prevailing economic conditions. Nevertheless, these moves might potentially impact the amount of popular support that the administration receives. Populist governments have exerted political influence on their respective central banks. However, in both nations, the presidents of the central banks stepped down and were replaced by individuals who showed more enthusiasm in carrying out the directives of their respective governments. To retain popular support, governments often attempt to exert control over central banks, pressuring them to implement policies that may contradict current market conditions. The precedence is not given to the economic interests of the nation. Both countries have employed the application of high interest rates as a strategy to reduce the decline in the value of their currency. The development of monetary policy is mostly affected by political pressures imposed on obedient central banks rather than being led by autonomous central banks. Additionally, credit allocation is directed toward satisfying populist targets. When combined with continuous expansionary fiscal actions, this method has many constraints. Within the framework of expansionary policies, the ongoing increase in interest rates presents a formidable obstacle. Thus, it is essential for governments to consider other approaches, such as adopting a deposit indexing system that is tied to the fluctuations of foreign currency over a period of time.

Argentina had persistent macroeconomic imbalances throughout the 2020s. The inflation rate exceeded 100%. The IMF-government negotiating process failed to achieve a timely accord. The devaluation of the peso was significant. Due to the economic turmoil, the central bank adopted actions that included raising the interest rate. On 27 April 2023, the overvalued currency system was severely impacting the Argentinian economy. Politicians who followed populist measures were the ones who were responsible for the phenomena of inflation. The central bank enacted a significant increase in the interest rate, elevating it from 81% to 91%. The observed phenomena may be described as a gradual increase in the interest rate, used to affect the currency, which was unable to support expansionary actions. The interest rate was much higher compared to the majority of rates worldwide. The execution of this approach exemplifies the central bank's dedication to combating inflation and mitigating the deteriorating consequences of the economic downturn. This decision was executed in an effort to restrict the rate of exchange between the peso and the US currency. Due to the prevailing dominance of the dollar in the economy, the central bank's policies proved insufficient in effectively addressing the problem. The most significant event after President Alberto Fernandez's tenure was a substantial depreciation of the peso. The peso experienced a depreciation of 118% against the US dollar on 12th December.[7] The populist administration seized control of the central bank and maintained an artificially high exchange rate to prevent the economy from breaking down any worse. Attempts were made by the central bank to create swap agreements with countries that had considerable reserves of foreign currencies, such as China.

The announcement made by the minister of Sergio Massa indicated the implementation of economic measures aimed at stabilizing the situation and mitigating the depreciation in the exchange rate. In the field of institutional economics, the establishment of rational values is crucial, as shown by Commons' emphasis on this notion. Alternatively, the implementation of conflicting economic policies would likely lead to an unavoidable confrontation. When implementing expansionary policies, it is apparent that the exchange rate may not be able to withstand the pressure exerted by increasing the money supply to stimulate domestic demand. The escalating costs of goods and food items on a daily basis provide a remarkable challenge in curbing the inflationary pressures on foreign reserves. The fundamental principles of economics dictate that money serves three primary functions: As a medium of trade, a unit of account, and a store of value. In light of increasing inflation, the efficiency of national money diminishes. This serves as a first step toward the implementation of a dollarization policy. Hence, in the absence of fiscal policy control, the implementation of monetary authority–driven interest rate hikes can only provide a temporary resolution for the economy. The populist administration demonstrates its efforts to combat inflation. However, it is comprehensible that this fight is not a genuine conflict but rather a staged performance. The media and news sources suggest that the administration is displaying a strong commitment toward implementing this strategy. The absence of institutional complementarity will exacerbate the issue, leading to a deferral of the solution until the subsequent administration.

The significance of central banks is emphasized by industrialized nations and economic institutions. The autonomy of this institution facilitates the implementation of macroeconomic policies aimed at achieving market stability and reducing inflation. In both Argentina and Türkiye, there has been a notable escalation in inflationary pressures. The currencies of both nations experienced volatility subsequent to the intensification of deregulation initiatives throughout the 2000s. The changing exchange rate system affords governments the ability to mitigate the effects of currency devaluation. Open economic policies have the propensity to attract a substantial influx of capital, resulting in an overvaluation of the currency rate. Despite both nations experiencing a substantial depreciation in their exchange rates, the implementation of the new exchange rate system has aided in mitigating the impact of the currency on the economy. In the context of the floating exchange rate system, it is important to note that depreciation does not occur suddenly but rather manifests as a progressive decline in the value of a currency. The fall of the fixed exchange rate regime resulted in severe economic crisis and bankruptcies. In the absence of institutional complementarity, neoliberalism promotes a free market economy, in which the values of currencies and labor are determined by market forces. Alternatively, the implementation of expansionary policies may lead to adverse outcomes, such as significant devaluations that amplify the debt burden of domestic enterprises, diminish purchasing power due to drops in real wages, increase unemployment, foster high inflation, and further worsen economic slump.

The implementation of inflation targeting has brought about a substantial institutional change in the historical evolution of the countries. Both countries were forced to initiate inflation-targeting programs due to a prolonged period of currency devaluation and ongoing inflationary pressures. In 2006, Türkiye implemented the strategy of inflation targeting at a rate of 5% after its economic crisis in the years 2000–2001. Argentina used an inflation-targeting program during the 2010s. From an institutional perspective, the introduction of new forms should lead to a condition of complementarity. In the absence of institutional complementarity between fiscal policy and monetary policy, it is impossible to make any predictions about the effectiveness of reform efforts. In both countries, the adoption of economic populism weakened the success of inflation-targeting strategies. The use of expansionary measures, along with a lack of coordination between monetary and fiscal policy, led to the development of ineffective institutional reforms. The modifications were announced by the governments or central banks, but the possibility of political disapproval and the tendency for the program to remain unchanged due to previous decisions made it ineffective and limited its implementation to theoretical existence only. The phenomenon of rising prices is frequently regarded as a prominent characteristic of populist movements. Populist parties tend to prioritize their short-term gains. The character that they have is one that is marked by a lack of patience. Controlling inflation is a difficult task for both developed and developing countries. To effectively reduce inflation, it is essential to adopt a systematic strategy. By contrast, populist governments do not exhibit this pattern. To reduce inflation, it might be necessary to apply elevated interest rates together with strict austerity measures for a certain period of time. A government should endeavor to mitigate the significant political risk involved with formulating such a policy. Thus, populists exhibit a deficiency in the essential determination and guidance required for proficiently handling inflation. Usually, after the election triumph of a populist government, there is a noticeable pattern of increased inflation that tends to arise. Inflation poses a significant challenge to the maintenance of macroeconomic stability as well as the promotion of equality and the alleviation of poverty. While governments may make commitments to address these concerns, they often struggle to effectively tackle the issue of inflation. Modern democratic economies often strive to steer clear of economic populism, but they may still be susceptible to the influence of neopopulism. Both these economies are aware of the fact that implementing high expansionary policies might lead to more detrimental outcomes. It is assumed that the establishment of a conducive environment for investments and the implementation of economic incentives are essential components of a functional free market economy. These characteristics may effectively maintain productivity levels and facilitate economic expansion. Engaging in the practice of romanticizing previous eras of economic success under different regulatory systems may worsen present challenges and impede a nation's advancement, leading to a lag behind both developed and developing economies.

The increasing price levels provide a substantial issue for governments. Calculating the consumer price index may be a subject of controversy for regions with high levels of inflation. Particularly, when there is a rise in food prices, governments may be motivated to directly intervene in the market. This statement is in direct opposition to the ideas of liberal economics. Developed countries employed this strategy to address the problem of stagflation. However, the intrinsic attributes of the free market make it resistant to artificial interference. Both Argentina and Türkiye experienced difficulties in effectively addressing the problem of rising inflation. They have focused on managing statistical institutions to control price levels by adjusting the weights of items and services utilized for calculating inflation. The accuracy of the inflation rate is a subject of substantial debate in both countries. The prices collected from online retailers may be used to generate daily price indexes that serve as a supplementary source of information alongside official data. The research investigated the accuracy of official inflation figures in five Latin American countries, with a specific focus on Argentina, where there has been much doubt about the reliability of official data. The figures were gathered from the leading supermarket in each country. The online price indexes in Brazil, Chile, Colombia, and Venezuela accurately mirrored the magnitude and main patterns of official inflation. Conversely, the internet inflation rate in Argentina was around three times higher than the official estimate (Cavallo, 2013). Autonomous groups are endeavoring to evaluate the actual level of inflation. The requirement to display inflation rates at significantly reduced levels arises from the impact of conflicts with different factions and public dissatisfaction, prompting administrations to raise wage growth to a minimum threshold that corresponds with inflation. The rising inflation rate presents a potential threat to macroeconomic factors, such as the instability in currency exchange rates, resulting in an upsurge in the prices of imported commodities. Hence, the working class articulates a compelling demand for an increase in wages that exceeds the inflation rate. The issue of whether to execute policies that are irrational or to undertake institutional reforms that are favorable puts governments in the position of having to choose between two different approaches. It is possible to classify the phenomena as a symptom of economic populism, which is characterized by the presentation of genuine data information in a way that obscures the underlying truth and lacks fundamental institutional reform. Populist political tactics had instead chosen to speculate about possible flaws in the consumer price index's calculation rather than understand the problem and implement significant institutional reforms. Altering the weights that are provided to consumer products inside the index might be accomplished via the adoption of an initial technique. It is possible that the computation of the inflation rate will differ from the actual impression of the market in this kind of way. To reflect a smaller statistical measure of inflation, it is feasible that more emphasis may be placed on items that experience only modest increases in price. In light of this, it is possible to bring about a decrease in the level of social dissatisfaction. The probable existence of the problem is not likely to be linked only to the actions taken by the government to combat inflation, given that the situation may be more complicated than was recognized. As an outcome, it is of the utmost importance to acknowledge the existence of opponents, whether they are domestic or international, who actively contribute to the escalation of inflation rates or participate in the practice of offering goods at inflated prices. There is a common occurrence of governments initiating conflicts against economic entities.

The advancement of industrialization necessitates the implementation of protective measures aimed at supporting domestic enterprises from the fierce competition created by foreign corporations, which possess the potential to undermine the productivity of emerging organizations. Following the preliminary phase, it is essential for these sectors to be adequately prepared to engage in competition within both local and foreign markets. Otherwise, their ability to maintain productivity and competitiveness would diminish over time. However, to facilitate robust industrial growth, it is essential to take into account the role of wages. Industries may have a predictable trajectory under good macroeconomic conditions. In nations where wages are indexed to past inflation rates, the effectiveness of this approach in mitigating the decline in purchasing power remains limited. The reason for the inability to enhance productivity in an economy lies in its susceptibility to business cycles as well as economic and political turbulence. When productivity fails to meet expectations, it may lead to an increase in inflation. Consequently, wage costs may increase in the following year. Developing nations often lack robust strategies for their industrial processes. The output of domestic industries may be diminished by the presence of established and multinational corporations. Given the intense competition, it is difficult to envision that production can reach its maximum potential. When economic growth in a nation slows below its potential rate, inflation rises. Hence, in emerging economies, where wages are tied to inflation, there is a possibility for inflation to keep rising each year, as long as these nations continue to adjust wages based on previous inflation rates. This phenomenon does not result in an increase in the ability of individuals to purchase goods and services. While individuals may experience temporary satisfaction from a rise in their wages, it is important to recognize that this sense of contentment is likely to be short-lived. The practice of wage indexation to inflation can become a prevalent phenomenon, leading to a persistent inflationary issue and self-destructive consequences.

Commons (1925b) astutely identified the phenomenon of inflation and its associated false sense of affluence among the working class. However, he elucidated that this illusion might be understood as a social condition. According to his perspective, achieving stability is contingent upon the collaboration of companies, workers, and farmers who bear the brunt of economic challenges since they must collectively exert sufficient pressure on politicians. Therefore, individuals have the ability to use their authority to establish economic stability by distancing themselves from deceptive practices. Any broad increase in prices or salaries is the illusion of general scarcity if it is assumed that all available labor could be fully engaged. This would result in the creation of the illusion of prosperity. This is an illusion that is formed from the perspective of society, not the perspective of the individual. The phenomenon under consideration is the redistribution of wealth from individuals due to the escalation of price levels rather than via the implementation of economic processes that generate income. Once the illusion of societal affluence is dispelled, it will concurrently eliminate the perception of excessive output. It was pointed out that due to the illusion of wage per hour that climbed three-fold and the output that reduced two-thirds, which is the illusory prosperity created four factors for organized and unorganized labor under the illusion of widespread scarcity. These include excessive wages, poor productivity, decreased production, and a lack of discipline or accountability in the workplace. The illusion generated by statistics institutions only served to promote a false sense of economic well-being, making it seem as if prices were low and workers were enjoying significant salary increases. Nevertheless, it might be claimed that this was only a deceptive tactic employed to mitigate any political risks within the societal framework. Hence, it may be inferred that this issue transcends individual actions and instead pertains to the broader societal perspective around the governance of populist regimes. In the context of class disputes between employers and employees, it is essential to consider the factors of salaries and dividends, and then give necessary modifications. The prevailing economic circumstances create an illusion that makes the working class perceive that wage growth is higher than the rate of inflation. In essence, the government ensures that all aspects are effectively managed and regulated. Consequently, the absence of available capacity for institutional adjustments may impede the working class from contemplating the fiscal debt and the potential ramifications of expansionary policies. The increase in fiscal expenditure engenders an illusion among the working class that is predicated on the statistical apparatus.

Notes

1 Source: IMF Executive Board Approves 30-month US$44 billion Extended Arrangement for Argentina and Concludes 2022 Article IV Consultation, Press Release, No: 22/89, the IMF.
2 Source: Minimum wage is derived from Ministry of Labor and Social Security.
3 Source: Inflation, Consumer Prices, World Bank.
4 Source: Buenos Aires Times "Cristina Fernández de Kirchner attacks Milei dollarisation plan, blames IMF for inflation" 27 April 2023.
5 Source: CNN 'Tens of thousands protest as Milei's austerity measures hit Argentina's public universities' 24 April 2024.
6 Source: Consumer Price Index, TurkStat.
7 Source: US Dollar Argentinian Peso, www.investing.com.

10 Why is there economic populism?

There are various types of populism that can be witnessed, and they might originate from intellectual, cultural, or religious foundations. The economy has a central position within the fabric of societal existence. The significance of this phenomenon cannot be overstated in the context of contemporary politics. When nations embarked on the process of industrialization, they were confronted with the harsh economic realities. Government can face potential risks in the realm of political economy when an economy undergoes a process of increased centralization and connectivity via institutional reforms. The emergence of the working class can be attributed to the advent of industrialization. Over time, government policies have had a growing impact on individuals, leading governments to utilize economic populism to control institutions and gain credibility with the general public. In a competitive political environment, governments employ economic populism as a tactic to bolster their own political position in relation to other parties, which ultimately has adverse effects for the economy. Governments are aware that implementing populist policies leads to high inflation, currency volatility, and persistent macroeconomic issues. Nevertheless, they acknowledge that implementing policies that are in line with market reality might quickly jeopardize their control on power.

Multiple factors contribute to the rise and progression of populism. Populist tendencies emerge as a result of the deficiencies exhibited by dominant economic, social, and political institutions. The appeal aims to alter current economic institutions, establish innovative social and economic systems, and foster new economic connections and identities. It has both political and economic dimensions (Panizza, 2005). The phenomenon of populism arises as a manifestation of a crisis in the realm of political representation. In the event that the current system proves inadequate in meeting the needs of the people, politicians may use the system's vulnerabilities as a means to garner public support. This is a problem with the institutional form. The phenomenon under consideration has the potential to amplify political risks and incentivize populist leaders to make irrational actions to appease the people. The reduction of pluralism might lead to the emergence of an adversarial connection between political and economic identities. Consequently, those who experience exclusion and marginalization due to their political affiliations, ethnic backgrounds, or ideological convictions endeavor to discover other forms of representation. In the realm of economics, those who are not adequately represented in

DOI: 10.4324/9781003438090-10

terms of their demands, such as minimum wage earners, private sector employees, or public servants, can explore alternative political affiliations to have their voices acknowledged and taken into consideration. The presence of stagnant wage growth, elevated taxation rates, and costly educational and healthcare services might serve as incentives for a political party to adopt populist strategies.

The emergence of populism could be attributed to institutional changes inside the system. The novel technology has the capability to generate lobbyists autonomously. Subsequently, the task of formulating new changes would become very arduous. The erosion of public trust in the government's efficacy in addressing societal challenges may inevitably compel individuals to explore other solutions. The presence of corruption propagated by the privileged class leads to the emergence of a different social faction referred to as the 'others,' who identify themselves as the general people. When pervasive corruption and the deterioration of institutions affect a significant portion of society, there is an increasing need for governmental and constitutional reform. The phenomenon of economic populism arises as a result of the alteration of growth patterns, culture, society, or technical development. The development of increasing urbanization throughout the 1950s and 1960s facilitated the emergence and implementation of populist programs. Technological advancements have the potential to disrupt and dismantle established institutional ideas and cultural norms on a global scale. The progress of technology, especially in the field of information and production technologies, has caused a significant change in the way society functions. Democracy, culture, and social order are all evolving notions. There have emerged new political factions and individuals who want to foster a society characterized by increased levels of tolerance.

The depiction might be observed at any given period within political works that examines the concept of populism. The majority of scholarly literature on populism tends to center its analysis on political leaders as a means to assess the implementation of populist agendas. Nevertheless, the presence of institutional structure serves as compelling evidence that populism may exist independently of the incumbent leadership. Even in the absence of a leader, the phenomenon of populism has the potential to persist through subsequent regimes. Panizza (2005) provides an illustrative case of the Peronist party in Argentina, which managed to endure and maintain its existence after the death of its leader. Although the impact of institutional structure is not directly addressed, it is recognized that the policies under discussion may not always be related to a specific populist leader who is in power. As a consequence, populism is regarded as a longstanding practice deeply rooted in the Peronist party's nostalgia, myths, institutions, and rhetorics. Throughout the years, the party, its goals, and its members have been shaped by the persistent impact of Peron's principles. However, the basic issue of economic populism is concealed within the institutional reforms that occurred during the period of import substitution industrialization. Even in the event of a populist party's loss of power, there remains the possibility for a subsequent opposition party to adopt and enact populist ideas. This was accomplished by the adoption of expanding policies, considerable wage increases, and the maintenance of an overvalued currency rate. After the import substitution industrialization, the government implemented a policy of deregulation, albeit the extent and effect of this move were rather limited. Rather than implementing measures to reduce manufacturing costs and facilitate export-driven economic development, the government only focused on adopting policies aimed at appealing to broad segments of the population. The populist discourse remained consistent throughout different time periods, as political parties maintained to adhere to the ideology despite changes in economic circumstances. This pertains to institutional reforms rather than their ideological position. During the Atatürk era, Türkiye experienced a low inflation rate and significant development in productivity (Ünal, 2018). During the 1960s, the implementation of institutional reforms based on new economic conceptions allowed political parties to strategically use economic instruments to achieve their political objectives. Hence, there is a conspicuous lack of a distinct correlation between the leader and populist policies. On the other hand, there is a considerable association between institutional forms and the implementation of populist policies.

The role of the working class in populism

The core of economic populism lies in the nexus of interactions between the working class and the government. As governments work to nurture public support for their political choices, workers struggle to preserve their financial and employment stability in the face of the unexpected impacts of liberal policies, trade disruptions, and immigration (Barone and Kreuter, 2021; De la Torre, 2017). The working class has the potential to emerge as a crucial element within a populist coalition, contingent upon the implementation of wage-setting policies that are advantageous to their interests. The prevalence of economic populism may be attributed to a longstanding symbiotic relationship between the government and the working class. The government is hesitant to reduce its political maneuverability by enacting more modifications that might put limitations on the ambitions of the working class. To successfully achieve its objectives, the government would require an economic tool to obtain and maintain popular support. The working class comprises a considerable segment of the population, offering important assistance to the government. Hence, the government demonstrates a lack of enthusiasm to adopt institutional reforms in wage–labor relations since these adjustments would reduce its power within the political sphere. In addition, the working class demonstrates resistance to giving up its socioeconomic position due to deregulation policies that might possibly create a labor market characterized by fierce competition and lack of government involvement. The determination of wages under a deregulated system would be independent of government intervention and instead be influenced by prevailing market forces. Consequently, the working class would experience a loss in its bargaining power, perhaps leading to a decline in its purchasing power. It is important to highlight that governments have been known to execute wage growth even when the economy was in a state of crisis. There are intrinsic restrictions that are placed on industries within the context of this bilateral alliance between the government and the working class. This situation hinders their ability to attain circumstances that are advantageous to their specific objectives. It may be argued that the implementation of a tripartite coalition is ineffective due to the absence of a suitable environment for industries. The process of wage negotiation between the government and labor regularly takes into account the impact of inflation. This technique is regarded as a norm within the national economic framework. However, the act of connecting wages to inflation has been shown to lead to a rise in inflation. The working class wants to maintain its ability to purchase goods and services, while the government aims to prevent the creation of negative attitudes toward its programs. Thus, it can be claimed that economic populism is based on the practice of connecting wages to inflation. This tactic became more common, as the working class gained importance and formed an alliance with the governing authority. Inflation is recognized as the factor that determines wage increase by both entities rather than taking into consideration the rise of productivity in industries. Because of this, it is reasonable to assume that a wage increase that is lower than the rate of inflation can have a negative effect on the support generated by the people.

The rise of economic populism can be attributed to institutional reforms in the wage–labor dynamics. Economic populism is a dominant and powerful political trait in developing countries, despite changes in leadership and political parties. Peronism has become the dominant political force in Argentina, exerting substantial influence. Since its establishment in 1945, the movement has the capacity to exercise control over the country for several decades via its successors. A considerable number of votes were also cast for political parties that adhered to the Peronist ideology. The establishment of the wage–labor relationship during the post-1940s significantly contributed to this success, despite the suboptimal functioning of the economy. Both the government and the people adamantly refused to relinquish their own interests in favor of the collective welfare of the country. The mobilization of the working class contributed to the widespread endorsement. It was possible to exercise influence over the people and cultivate their allegiance via the utilization of trade unions. Clientelistic techniques were effective even under the administrations of Menem and Kirchner. This technique fostered a strong connection that encouraged solidarity among the working class residing in rural regions and provinces mostly populated by people from moderate socioeconomic backgrounds.

Removing barriers to global trade is anticipated to result in greater prosperity inside nations, mostly due to the enhanced productivity witnessed in export sectors. As output levels rise, wages can also grow in proportion. At this point, it is essential to reallocate workers who were previously assigned to certain activities to facilitate their deployment in alternate areas. The anticipated rise in productivity in the export sectors is expected to result in a favorable effect on employment in these areas. Hence, it is necessary to possess labor flexibility to enable the efficient transition of workers across different industries. The existence of major state enterprises is a factor that contributes to the rigidity of the labor market, which in turn creates difficulties for workers who are looking for employment opportunities in alternative production facilities. Nevertheless, this might be a substantial obstacle for those in the working class. The rationale behind this is that individuals would encounter reduced earnings in sectors characterized by lower levels of productivity.

Hence, it is important for them to embrace a position opposing the increasing patterns of globalization and liberalization. Moreover, the process of globalization involves the transfer of capital from countries with lower levels of productivity to countries with greater levels of productivity. Global firms have been lured by the appealing potential for increased productivity in China, prompting them to expand their operations inside the nation. Trade unions should advocate for the interests of workers, regardless of their membership status. Industries have the ability to concentrate their efforts on improving their competitiveness and promoting innovation. The industrial class has a stronger propensity for individuality, competition, and a concentration on economic endeavors. Nevertheless, trade unions relied on the principles of mutuality and solidarity, which fluctuated in accordance with the fortunes or setbacks experienced by the working class. Industries exhibit a reluctance to depend on mutual agreements, but the working class is fundamentally grounded on the principle of mutuality. The class engages in collective efforts to enhance their economic and social progress, while firms strive to enhance innovation and productivity (Commons, 1925b). Hence, it may be argued that politicians are predisposed to implement policies that cater to the needs of the working class, a cohesive and supporting segment of society that has more influence over policy formulation in comparison to specific sectors. One potential approach to reducing the occurrence of crises similar to those experienced in populist countries is to develop and implement contemporary economic policies that prioritize deregulation, openness, and the advancement of international competitiveness. The process of deregulation started prior to the 2000s in Argentina and Türkiye. Nevertheless, every attempt to implement reforms was met with unfavorable reactions from trade unions, including healthcare professionals, civil workers, and public employees. Administrations have challenges in gaining support, even from inside their own party, due to rising political risks and social animosity. Both countries failed to establish a competitive and liberalized system for public workers by integrating them into a market that is characterized by competition.

Wars, economic crises, social difficulties, and globalization have been viewed to contribute to the polarization of societies. There exists a strong correlation between populism and polarization. The argumentation and communicative style used in this context exhibits a Manichean framework, whereby the pronoun ‘us’ refers to the sovereign and righteous individuals, while ‘them’ denotes those who are regarded as negative and external (Anselmi, 2018). Populism engenders agreement among the people via the use of oppositional techniques. The phenomenon of polarization manifests itself in opposition to both elitist and pluralist perspectives. Populism fosters a pronounced division among political identities. Populist regimes often employ a rhetorical strategy, whereby they portray their opponents as adversaries who pose a threat to the collective interests of the people. Polarization may arise as a result of economic conflicts. Populist administrations may endeavor to cultivate the notion that an alternative political party will exacerbate the socio-economic well-being of the people. Polarization therefore appears in the economic sphere. Populists advocate for the need of a conflict between forces representing moral righteousness and those embodying moral depravity. The elites and affluent minority groups might potentially be regarded as adversaries to the general populace. Populist factions assert that they are engaged in a struggle against privileged groups that oppose the desires and preferences of the people. The primary objective of this administration is to generate legitimate assertions against long-standing established institutions. Thus, populists have the potential to attract widespread appeal and get substantial support. The phenomenon of economic populism engenders a state of division between those who get advantages from the prevailing policies and others who encounter barriers in accessing the market. Economic populism stands in opposition to the principles of economic democracy. The economic agents do not possess equitable chances to access the market in an equal manner. The market encompasses various fields, including the labor market, investments, and industries. The government establishes a distinct delineation between the factions that support its programs and those that do not. However, this phenomenon also gives rise to a faction inside the government that might be characterized as elitist. A subsequent political faction adheres to a set of principles by publicly criticizing the prevailing institutions and their respective elite classes. Hence, the phenomenon of populism has the potential to incite political discord. When populism is oriented toward the promotion of democratic ideals and the mitigation of societal tensions, it has the potential to strengthen the foundations of democracy. Nevertheless, it is important to note that this issue is not exclusive to politics; rather, it is a fundamental problem inherent in institutional forms.

The existence of a significant divide between the working class and industry may be attributed to the actions of the government. The prevailing image conveyed by media, newspapers, and social media is that the reason for rising prices is not primarily attributed to the cost of manufacturing resulting from economic populism but rather to profit-seeking behaviors shown by industries. While it is true that certain industries or firms may set prices above the natural price in response to high inflation, it appears that markets operate based on the anticipation of future price increase. Consequently, they may implement higher prices to align with their costs. High levels of inflation can have detrimental effects on an economy. Türkiye did not demonstrate considerable market distortions during the 2000s. The government implemented measures to reduce the practice of dollarization, which had been used as a strategy to alleviate inflationary pressures in the market. During the 2010s, the government implemented a policy that mandated the use of the lira. In the marketplace, the dollar and the euro have begun to supplant the lira as prominent currencies. Residential properties, automobiles, and rental accommodations are denominated in foreign currency. Alternatively, an increased demand for foreign reserves may exert pressure on the exchange rate. Therefore, it seems that the market is mostly operating with the assumption that the future value of the national currency may experience a substantial depreciation, resulting in higher prices. Consequently, Türkiye has undergone a transformation into a nation characterized by high costs. Certain goods in less developed nations may continue to exhibit higher price levels compared to those in developed ones. These categories may include electronics, motor vehicles, real estate, and staple foods. The government makes efforts to persuade the working class that their actions are aligned with the interests of the people while attributing any hindrances to their progress to the influence of the industrial sector. The existence of polarization and division between the working class and industry makes nations less appealing to investments and private enterprises. Liberal economics is predicated upon the principles of a free market framework and individual entrepreneurship. In nations characterized by significant division, there exists a view that such countries are not conducive to private enterprises, as their success becomes dependent not on market dynamics but on governmental determinations. Furthermore, the corporations themselves may become susceptible to economic populism, as they grapple with the challenges of elevated inflation, increased production costs, overvalued exchange rates, and a less efficient workforce.

How to reduce economic populism via institutional reform

Individual actors in the field of economics place a strong emphasis on the fulfillment of their own personal desires and requirements, often neglecting the larger collective interests of the nation as a whole. Putting an emphasis on their own interests is one of the ways that populist regimes attempt to establish legitimacy for their government. The focus of the working class, on the other hand, is to maximize their income without placing a significant amount of attention on production. In the meanwhile, industries are struggling to maintain output within surroundings that are protected and less competitive, and this struggle often comes at the expense of exploiting people. Commons (1925a) raised a critical inquiry on the ability of companies and the working class to have a shared interest. This topic has persisted for over a century. It was mentioned that discerning disparities between those who generate profits and those who got wages is challenging. These two entities are self-interest factions that actively pursue maximizing individual gains while minimizing benefits for others. The dilemma arises as to how the universal selfishness inherent in human nature may be effectively coordinated, given that each individual actor is driven by their own self-interest and, unintentionally, may inadvertently contribute to the collective benefit. Institutional economics aims to establish deliberate mechanisms that facilitate the realization or advancement of shared objectives. The advancement of human nature and its economic systems necessitates a greater reliance on scientific perspectives rather than relying only on natural processes. To mitigate the prevalence of economic populism, it is essential to implement substantial and transformative institutional reforms that effectively eradicate path dependency and establish a framework of institutional complementarity within economic policy. Undertaking this endeavor is challenging due to the potential consequences faced by each government, as they run the threat of losing their positions of authority. The political risk associated with initiating institutional reforms becomes significant in situations when the working class has a favorable position in the balance of power. Nevertheless, historical evidence demonstrates that nations have the capacity to enact institutional reforms in response to extreme situations. In the United Kingdom, throughout the 1980s, the government led by Thatcher demonstrated resistance toward the organized working class and proceeded to enact significant institutional reforms that facilitated the transition toward a free market–oriented economic system (Gregory, 1998). While the United Kingdom differs significantly from economically populist countries such as Argentina and Türkiye, it serves as an illustration of how change can be achieved by prioritizing the overall economic interests without being swayed by concerns about potential negative political consequences. This suggests that economic populism can persist in the foreseeable future until a politically dominant movement with resolute determination attains power. In other words, the initiation of institutional reform requires a strong political will.

Institutional change may be triggered by a profound acknowledgment of a societal issue, a reaction to an abrupt disaster like a financial crisis, or a coalition of interests trying to maintain or enhance their own authority. Furthermore, the process of institutional transformation is influenced by other elements, such as the influence of different groups, their strategies, and the strength of their ideas. For economic players involved in economic operations, it is essential to comprehend the nature of international or social consensus, public opinion, and institutions, as well as their evolving trends. To enhance their influence in the market, firms and workers must effectively interpret institutional dynamics and adapt accordingly. They may possess the capacity to participate in political lobbying with political parties, governments, and local authorities to advocate for a modification in the existing system that better corresponds with their objectives of expanding their own power and control. The justification for implementing political decisions might be based on popular opinion or the decision of the majority. These factors can be persuasive and empathetic to the working class and political authorities. Nevertheless, this dispute does not indicate the validity of an agreement in which one party asserts its superiority over the other. When undergoing institutional change, it is important to take into account the ethical standard for the process. This criterion should be determined by consensus and should not exclude players who lack authority. To make an appropriate choice, it is essential to have the consensus of different parties. However, it is important to note that public justifications for the legality of a decision may also have weaknesses. It is essential to convey the principles of scientific methodology to convince participants in institutional negotiations to reach an agreement that encompasses a wide variety of entities. The existence of the persuasion of the opposing party or interest groups with significant support or membership is possible. Hence, it is critical to present the most advantageous choice to both society and industry. The decision might get support from a significant portion of interest groups. The use of scientific methodologies in a justification case is necessary to establish the rationality of the institutional transformation (Fujita et al., 2023). Nevertheless, the mere act of communicating scientific data did not have the power to alter the choices made by economic actors. Therefore, a significant governmental decision should endorse the arguments and be employed to foster a consensus between the people and the industrial entities.

Argentina and Türkiye possess expansive territories, substantial populations, and abundant natural resources. Nevertheless, in the absence of significant institutional reforms, it seems improbable that these states can be capable of attaining the status of industrialized countries. Furthermore, if these nations persistently fail, it is likely that other countries with robust institutional frameworks would attain economic progress and surpass these economies. This suggests that these two countries may experience a relative lag or decline in contrast to others. Nevertheless, it is difficult to enact practical reforms within the current policy framework. If there is a lack of determination to establish a harmonious interaction among institutions, it is recommended to at least create settings that promote free market principles for workers, firms, and other participants in the economy. Establishing regulatory frameworks that effectively reward investment activity is crucial. It is imperative that governments that are accountable for the implementation of investment and welfare programs adjust their approach to satisfy the requirements of the circumstances. It is necessary to diminish the influence of lobbying organizations to establish an environment that promotes economic policies in the best interest of a nation. Furthermore, it is essential to structure domestic markets in accordance with global competitiveness. It is important to encourage foreign investments that have the potential to enhance productivity and foster innovation and imitation. Maintaining exchange rate stability in an economy characterized by a historical pattern of significant volatility and devaluations poses considerable challenges. The instance of Ecuador exemplifies this phenomenon. The nation underwent a significant institutional transformation by formally adopting the US dollar as its official currency in response to persistent inflation. Consequently, the influence of the exchange rate on inflation diminished. The nation successfully mitigated its inflationary issue, which had been exacerbated by fluctuations in its currency. Despite the stabilization of the exchange rate, the effects of wages may still be evident (Köse and Ünal, 2024). It is essential to implement substantial institutional modifications. The exchange rate may either be freely floating, devoid of any intervention or control, or it can be managed to promote productivity and investment. Furthermore, the acceptance of an official or alternative currency might serve as a means to mitigate the political influence exerted on the exchange rate. Ecuador's monetary system underwent complete dollarization. The nation that had significant challenges due to its corrupt exchange rate system witnessed a notable improvement in its macroeconomic performance, resulting in more stability.

In the realm of scholarly inquiry, it is often observed that populist research often lacks substantial recommendations for mitigating the prevalence of populism. The provided responses lack specificity and cannot be considered in a targeted manner. However, while examining the phenomenon of economic populism, it becomes much more feasible to locate the solutions. To address the issue of path dependency in developing nations' import substitution industrialization phases, it is imperative to implement institutional changes. These reforms should aim to reduce the reliance on previous patterns and establish a framework of institutional complementarity. It is essential to establish a stronger correlation between the rates of wage increase and productivity growth. The consideration of pluralism is warranted in the context of economic policy. Industries represent the upper echelons of the economic hierarchy. The working class comprises those who are engaged in labor-intensive occupations. The government fails to recognize the need of maintaining a balance of power among market participants. Therefore, it is essential to consider democracy while formulating economic policy. The neglect of industries and the consolidation of the working class are outcomes of policies pertaining to wages, currency rates, prices, and other macroeconomic imbalances. It is essential for governments to implement substantial institutional reforms to reinstate mediation within economic relationships. The implementation of radical institutional amendments resulted in the reinforcement and institutionalization of the wage–labor relationship. An explicit connection between the governing body and the people materialized. The creation of novel mediation mechanisms should be undertaken in accordance with the consideration of power dynamics.

Due to a lack of economic knowledge, individuals may support policies that are disadvantageous. Thus, it can be argued that populism attracts those who do not possess the requisite understanding to grasp the essential connection between the wage-inflation spiral and the economic growth patterns inside a country. Implementing impractical economic policies is more viable in a less informed society than in a democratic one. Therefore, it is necessary to have a thorough comprehension of economics to counteract the populist misuse of economic instruments. Populist governments begin their term by expressing their goal to strengthen economic growth, increase real earnings, and reduce unemployment. After the change in leadership, both markets and people may have an optimistic view of the future direction of the economy. It might be deemed that the basic policies were successfully implemented. For a short period of time, it may be possible to successfully control inflation and maintain currency rate stability. The issue at hand pertains to the tendency of politicians to formulate policies based on popular opinion. It is not permissible to express dissatisfaction over this matter. It is essential for the politician to exhibit responsiveness to the demands expressed by the people. This is a fundamental characteristic of democracy. Leaders aim to maintain the continued robustness of support for their government. It is essential for political representatives to not disregard the desires of mass constituents. Nevertheless, a significant concern arises from the fact that populist administrations employ economic instruments based on their own objectives, occasionally neglecting the potential consequences. The rationale for the infeasibility of policies and the ensuing consequences need elucidation. It is arguable that politicians may be misguided in their decision to embrace legislation aimed at mitigating political risks. The advocacy for economic populist measures may have significant appeal during electoral campaigns. It is possible to argue, on the other hand, that it would be unfair to impose the adverse effects of consequences on the working class. The adherence to rationality is vital. It is important to have policies that are supportive of scientific advancements and technological innovations.

The market consists of three participants. One prominent strategy employed by governments is the utilization of economic populism as a means to enhance their electoral influence. The working class constitutes a significant portion of the demographic that aligns with the demand side of populism. This course consistently advocates for the attainment of benefits and salary expansion without necessitating any kind of compromise or sacrifice. The corporate or industrial class, which is influenced by elitism, opposes the interests of the working class. Hence, Veblen postulates the emergence of a confrontation between the proletariat and the bourgeoisie, as envisioned by him, which has the potential to disrupt established societal structures and pave the way for the development of a technocratic regime. In the event of a prevailing industrial hegemony, that authority has the capacity to shape the market in alignment with its own vested interests. Nevertheless, to mitigate the predatory actions shown by politicians, elites, or the working class, it is critical to prioritize institutional reform rather than relying only on technocrats who lack the ability to obtain widespread support or effectively execute an alternative system. Commons highlighted the significance of power equilibrium and the division of power. In this scenario, it is imperative to acknowledge that the absence of a dominant actor necessitates the implementation of institutional reform to maintain equilibrium. The centralization of power in the hands of the government is essential for effective market regulation. The implementation of institutional change is expected to provide advantages for the government as well. To mitigate the presence of populism within the economy, it is essential to employ reasonable bargaining, foster institutional complementarity, and adopt a favorable growth model. This approach aims to foster scientific collectivism within the economy by diminishing the concentration of power and creating institutional power as the only governing structure. This type needs the endorsement of the working class or an in-depth understanding of the people.

The objective of enhancing trade unions was pursued to strengthen domestic consumption, leading to a subsequent increase in both the occurrence of strikes and the number of workdays missed due to strikes over time. Despite the significant increase in wages, the inflation rate increased due to the relative modest rate of domestic productivity growth. Due to this issue, deregulations significantly increased in developed countries. The main objective was to reduce the power of trade unions and move toward a more flexible mode of production. The United Kingdom was one of the leading countries to adopt deregulation measures under the control of Thatcher policies. In the 1980s, there was a significant rise in the adoption of liberal measures. As a part of this tendency, the minimum wage was eliminated until the late 1990s. Consequently, the United Kingdom had achievement in reducing the inflation rate (Ünal and Köse, 2019). Thatcherism successfully abolished wage and price controls by reducing government intervention in the market. These changes were brought about by the introduction of deregulation policies and the restriction of trade unions, with the goal of developing an economic system where price adjustments occurred within the context of a free market. The enactment of minimum wage legislation in the United Kingdom during the late 1990s was relatively uncomplicated when compared to Türkiye, where the presence of weak trade unions impeded the construction of efficient income rules. After the adoption of deregulation measures in the United Kingdom, trade unions, who had considerable influence on the economy, tried to resist newly enacted reforms. There was a perception of a state of confrontation between the government and the trade unions. From 1979 to 1990, the government that was headed by Thatcher implemented measures that significantly decreased the influence and strength of trade unions.

Income policies were introduced in Sweden at a period when trade unions had little power and were primarily engaged in collective bargaining. Consequently, the effect of trade unions on income policies was constrained. Additionally, the adoption of inflation targeting in 1993 was also taken into account. Even though Sweden does not have a minimum wage policy, the country has been able to maintain a favorable level of international competitiveness due to income policies that formed under wage increase following the productivity growth of export goods. This condition also indicates a prevailing agreement within the collective bargaining framework between trade unions and employer organizations over income programs. Even though Sweden experienced high inflation rates comparable to those experienced in the United Kingdom, the trade unions in Sweden were not the same as the trade unions in the United Kingdom. This is because Sweden was able to significantly restrain trade unions by enacting a social agreement that produced wage increase. Trade unions in the United Kingdom were not restrained in this way. In contrast to the United Kingdom, Sweden had a greater trade union density, indicating a larger percentage of its workforce being affiliated with labor unions. During the early 1990s, subsequent to Sweden's economic crisis, the government implemented measures to curtail industrial strikes and militancy shown by trade unions as well as to diminish the strength of social systems. Throughout the 1990s, there was a notable decline in the percentage of those employed in trade unions. As a consequence, the influence of trade unions in Sweden diminished throughout the 1990s (Ünal, 2017).

The first phase of a populist government is defined by the execution of expansionary policies, the supply of transfers and benefits, and a considerable rise in wage growth either during or after elections. The economy will ultimately reach a threshold where it becomes unable of enduring these practices for any longer. The simultaneous occurrence of rapid wage growth and an overvalued exchange rate might result in a bottleneck as an outcome of the exhaustion of foreign currency reserves. The central bank can employ currency depreciation as a strategy to tackle certain macroeconomic imbalances such as trade deficits. Alternatively, foreign reserves might be considered to maintain exchange rate stability, hence necessitating higher interest rates. However, it should be noted that this approach cannot be a comprehensive solution. The use of high interest rates has always been a strategic instrument in political discourse. If the central bank raises the interest rate by an amount greater than the rate of inflation, it will only have a temporary effect in reducing both inflation and the value of the currency. The challenge lies in the scarcity of foreign reserves inside the domestic economy, which is exacerbated by the implementation of expansive policies and escalating production costs. During periods of high inflation, the working class, who get the advantage of a policy that adjusts their wages to compensate for inflation, can request an increase in wage growth from the government. This can lead to a rise in economic expenses. There can be a depletion of the central bank's budget and reserve. One such strategy may be raising the interest rate to strengthen reserves or attract further speculative capital inflows. Ultimately, regardless of the chosen approach, the central bank should make the decision to devalue the currency.

The phenomenon of economic populism leads to the gradual decline of transient prosperity. Due to the implementation of expansionary policies, it becomes apparent that the budget deficit could not be adequately covered by tax revenues. Despite the government's efforts to address inflation and mitigate the depreciation of the currency rate to address the trade deficit, the wage policy remains unchanged. Therefore, inflation becomes a persistent component of the economy. The market is unable to sustain the implementation of unrealistic policies that have a negative effect on economic performance. At this juncture, a subsequent populist party asserts its intention to discontinue heterodox practices, instead advocating for the adoption of more advantageous policies by the government. Nevertheless, the subsequent administration, beginning its tenure with conventional policies, has to find sources of funding to enhance the prevailing economic circumstances. Wage growth is anticipated to experience a temporary period of suppression. Discontinuing populist initiatives would lead to a significant political change. The working class consents to these institutional and political changes because they consider the negative economic consequences of alternative economic policies to be even more unfavorable. In instances when a government assumes authority, the presence of political risk stemming from an imbalance of power may incentivize the opposing political party to implement economic populism as a strategy to secure political control. The recurrence of populist policies is contingent upon the absence of substantial institutional transformation. During the 1990s, the implementation of populist economic policies proved to be ineffective, ultimately leading to severe economic issues in Türkiye. The emergence of the economic crisis during the tenure of the left-wing party, namely during the Ecevit administration, resulted in a subsequent transfer of power to the succeeding government, which intended to establish equality, prosperity, liberal economic policies, and economic fairness.

Argentina and Türkiye have shown significantly improved performance throughout the 2000s. The nation witnessed an unprecedented surge in economic growth. The expansion of Türkiye had a striking similarity to that of China. Türkiye was presented as a model for other emerging nations in the Middle East and Europe. The country's economic success is not the only determinant of its overall standing, as its political structures, democratic institutions, and adherence to established laws all play significant roles. During that period, Türkiye fostered much stronger ties with the EU and other economically advanced nations worldwide. Both nations have had economic growth above 8%. This exceeded their potential rate of progress. The increase in exports led to a widening of the growth, emerging as a significant catalyst for economic development. However, after the global crisis of 2008, the nations experienced a decline in their economic performance. The trade imbalance witnessed a significant increase, particularly in the case of Türkiye, reaching an unprecedented level in 2011. The strong economic performance faded in the 2010s. The pace of growth experienced fell below their anticipated potential. Two nations have unequivocally failed to sustain favorable policies aimed at fostering innovation and modernization inside their respective economies in the global arena. Resentments within the society were instigated by a decline in economic performance. Consequently, administrations with populist tendencies attempted to attribute responsibility to international organizations while adhering to conspiracy theories. Nestor Kirchner and his wife Cristina Fernandez de Kirchner held foreign investors accountable and made limited efforts to diversify the country's economy beyond its heavy reliance on primary commodities. The scenario for Türkiye was similar. Moreover, global multinational firms witnessed a change in their decision-making process regarding the selection of their business locations in different countries. Furthermore, several multinational corporations decided to move to other locations. Insufficient evidence exists to support the adoption of practical techniques to improve institutional transformation and increase productivity via investments or technology transfers. Currently, there is no apparent plan to reduce the power of the working class and other interest groups that oppose reforms on the connection between wage and labor. Consequently, it is expected that there would be limited alteration in the composition of macroeconomic indicators in both countries.

Periodically, there appears to be a temporary decrease in populism within these countries. Nevertheless, it is certain that populism will often reemerge in the future. When the influence of populism has decreased, there is a clear disparity in the degree of involvement compared to nonelection years. Administrations often make a number of promises of generous policies over the course of the election campaign, which they hope to put into effect after they are elected by the people. Historical data indicate that it is too optimistic to assume that another political party can consistently embrace policies that are more advantageous and rational. The absence of institutional reform will result in a lack of discernible differentiation. It is difficult to conceive that a future administration would successfully address these issues and macroeconomic imbalances without enacting substantial changes. In those countries, it is anticipated that export prices will remain at elevated levels, while inflation is expected to continue as a persistent issue. Consequently, the implementation of populist measures will have detrimental effects on the working class. Individuals will experience the effects of reduced purchasing power, high inflation rates, and high unemployment rates. Two nations will maintain their current economic and GDP per capita levels without achieving any progress. Nevertheless, it is certain that emerging nations that exhibit more economic discipline, efficient organizational structures, and improved political systems would experience accelerated progress and enhance their influence within a very little timeframe. Political parties may be hesitant to confront political risks when it comes to making institutional reforms aimed at improving living conditions and stimulating productivity development. Populist leaders and political consultants may have a profound comprehension of the fact that the interventions of the government in the market, the exercise of control over economic tools, the diminisment of democratic processes, the disregard of institutional structures, and the adoption of particular rhetorical strategies are not the methods by which persistent issues can be addressed. Nonetheless, they are unwilling to undertake the necessary institutional reforms that are essential for the efficient transformation of the economy. Although the administration may maintain its position, it is crucial to recognize that it lacks the capacity to perform remarkable achievements that may radically change the conditions of the working class and the economy. Economic democracy may be limited in its extent. These countries lack the ability to successfully attract FDI and ease the transfer of technology necessary for the manufacturing of sophisticated industrial goods.

The emerging economies have more potential for growth compared to the industrialized economies that have already attained technological frontiers. Developed nations are actively looking for alternative avenues to foster innovation and embark on a new trajectory of technical advancement to reinvigorate economic growth. This phenomenon might be interpreted as Schumpeter's concept of creative destruction. Countries that strive for methods to enhance productivity are more likely to experience accelerated growth and wealth. The Chinese economy has been able to achieve this level of achievement during the last three decades. When examining the historical context of Argentina and Türkiye, it becomes evident that their economic development has consistently lagged behind that of East Asian nations. There are two approaches that might be examined to enhance production. The first step is generating demand from other nations. The initiative is expected to facilitate the expansion of exports in the realm of products and services. The use of high-tech items is not always a must. The increasing competitiveness within the low- and medium-tech product category is expected to result in a corresponding growth in export activities. To achieve the desired outcome, it is essential to formulate a growth model that is in line with institutional reforms that are intended to improve economic development. Another crucial factor to take into account is the inclusion of provisions for technological transfer. FDI may be attracted via the implementation of vertical integration strategies. Enforcing these policies may facilitate the development of the country.

In the absence of establishing equilibrium among economic actors, there exists the potential for the government to adopt populist policies in elections. Furthermore, parties possess the ability to modify the constitution and galvanize society toward more assertive and regressive approaches. Argentina and Türkiye have a lengthy historical record characterized by periods of unrest and crises. Holding a political identity is considered necessary to have sufficient courage to implement institutional reforms that drive countries toward becoming industrialized economies. Both nations possess abundant resources, significant development potential, and a youthful demographic that may propel their respective economies toward progress. It is recommended that governments undertake measures to diminish the influence wielded by interest groups, such as trade unions, extremist and populist ideologies, and elites who oppose the principles of pluralism and scientific collectivism. If the requisite institutional reforms are implemented, nations can expect a substantial surge in economic development, an increase in purchasing power, and a rise in employment opportunities.

Institutional decision-making should be grounded on the principles of representativeness, independence, transparency, and research capability aligned with the scientific process. Scientific methodology should be strictly adhered to by an independent commission. Therefore, the analytical formulation would serve as a solid foundation for policy formation, and ethical considerations regarding national interests would be necessary. Ethical concerns would diminish the actions aimed at advancing political objectives. This would lead to a reduction in the influence exerted by interest organizations and lobbyists. Therefore, researchers who follow scientific methodologies must reveal their identity and maintain neutrality to make essential contributions to society. Authorities have the ability to intervene in the decision-making process if there is a lack of scientific and compelling evidence in developing nations with weak institutional and social structures. A fundamental constraint of democracy is its inherent time limitations (Fujita et al., 2023). During fierce competition, political parties give more importance to their campaigns rather than focusing on resolving institutional issues that need a prolonged process of building consensus, particularly at the national level. The wage–labor relationship is an essential structure that requires a substantial amount of time to undergo institutional transformation and effectively assure the working class that their purchasing power would be protected. Political identities strive to evade implementing institutional reforms that would foster a more transparent, equitable, and evidence-based approach. Another crucial concern is the potential political risk. Implementing institutional reform can lead to discontent among certain factions who remain unconvinced about the actual state of the economy. The enduring nature of the unresolved political risk makes it a substantial and persistent concern. The issue pertains to the socioeconomic conditions. Institutional reforms may provoke societal resentments if they are implemented with the intention of diminishing the economic advantages of certain groups. The objective of neoliberalism is to diminish the influence of lobbyists or interest groups with divergent values in the market. Consequently, neoliberalism does not support democratic identities from the point of view of institutional economics, which tries to establish a consensus between various groups that are present in the market. In neoliberalism, there is no concern about the time constraint the democracy needs. Neoliberalism promotes the adoption of deregulation measures, the endorsement of free trade and competition, and the diminishment of state involvement in the market. Nevertheless, despite the Japanese economy's efforts to deregulate its market and establish huge global firms, it still faced significant economic stagnation for several decades. Given the absence of any potential for more deregulation, the ability to stimulate the economy has become limited. The frailty of democracy necessitates the establishment of institutional economics to bring about coordination and new reformation in the market (Fujita et al., 2023). Authoritarian governments have the capacity to promptly enact policies, even without the ability to develop a consensus or a realistic mechanism for initiating institutional reform. However, the implementation of institutional reforms requires the utilization of scientific methodology, a commitment to openness and transparency, the establishment of independence, the use of persuasive techniques, and the pursuit of a balance of power between different values. Therefore, political risks may be mitigated to pave the way for fundamental institutional reforms that would facilitate future advancement, even in the event of a change in the governing party. This approach might potentially reduce the long-standing issue that has persisted for decades when various political parties have obtained power but have been hesitant to enact institutional reform.

The reason why the pluralist worldview increases the chance of undesired lawmaking is due to its inherent nature. In republican approaches to politics, laws must be justified by logical reasoning and rational justifications. They cannot simply be advocated for or be the result of self-interested negotiations. Legislation cannot be solely justified based on arguments that just concern an individual's private interests. Political actors are required to provide a rationale for their decisions by appealing to a wider concept of the common good. This condition imposes a regulatory influence on the kind of initiatives that may be suggested and implemented. The inclusion of an obligation to provide arguments that are relevant to the public interest may increase the probability of the successful implementation of legislation. In this perspective, it is crucial to ensure that socioeconomic groups, particularly those who are disadvantaged, are not hindered from asserting their own interests in the political sphere. The primary objective of political discourse is to empower these organizations to achieve change by exactly engaging in such activities. The idea of a civic public relies on rejecting diversity and embracing the notion of transcending one's circumstances. These unrealistic expectations hinder the possibility of achieving positive change. An approach to politics that aims to exclude such matters from the political sphere, to function based on a fiction of shared identity, and to eliminate interests that exist outside of politics leads to unproductive outcomes. The opposite of deliberation is the imposition of results by private groups with self-interest and political power. The republican approach highlights that deliberative processes are frequently undermined by intimidation, strategic and manipulative actions, collective action issues, adaptive preferences, or, more generally, disparities in political influence (Sunstein, 1988). The discussion criterion is intended to guarantee that political results are endorsed based on a consensus or, at the very least, a widespread agreement among individuals with equal political standing.

To avoid the influence of interest groups and pursue a more objective approach, one strategy is to establish a commission tasked with identifying an appropriate justification and rationality. The commission is an institutional approach employed by Commons to deal with the economic challenges in Wisconsin.[1] Commons aligned more closely with Veblen's perspective, with a heightened focus on the issues faced by the working class throughout the twentieth century. Industrial accidents resulting from increased industrial output and technical breakthroughs led to significant social and economic losses. Commons was appointed as an actor to assess the issue. The institutional form employed an advanced form by merging safety standards with an insurance program to improve cost savings and safety conditions. Another innovation was the implementation of a legal system that operates under the authority of a commission. The new institutional entity had the authority to modify legislation in accordance with safety regulations, which might result in cost reduction. Industries expressed opposition to these reforms due to their concerns. Nevertheless, the commission members were able to identify and mitigate the hazards without causing any extra security issues. Public campaigns were created to enhance workplace safety. Furthermore, this commission had a major role in the development of the unemployment insurance legislation (Fujita et al., 2023). The commission should ensure its independence by autonomously choosing its members rather than allowing authorities and lobbyists, who may exert influence over the negotiating process. The commission's independent scientific approach should aim to enhance consensus and discussions among parties involved in economic issues. The independent commission approach may serve as a robust institutional method to foster agreement and facilitate the decision-making process. However, this approach also has its limitations since the independent commission may not always be really independent, especially in nations with a powerful working class and a government that has a solid institutional foundation. Thus, it is crucial to establish a commission in these nations that can adhere to a rigorous scientific approach grounded on a well-defined framework. Therefore, it is essential to support the institutional form in these nations with market dynamics and strategies that may minimize the influence of political parties. An autonomous institutional commission naturally expands its scope beyond economic and technical assessments to include social and ethical considerations. The ethical dilemmas may be examined on a nationwide scale, including both the industries and the people within the community. In other words, the decision-making process should prioritize the welfare of the country rather than the interests of a certain group or political entity.

The current macroeconomic conditions are inadequate in terms of enhancing the competitive standing of nations vis-à-vis their trade counterparts and fostering a favorable position in Argentina and Türkiye. The conditions give rise to elevated levels of inflation, increased volatility in the currency rate, a substantial trade imbalance, sluggish growth in exports, and diminished competitive power. These outcomes are inadvertent ramifications of pursuing a steady development trajectory. The majority of the partner nations had more favorable and competitive macroeconomic conditions. The issue that emerged was the escalation of production costs due to the rapid increase in wage rates, which exceeded the growth in productivity of exported goods. Additionally, the implementation of monetary policies, along with income policies, resulted in the overvalued currency. The unsatisfactory outcomes of macroeconomic factors can be attributed to a power asymmetry among the government, trade unions, and employer' associations. These entities constantly emphasize their own interests instead of collaborating toward a common objective, which can be achieved by a mathematical-based social contract referred to as tripartism. The high production costs might be attributed to the absence of a social contract among the three actors, which is a result of path dependency and sluggish institutional reforms. The countries need to adopt new institutional reforms in their income policies and exchange rate systems to converge toward a shared objective, therefore mitigating the influence of individual interests and taking into account the global standing of their respective economies. To address the economic challenges faced by nations arising from the absence of complementarity in wage–labor relations and the exchange rate system, it is possible to organize the political ramifications of these issues within the framework of a mathematical-based social contract. This economic approach provides two distinct advantages. To begin with, the reduction of the currency's volatility in connection to overvaluation, which is driven by short-term capital inflows, can be achieved via institutional adjustments in wage–labor relations. This can result in a more stable exchange rate. Furthermore, the implementation of the institutional reform would enhance the competitive capabilities. However, to successfully adopt such a system, both nations need to undergo significant institutional transformations in their wage–labor relations. The establishment of institutional complementarity between exchange rate and wage growth policies is crucial for addressing economic vulnerability. Neglecting to take action might result in a decline in the PPP and perhaps lead to the breakdown of controlled exchange rate regulations, worsening the economic difficulties experienced by these nations. Effective implementation of wage growth programs requires a mathematical framework that is firmly rooted in a social compact between the government, trade unions, and employers' associations. This social contract is the outcome of a tripartite negotiation process.

The use of a mathematical foundation in the formulation of a social contract becomes imperative in facilitating institutional transformations due to the identified issue of disproportionate wage rate increase within the economy, coupled with concurrent political obstacles. The issue of power asymmetry in income policies arises from multiple factors, including the actions of trade unions, which employ strikes and advocate for industrial action in addition to exerting political and social pressure. Furthermore, the government's continued presence and control over national-level income policies also contribute to this problem. The government's substantial involvement in income policies, which has had a significant impact, ought to have been designed in accordance with inflation targeting. However, this endeavor was unsuccessful as a result of social and political movements. Governments have historically pursued populist wage growth policies primarily driven by their own self-interests, such as securing votes. These short-term wage growth measures have failed to establish the required institutional complementarity that strikes a balance between the growth of wage rates and the productivity growth of export goods. This lack of institutional complementarity undermines the effectiveness of these policies in achieving optimal outcomes. The government's decision-making process was impacted by social and political movements spearheaded by trade unions due to their significant influence in income programs. Consequently, the government has become a prime target for demands to boost wages. Because of this issue, there was persistent inflation, which was further fueled by high manufacturing costs and significant devaluations. The government continues to have a significant role in an economy characterized by rigid wage increases that surpass those observed across multiple nations. Hence, it is essential to implement novel institutional reforms aimed at mitigating economic fragility and addressing the issue of inflation. These reforms should aim to establish a more equitable distribution of power among players involved in income policies, thereby fostering the development of a more robust and inclusive economy that minimizes disadvantages. To effectively address economic challenges, it is essential to implement substantial institutional reforms within the framework of tripartite negotiations. The negotiation of tripartism should be structured in an approach that aligns with the growth of wage rates associated with the productivity growth of export goods. An enduring institutional norm has been established between the government and the working class, which has been deeply rooted in the economy for decades. The prevailing standard is that the policy for determining wages should be based on the inflation rate. The drawback of this institutional form is that it might lead to a wage-inflation spiral during periods of sluggish economic growth. Hence, it is vital for the government to implement an institutional reform that aligns wage growth with productivity. There is a need to establish an institutional reform that is founded on a strong scientific agreement that takes into account productivity growth via a mathematical resolution. This approach aims to mitigate the individual interests of the involved parties and facilitate the implementation of a cohesive income policy that can establish an adjustment mechanism within the exchange rate system. Furthermore, this mathematical foundation of a social contract can be employed in international trade, taking into account economic and political circumstances, to provide benefits for all three parties involved in determining the growth of wage rates.

Although wage-setting policy may not successfully reduce the competitive gap between a strongly export-oriented country and populist countries, its adoption might be regarded as a strategy to improve competitiveness versus other nations. This may be accomplished by reducing the rise of ULC in the export industry to a certain degree, thereby better aligning it with current economic realities. Applying mathematical methods to create a social contract can offer valuable insights into the inquiries. Specifically, formulating income policies grounded on a mathematical framework of the social contract has the potential to foster a beneficial economic environment. First, it is anticipated that this suggested institutional change would result in a reduction in the growth rate in the ULC for export goods. Second, there is potential for trade unions to embrace this change as it promotes convergence among individuals. Third, the introduction of this modification can enhance the stability of the exchange rate by protecting it against extreme devaluation or overvaluation via the creation of a defined range. Fourth, it has the potential to mitigate inflation to some extent and reduce the excessive consumption of imported goods. Fifth, it could enhance the competitive advantage of countries and contribute to the growth of export goods. Finally, while it may not offer a comprehensive solution to the trade-deficit problem faced by export-led growth countries, it does present a potential avenue for reducing the trade deficit and alleviating the current account deficit to a certain degree.

Note

1 United States Commission on Industrial Relations (1916) Industrial Relations. Final report and testimony, Vol. 1, Washington, U.S. Government Printing Office.

11 Conclusion

Populism stands in contrast to liberal economics, communist economics, and institutional economics. The tenets of economic populism are in opposition to the preferences and mechanisms of the market. In the presence of economic populism, the pursuit of institutional improvements becomes ineffective due to the probability of path dependency and an absence of institutional complementarity. The ultimate objective of economic populism is to exercise control over all institutional forms to mold the economy in the service of gaining political popularity. In the end, if there is no balance of power among players, it prevents the formation of an advantageous condition at the national level. The prolonged duration of this phenomenon may be attributed to the existence of dysfunctional institutional forms. To create institutional reform, it is essential to make radical, courageous, and revolutionary actions, while relying just on authority is insufficient to accomplish this objective. The need for institutional reform should not be misconstrued as endorsing the elimination of unionization and left-wing activities. The current strategy being used is deemed inadequate. Furthermore, it is not indicative that liberalism ought to exert hegemony over economic interactions. This book demonstrates the need of establishing a system that ensures a proper equilibrium of power and delineates clear boundaries between economic participants. When one economic actor acquires influence over others, it tends to diminish the pluralistic nature of the interaction. The potential implementation of radical deregulation policies and exclusive support for industrial economic activity may not directly result in economic populism. However, it is important to recognize that such policies might give rise to a distinct kind of economic populism characterized by reduced salaries, increased tax burdens, unemployment, immigration challenges, and heightened risks. Therefore, it is critical to implement a strategy that ensures an equilibrium of power among the entities. Otherwise, government control over economic instruments can continue to exist. To mitigate this issue, it is imperative to develop a social contract grounded in mathematical principles. Utilizing a scientific methodology in the pursuit of institutional transformation has significant potential for effectively addressing economic imbalances within a given nation.

The wage is a significant political instrument that may be effectively employed by both the government and trade unions. The primary objective of political parties is to secure electoral support or address societal dissatisfaction via the use of wage mechanisms. However, this approach might inadvertently exacerbate social

DOI: 10.4324/9781003438090-11

discontent, as an excessive rise in wages disconnected from productivity growth rates can further stimulate macroeconomic challenges. The primary objective of trade unions is to endeavor to maintain a high rate of wage rise. To achieve this objective, organizations often strive to maintain a high level of employee engagement by using the inflation rate as a basis for determining compensation increase, aiming to surpass the inflationary threshold. In contrast, employers' associations endeavor to maximize employer satisfaction by advocating for minimal wage increase. Due to this rationale, the players engaged in a conflictual dynamic as they endeavor to protect their own interests while determining the pace of wage growth. This phenomenon has the potential to adversely impact the economy and diminish the country's competitive edge in the global trade arena. Therefore, it is essential to construct a mutually acceptable agreement that effectively addresses the issue among the three parties involved and meets the individual needs and interests of each party. The proposed solution to address the interests of all actors, maintain equilibrium in global trade, and promote the establishment of a stable currency rate and minimal inflation is the Mathematical Based Social Contract. This contract posits an agreement, whereby the rate of wage growth is advocated to be contingent upon the rate of increase in export productivity (Ünal, 2017, 2021a). The institutional norms that dictate wage increase in accordance with inflation provide a significant barrier to addressing the issue of inflation. Indexing wage growth with the inflation rate might lead to a wage-inflation spiral. Specifically, during a time of sluggish economic growth, inflation might be further boosted. This implies that the issue of chronic inflation may persist for decades. Therefore, it is essential to implement institutional reforms to alter the view of the relationship between wage growth and inflation. Instead, institutional reform should implement a very effective alternative that prioritizes productivity growth above inflation. While examining wage growth in a nation, it is important to take into account the increase in productivity or output.

The strategy that connects wage growth rates to export productivity growth rates is regarded as a suitable approach in the context of international trade. This policy ensures that export prices remain stable and that the exchange rate maintains equilibrium over an extended period. One of the primary concerns is the absence of a strong correlation between the rate of wage growth and the growth rate of export productivity. Maintaining wage growth at a level consistent with the pace of export productivity can effectively mitigate the macroeconomic imbalance. The gap between the wage growth rate and the domestic productivity growth rate may be narrowed by basing wage increase on export productivity growth. Therefore, it is anticipated that the inflation rate will continue to be at a low level, enabling trade unions to get a wage rise that surpasses the inflation rate. Furthermore, this agreement serves to address macroeconomic imbalances and foster a heightened level of economic stability. It may no longer serve as a detrimental element impacting politicians and will effectively mitigate societal unhappiness stemming from macroeconomic instability. Employers' associations play a crucial role in curbing the independent rise of labor cost growth in relation to export productivity growth. This is achieved via the implementation of balanced wage increase, which protect industries against the loss of competitiveness in the realm of international trade. Consequently, these unions contribute to the establishment of favorable economic circumstances.

The prospect of revolutionary change rests on either a political party willing to embrace strategic risk-taking or on the people who are willing to relinquish populist notions that perpetuate socioeconomic disparities and inequality. The existing system has a multitude of adverse effects on the people. There are times when it may be essential to contemplate terminating the employment of certain individuals, especially when the pace at which wages increase exceeds the rate at which productivity increases. The escalation of unemployment is an inevitable consequence. In other words, it is anticipated that a considerable degree of inequality would ensue, resulting in a reduction in purchasing power parity for people belonging to the working class, attributable to inflationary pressures. Hence, it is imperative to persuasively sway politicians across the ideological spectrum, including both the left and right, to adopt policies that promote economic liberalization and are in harmony with prevailing economic frameworks. When contemplating ways to increase productivity, one effective strategy is to reduce wage growth. Governments should undertake steps to boost production and stimulate demand for domestically produced items. It is crucial to prioritize competitiveness, efficiency, and innovation. Policymakers should take into account democratic principles, societal advancement, and strict adherence to legal principles. There is a need for enhancements in these particular domains.

Populism is characterized by its opposition to the pluralistic nature of Commons and the elitist tendencies identified by Veblen. Veblen posited the notion that the economy is subject to the influence and control of technologically proficient engineers or workers. While he did not explicitly address the issue of technocratic elitism, his perspective on the contemporary technology revolution has the potential to foster the emergence of a dominant social class that may exclude other societal groups. Veblen's implication might be characterized as a kind of scientific collectivism. He did not specifically state that the working class would be disregarded since they were unable to ascertain a viable means of ensuring the inclusion and representation of this socioeconomic group. The discussion of Commons revolved on the significance of institutional economics in establishing and maintaining a state of equilibrium in power dynamics. The concept of the division of power is important to establish a state of equilibrium. Therefore, the establishment of a balanced distribution of authority across the several identities is critical to achieve a scientifically cohesive society. From a theoretical standpoint, institutional economics may be characterized as a pluralistic discipline that tries to identify an optimal equilibrium between players who possess varying degrees of power. Implementing institutional changes might be employed to assess the exertion of more power on a different party. This action has the capacity to destabilize the balance of power. Populism emerges in this scenario when a ruling entity deliberately works to strengthen its own power and advance its own interests to implement institutional reform. Therefore, the rise of economic populism can be credited to the introduction of institutional changes. Economic populism develops as a consequence of the birth of institutional changes. Hence, it is necessary to implement institutional reforms to achieve compromise among the players in that particular situation. The implementation of institutional reform has the potential to establish a harmonious distribution of authority and division of authority via the establishment of a system of scientific collectivism in the realms of production and consumption. In both nations, wage growth is determined by taking into account inflation. Populist administrations endeavor to augment wages at a higher rate than the prevailing inflationary levels. This phenomenon contributes to the occurrence of a wage-inflation spiral. Furthermore, a lack of power equilibrium exists among the government, the working class, and industry. The government has the ability to employ economic tactics at any given moment to appeal to the people and strategically influence them for their political objectives. Ultimately, these nations are unable to achieve growth and advancement comparable to countries at the forefront of technological frontiers. To successfully accomplish institutional reform, it is essential to adopt both a scientific collectivist approach and a balance of power. It is suggested that the two nations discontinue the implementation of traditional wage-setting policies. It is not appropriate to associate wage growth to inflation. This phenomenon leads to an increase in the price of exported goods as well as non-tradable goods. They need to come up with a method that is supported by greater scientific evidence. In essence, the implementation of wage-setting policy should align with the rate of productivity increase. The implementation of wage growth aligned with productivity growth has the potential to enhance competitiveness in the realm of international trade. Furthermore, it is essential to pursue institutional reforms that have previously been constrained to dissolve the connection between populist governments and the working class. There should be a broad consensus to implement new institutional reforms aimed at reducing the excessive influence of the government on the working class to address economic issues. In this way, the principle of the separation of powers may be maintained, facilitating the establishment of a delicate equilibrium among the government, the working class, and industries. Alternatively, if populist governments persist in using minimum wage, pensions, bonuses, transfers, and taxes in the economy without adhering to a scientific methodology, certain consequences may ensue.

This book endeavors to elucidate the distinct challenges faced by populist economies. It aims to establish a framework for implementing novel institutional reforms pertaining to wage–labor relations and an exchange rate system. These reforms are based on a macroeconomic model that is tailored to foster wage rate growth and enhance productivity. Nevertheless, it is important to note that the examination of nations should not be confined just to these elements within the context of institutional economics, since this discipline comprises a wide range of ideas and theoretical approaches. Understanding the foundational principles of institutional economics, as established by Commons and Veblen, is crucial for effectively describing the current state of affairs.

References

Abrams, B.A. and Butkiewicz, J.L. (2017) The Political Economy of Wage and Price Controls: Evidence from the Nixon Tapes, *Public Choice*, 170: 63–78.

Aglietta, M. (1979) *A Theory of Capitalist Regulation: The US Experience*, Trans. David Fernbach, Verso, London.

Amable, B. (2016) Institutional Complementarities in the Dynamic Comparative Analysis of Capitalism, *Journal of Institutional Economics*, 12(1): 79–103.

Amin, A. (2000) *Post-Fordism: Models, Fantasies and Phantom of Transition, Post-Fordism: A Reader*, Blackwell Publishers, Oxford.

Anselmi, M. (2018) *Populism: An Intorduction*, Routledge, New York.

Atkinson, G. (2007) Pecuniary Institutions: Their Role and Effects, in J.T. Knoedler, R.E. Prasch and D.P. Champlin (eds.) *Thorstein Veblen and the Revival of Free Market Capitalism*, Edward Elgar Publishing, Cheltenham, pp. 69–86.

Aytaç, S. and Öniş, Z. (2014) Varieties of Populism in a Changing Global Context: The Divergent Paths of Erdogan and Kirchnerismo, *Comparative Politics*, 47(1): 41–59.

Balassa, B. (1964) The Purchasing-Power Parity Doctrine: A Reappraisal, *Journal of Political Economy* 72(6): 584–596.

Barr, R.R. (2009) Populists, Outsiders and Anti-Establishment Politics, *Party Politics*, 15(1): 29–48.

Barros, S. (2005) The Discursive Continuities of the Menemist Rupture, in F. Panizza (eds.) *Populism and the Mirror of Democracy*, Verson, New York.

Barone, G. and Kreuter, H. (2021) Low-Wage Import Competition and Populist Backlash: The Case of Italy, *European Journal of Political Economy*, 67: 101970.

Bazdresch, C. and Levy, S. (1990) Populism and Economic Policy in Mexico, 1970–1982, in R. Dornbusch and S. Edwards (eds.) *The Macroeconomics of Populism in Latin America*, The University of Chicago Press, Chicago and London.

Beccaria, L. and Carciofi, R. (1982) The Recent Experience of Stabilising and Opening Up the Argentinian Economy, *Cambridge Journal of Economics*, 6(2): 145–165.

Beccaria, L. and Groisman, F. (2015) Informality and Labour Market Segmentation: The Case of Argentina, *CEPAL Review*, 117: 121–136.

Beckerman, P. (1995) Central-Bank 'Distress' and Hyperinflation in Argentina, 1989–90, *Journal of Latin American Studies*, 27(3): 663–682.

Bernanke, B.S. (2012) *Opening Remarks: Monetary Policy Since the Onset of the Crisis*, Jackson Hole Economic Policy Symposium, Federal Reserve Bank of Kansas City.

Boyer, R. (1990) *The Regulation School: A Critical Introduction*, Trans. C. Charney, Columbia University Press, New York.

Boyer, R. and Hollingsworth, J.R. (1997) The Variety of Institutional Arrangements and Their Complementarity in Modern Economies, in R. Boyer and J.R. Hollingsworth (eds.) *Contemporary Capitalism: The Embeddedness of Institutions*. Cambridge University Press, Cambridge, UK, pp. 49–54.

Boyer, R. and Yamada, T. (2000) Introduction: A Puzzle for Economic Theories, in R. Boyer and T. Yamada (eds.) *Japanese Capitalism in Crisis: A Regulationist Interpretation.* Routledge, London, pp. 1−16.

Boyer, R. (2005) Coherence, Diversity, and the Evolution of Capitalism-The Institutional Complementarity Hypothesis, *Evolutionary and Institutional Economics Review*, 2(1): 43–80.

Boyer, R. and Saillard, Y. (2002) A Summary of Regulation Theory, in R. Boyer and Y. Saillard (eds.) *Regulation Theory: The State of the Art*, Trans. C. Shread, Routledge, London, pp. 36–44.

Boxill, B. (1997) Populism and Elitism in African-American Political Thought, *The Journal of Ethics*, 1(3): 209–238.

Bromley, D.W. (2006) *Sufficient Reason: Volitional Pragmatism and the Meaning of Economic Institutions*, Princeton University Press, Princeton, NJ.

Burke, M. and Malloy, J.M. (1974) From National Populism to National Corporatism: The Case of Bolivia (1952–1970), *Studies in Comparative International Development*, 9: 49–73.

Campano, A.R. (1966) The Minimum Wage Act in Argentina, *International Labour Review*, 94(3): 237–254.

Canovan, M. (1981) *Populism*, New York: Hartcourt Brace Janovich.

Canovan, M. (1999) Trust the People! Populism and the Two Faces of Democracy, *Political Studies*, 47(1): 2–16.

Cavallo, A. (2013) Online and Official Price Indexes: Measuring Argentina's Inflation, *Journal of Monetary Economics*, 60: 152–165.

Chasse, J.D. (2017) *A Worker's Economist: John R. Commons and His Legacy from Progressivism to the War on Poverty*, Routledge, London.

Checchi, D. (1996) Macroeconomic Populism: A Formal Representation and A Suggested Interpretation of the Peruvian Experience (1985–1990), *Journal of International Development*, 8(4): 489–516.

Craig, B. and Waller, C.J. (2004) Dollarization and Currency Exchange, *Journal of Monetary Economics*, 51: 671–689.

Commons, J.R. (1924) *Legal Foundations of Capitalism*, The Macmillan Company, New York.

Commons, J.R. (1925a) Marx Today: Capitalism and Socialism, *Atlantic Monthly*, 136: 682–693.

Commons, J.R. (1925b) The True Scope of Unemployment Insurance, *American Labor Legislation Review*, 15: 33–44.

Commons, J.R. (1931) Institutional Economics, *American Economic Review*, 21: 648–657.

Commons, J.R. (1934) *Institutional Economics*, The Macmillan Company, New York.

Commons, J.R. (1936) Institutional Economics, *American Economic Review*, 26: 237–249.

Davidson, L.S. (1983) The Macroeconomic Impact of the Nixon Wage and Price Controls: A General Equilibrium Approach, *Journal of Macroeconomics*, 5(4): 399–420.

Davila, L.R. (2000) The Rise and Fall and Rise of Populism in Venezuela, *Bulletin of Latin American Research*, 19: 223–238.

De la Torre, C. (2017) Trump's Populism: Lessons from Latin America, *Postcolonial Studies*, 20(2): 187–198.

De la Torre, C. (2000) *Populist Seduction in Latin America: The Ecuadorian Experience*, Ohio University Center for International Studies, Research in International Studies Latin America Series, No: 32.

Dent, C.M. (2020) Brexit, Trump and Trade: Back to a Late 19th Century Future? *Competition & Change*, 24(3–4): 338–357.

Dornbusch, R. and Edwards, S. (1991) The Macroeconomic of Populism, in R. Dornbusch and S. Edwards (eds.) *The Macroeconomics of Populism in Latin America*, The University of Chicago Press, Chicago and London.

Edwards, S. (2010) *Left Behind: Latin America and the False Promise of Populism*, The University of Chicago Press, Chicago and London.

Etchemendy, S. and Garay, C. (2011) Argentina: Left Populism in Comparative Perspective, 2003–2009, in S. Levitsky and K.M. Roberts (eds.) *The resurgence of the Latin American Left*, The John Hopkins University Press, Baltimore, pp. 283–305.

Finchelstein, F. (2017) *From Fascism to Populism in History*, University of California Press, Oakland, CA.

Finchelstein, F. (2018) Fascism and Populism, in C.D. Torre (eds.) *Routledge Handbook of Global Populism*, Routledge, Oxon and New York.

Fujita, S., Kitagawa, K. and Uni, H. (2023) *Lectures on Modern Institutional Economics*, Nakanishiya, Kyoto.

Galiani, S. and Somaini, P. (2018) Path-Dependent Import-Substitution Policies: The Case of Argentina in the Twentieth Century, *Latin American Economic Review*, 27: 5.

Glückler, J. (2020) Institutional Context and Place-Based Policy: The Case of Coventry & Warwickshire, *Growth and Change*, 51(1): 234–255.

Goldfajn, I., Martínez, L. and Valdés, R.O. (2021) Washington Consensus in Latin America: From Raw Model to Straw Man, *Journal of Economic Perspectives*, 35(3): 109–132.

Greenspan, A. (2004) Risk and Uncertainty in Monetary Policy, *American Economic Review*, 94(2): 33–40.

Gregory, M. (1998) Reforming the Labour Market: An Assessment of the UK Policies of the Thatcher Era, *The Australian Economic Review*, 31(4): 329–344.

Groppo, A. (2009) *The Two Princes: Juan D. Perón and Getulio Vargas: A Comparative Study of Latin American Populism*, Eduvim, Villa Maria.

Gruncy, A.G. (1973) Law, Politics, and Institutional Economics, *Journal of Economic Issues*, 7(4): 623–643.

Harvey, D. (1991) *The Condition of Postmodernity: An Enquiry into the Origins of Cultural Change*, Blackwell Publishers, Cambridge.

Hawkins, K.A. (2010) *Venezuela's Chavismo and Populism in Comparative Perspective*, Cambridge University Press, New York.

Hicks, J.R. (1963) *The Theory of Wages*, Palgrave Macmillan, Toronto, pp. 1–22.

Hicks, J. (1989) *A Market Theory of Money*, Oxford University Press, New York.

Inglehart, R.F. (1977) *The Silent Revolution: Changing Values and Political Styles among Western Publics*, Princeton University Press, Princeton.

Inglehart, R.F. and Norris, P. (2016) *Trump, Brexit, and the Rise of Populism: Economic Have-Nots and Cultural Backlash*, Faculty Research Working Paper Series, RWP16-026, Harvard Kennedy School, Cambridge.

Ivaldi, G. (2019) Populism in France, in D. Stockemer (eds.) *Populism around the World: A Comparative Perspective*, Springer, Cham.

Jagers, J. and Walgrave, S. (2007) Populism as Political Communication Style: An Empirical Study of Political Parties' Discourse in Belgium, *European Journal of Political Research*, 46: 319–345.

Jackson, G. and Deeg, R. (2008) From Comparing Capitalisms to the Politics of Institutional Change, *Review of International Political Economy*, 15(4): 680–709.

Jessop, B. (1990) *State Theory: Putting the Capitalist State in Its Place*, Polity Press, Cambridge, pp. 74–76.

Jessop, B. and Sum, N.L. (2006) *Beyond the Regulation Approach: Putting Capitalist Economies in Their Place*, Edward Elgar Publishing, Cheltenham.

Jordan, D.C. (1977) *Argentina's Military Government, Current History, 72(424)*, University of California Press, Latin America.

Kaltwasser, C.R. (2018) Studying the (Economic) Consequences of Populism, *AEA Papers and Proceedings*, 108: 204–207.

Kaufman, R.R. and Stallings, B. (1991) The Political Economy of Latin American Populism, in R. Dornbusch and S. Edwards (eds.) *The Macroeconomics of Populism in Latin America*, The University of Chicago Press, Chicago and London.
Kenworthy, E. (1973) The Function of the Little-Known Case in Theory Formation or What Peronism Wasn't, *Comparative Politics*, 6(1): 17–45.
Krugman, P. (2009) *The Return of Depression Economics and the Crisis of 2008*, W.W. Norton and Company, New York.
Köse, N. and Ünal, E. (2021) The Effects of the Oil Price and Oil Price Volatility on Inflation in Turkey, *Energy*, 226: 120392.
Köse, N. and Ünal, E. (2024) The Effects of the Oil Price and Temperature on Food Inflation in Latin America, *Environment, Development and Sustainability*, 26: 3269–3295.
Köse, N., Ünal, E. and Gayaker, S. (2024) Time-Varying Effects of the Gold Price and the Oil Price on Imports in Turkey, *Asia-Pacific Journal of Accounting & Economics*: 1–20. https://doi.org/10.1080/16081625.2023.2298928
Levi, M. (1997) A Model, a Method, and a Map: Rational Choice in Comparative and Historical Analysis, in M.I. Lichbach and A.S. Zuckerman (eds.) *Comparative Politics: Rationality, Culture, and Structure*, Cambridge University Press, Cambridge.
Levitsky, S. and Loxton, J. (2013) Populism and Competitive Authoritarianism in the Andes, *Democratization*, 20(1): 107–136.
Lipietz, A. (1987) *Mirages and Miracles: The Crises of Global Fordism*, Trans. David Macey, Thetford Press, London.
Little, W. (1973) Party and State in Peronist Argentina, 1945–1955, *The Hispanic American Historical Review*, 53(4): 644–662.
Lyrintzis, C. (1987) The Power of Populism: The Greek Case, *European Journal of Political Research*, 15: 667–686.
Mahoney, J. (2001) *The Legacies of Liberalism: Path Dependence and Political Regomes in Central America*, The Johns Hopkins University Press, Baltimore.
Manzetti, L. (1999) Review: The Politics of Socioeconomic Change in Argentina, *Latin American Research Review*, 34(3): 166–178.
Moffitt, B. (2016) *The Global Rise of Populism: Performance, Political Style, and Representation*, Stanford University Press, Stanford.
Mouffe, C. (2005) The 'End of Politics' and the Challenge of Right-Wing Populism, in F. Panizza (eds.) *Populism and the Mirror of Democracy*, Verso, London, pp. 50–71.
Müller, J. (2016) *What Is Populism?* University of Pennsylvania Press, Philadelphia.
Mudde, C. (2004) The Populist Zeitgeist, *Government and Opposition*, 39(4): 541–563.
Mudde, C. and Kaltwasser, C.R. (2017) *Populism: A Very Short Introduction*, Oxford University Press, Oxford.
Mudde, C. and Kaltwasser, C.R. (2012) Populism and (Liberal) Democracy: A Framework for Analysis, in C. Mudde and C.R. Kaltwasser (eds.) *Populism in Europe and the Americas: Threat or Corrective for Democracy?* Cambridge University Press, Cambridge, pp. 1–26.
Muno, W. (2019) Populism in Argentina, D. Stockemer (eds.) *Populism around the World: A Comparative Perspective*, Springer, Cham.
Nakakubo, H. (2015) Industrial Action and Liability in Japan: A Legal Overview, *Japan Labor Review*, 12(2): 86–105.
Nataraj, G. and Sahoo, P. (2003) Argentina's Crisis: Causes and Consequences, *Economic and Political Weekly*, 38(17): 1641–1644.
Panizza, F. (2005) *Introduction: Populism and the Mirror of Democracy*, Verson, London.
Panizza, F. and Miorelli, R. (2009) Populism and Democracy in Latin America, *Ethics & International Affairs*, 23(1): 39–46.
Pappas, T.S. (2014) Populist Democracies: Post-Authoritarian Greece and Post-Communist Hungary, *Government and Opposition*, 49(1): 1–23.
Pion-Berlin, D. (1985) The Fall of Military Rule in Argentina: 1976–1983, *Journal of Interamerican Studies and World Affairs*, 27(2): 55–76.

Plotkin, S. (2012) Thorstein Veblen and the Politics of Predatory Power, in E.R. Reinert and F.L. Viano (eds.) *Thorstein Veblen: Economics for an Age of Crises*, Anthem Press, London, pp. 205–238.
Ricci, D.M. (2020) *A Political Science Manifesto for the Age of Populism: Challenging Growth, Markets, Inequality, and Resentment*, Cambridge University Press, Cambridge.
Richardson, N.P. (2009) Export-Oriented Populism: Commodities and Coalitions in Argentina, *Studies in Comparative International Development*, 44: 228–255.
Roberts, K.M. (2006) Populism, Political Conflict, and Grass-Roots Organization in Latin America, *Comparative Politics*, 38(2): 127–148.
Roberts, K.M. (2007) Latin America's Populist Revival, *SAIS Review of International Affairs*, 27(1): 3–15.
Rodrik, D. (2018a) Populism and the Economics of Globalization, *Journal of International Business Policy*, 1(1–2): 12–33.
Rodrik, D. (2018b) Is Populism Necessarily Bad Economics? *AEA Papers and Proceedings*, 108: 196–199.
Sachs, J.D. (1989) *Social Conflict and Populist Policies in Latin America*, NBER Working Paper Series, No. 2897, National Bureau of Economic Research, Cambridge.
Sagarzazu, I. and Thies, C.G. (2019) The Foreign Policy Rhetoric of Populism: Chavez, Oil, and Anti-imperialism, *Political Research Quarterly*, 72(1): 205–214.
Samuelson, P. (1964) Theoretical Notes on Trade Problems, *Review of Economics and Statistics* 46(2): 145–154.
Spithoven, A. (2018) The Legal-Economic Nexus from the Perspective of New Institutional Economists and Original Institutional Economists, *Journal of Economic Issues*, 52(2): 550–558.
Stabile, D.R. (1986) Veblen and the Political Economy of the Engineer: The Radical Thinker and Engineering Leaders Came to Technocratic Ideas at the Same Time, *The American Journal of Economics and Sociology*, 45(1): 41–52.
Stabile, D.R. (1987) Veblen and the Political Economy of Technocracy: The Herald of Technological Revolution Developed an Ideology of 'Scientific' Collectivism, *The American Journal of Economics and Sociology*, 46(1): 35–48.
Surel, Y. (2002) Populism in the French Party System, in Y. Meny and Y. Surel (eds.) *Democracies and the Populist Challenge*, Palgrave Macmillan, New York, pp. 139–154.
Sunstein, C.R. (1988) Beyond the Republican Revival, *The Yale Law Journal*, 97(8): 1539–1590.
Szusterman, C. (2000) Carlos Saúl Menem: Variations on the Theme of Populism, *Bulletin of Latin American Research*, 19: 193–2006.
Taggart, P. (2000) *Populism*, Open University Press, Buckingham.
Thelen, K. (2014) *Varieties of Liberalization and the New Politics of Social Solidarity*, Cambridge University Press, New York.
Tilman, R. (1972) Veblen's Ideal Political Economy and Its Critics, *The American Journal of Economics and Sociology*, 31(3): 307–317.
Tilman, R. (2007) *Thorstein Veblen and the Enrichment of Evolutionary Naturalism*, University of Missouri Press, Columbia and London, pp. 22–26.
Uni, H. (2007) Export-Biased Productivity Increase and Exchange Rate Regime in East Asia, *Kyoto Economic Review* 76(1): 117–138.
Uni, H. (2012) Comparative Analysis of Conditions for Monetary Integration: Europe and Asia, in R. Boyer, H. Uemura and A. Isogai (eds.) *Diversity and Transformations of Asian Capitalism*. Routledge, New York, pp. 287–305.
Ünal, E. (2016a) A Comparative Analysis of Export Growth in Turkey and China through Macroeconomic and Institutional Factors, *Evolutionary and Institutional Economics Review*, 13(1): 57–91.

Ünal, E. (2016b) How Can Turkey Be Part of the EMU? Turkey's Economic and Monetary Integration into the EMU and the Analyses of Macroeconomic and Institutional Factors by Export-led Growth, *Kyoto Economic Review*, 85(1–2): 2–41.

Ünal, E. (2017) Turkey's Current Account Deficit Problem and Integration into the Economic and Monetary Union of the European Union, *Kyoto Economic Review*, 86(1–2): 1–49.

Ünal, E. (2018) An Institutional Approach and Input-Output Analysis for Explaining the Transformation of Turkish Economy, *Journal of Economic Structures*, 7(3): 1–38.

Ünal, E. (2020) The Transformation of the Growth Regime and Populism in Turkey, in H. Uni, C. Yan and S. Fujita (eds.) *An Institutional Approach to the World Economy*. Nakanishiya Shuppan (in Japanese).

Ünal, E. (2021a) Economic Populism and Institutional Changes in Wage–Labor Relations, *Evolutionary and Institutional Economics Review*, 18: 407–433.

Ünal, E. (2021b) Industrial Growth Models by Input–Output Analysis and an Institutional Approach to the Automotive Industry in China and Turkey, *Evolutionary and Institutional Economics Review*, 18: 175–203.

Ünal, E. and Köse, N. (2018) The Impact of Workdays Lost by Strike on Wage Growth in Turkey, *Journal of Economic Structures*, 7(12): 1–19.

Ünal, E. and Köse, N. (2019) The Determination of Wage Growth in Turkey and the United Kingdom: The Role of Workdays Lost to Strikes, *Journal of Productivity (in Turkish)*, 2019(2): 143–168.

Veblen, T. (2004) *The Theory of Business Enterprise*, Charles Scribner's Sons, New York.

Waisman, C.H. (1989) Counterrevolution and Structural Change: The Case of Argentina, *International Political Science Review*, 10(2): 159–174.

Weyland, K. (1999) Neoliberal Populism in Latin America and Eastern Europe, *Comparative Politics*, 31(4): 379–401.

Weyland, K. (2001) Clarifying a Contested Concept: Populism in the Study of Latin American Politics, *Comparative Politics*, 34(1): 1–22.

Wortman, R. (1967) *The Crisis of Russian Populism*, Cambridge University Press, New York.

Zaslove, A. (2008) Here to Stay? Populism as a New Party Type, *European Review*, 16(3): 319–336.

Index

Page numbers in **bold reference tables.
**Page numbers in *italics* reference figures.

Kolibri 360 GmbH
Ferdinand-Jühlke-Straße 7
99095 Erfurt, Deutschland
produktsicherheit@kolibri360.de